First World War
and Army of Occupation
War Diary
France, Belgium and Germany

5 DIVISION
95 Infantry Brigade
Gloucestershire Regiment
12th (Service) (Bristol) Battalion,
Brigade Machine Gun Company
and Brigade Trench Mortar Battery
3 October 1915 - 31 July 1916

WO95/1580

The Naval & Military Press Ltd
www.nmarchive.com
Published in association with The National Archives

Published by

The Naval & Military Press Ltd

Unit 10 Ridgewood Industrial Park,

Uckfield, East Sussex,

TN22 5QE England

Tel: +44 (0) 1825 749494

www.naval-military-press.com

www.nmarchive.com

This diary has been reprinted in facsimile from the original. Any imperfections are inevitably reproduced and the quality may fall short of modern type and cartographic standards.

© Crown Copyright
Images reproduced by permission of The National Archives, London, England, 2015.

Contents

Document type	Place/Title	Date From	Date To
Heading	WO95/1580/1		
Heading	5th Division 95 Infy Bde. 12th Glosters 1915 Nov-1916 Dec		
Heading	32nd Division Transferred To 5th Div.-Dec. 26th Nov. 21st-Dec 31st 1915		
War Diary	Codford	21/11/1915	21/11/1915
War Diary	Boulogne	22/11/1915	23/11/1915
War Diary	Buigny L'abbe	24/11/1915	27/11/1915
War Diary	L'Etoile	27/11/1915	27/11/1915
War Diary	Bertangles	29/11/1915	01/12/1915
War Diary	La Houssoye	02/12/1915	02/12/1915
War Diary	Sailly Lorette	03/12/1915	03/12/1915
War Diary	Suzanne	04/12/1915	05/12/1915
War Diary	Maricourt	06/12/1915	08/12/1915
War Diary	Suzanne	09/12/1915	12/12/1915
War Diary	Sector A 2	13/12/1915	14/12/1915
War Diary	Suzanne	15/12/1915	16/12/1915
War Diary	Sector A 2	17/12/1915	18/12/1915
War Diary	Maricourt	19/12/1915	20/12/1915
War Diary	Sector A 2	21/12/1915	22/12/1915
War Diary	Suzanne	23/12/1915	24/12/1915
War Diary	Sector A 2	25/12/1915	26/12/1915
War Diary	Suzanne	27/12/1915	28/12/1915
War Diary	Sector A 2	29/12/1915	31/12/1915
Heading	95th Brigade 5th Division 12th Battalion Gloucestershire Regiment January 1916		
Heading	5th Div 12th G'cesters Vol. 3 Jan 16		
War Diary	Sector A 2	01/01/1916	08/01/1916
War Diary	Suzanne	09/01/1916	09/01/1916
War Diary	Sailly Lorette	10/01/1916	10/01/1916
War Diary	Allonville	11/01/1916	31/01/1916
Heading	95th Brigade 5th Division 12 Gloucestershire Regiment February 1916		
Heading	12th G'cesters Vol. 4		
War Diary	Allonville	01/02/1916	14/02/1916
War Diary	Coisy	15/02/1916	16/02/1916
War Diary	Riencourt	17/02/1916	24/02/1916
War Diary	Berteaucourt	25/02/1916	25/02/1916
War Diary	Hem	26/02/1916	29/02/1916
War Diary	Grand Rullecourt	01/03/1916	01/03/1916
Heading	95th Brigade 5th Division 12th Battalion Gloucestershire Regiment March 1916		
War Diary	Grand Rullecourt	01/03/1916	02/03/1916
War Diary	Dainville	03/03/1916	03/03/1916
War Diary	E Sector	04/03/1916	15/03/1916
War Diary	Agnez Les Duisans	16/03/1916	21/03/1916
War Diary	J. 2	22/03/1916	28/03/1916
War Diary	J. 2 (Spr)	29/03/1916	31/03/1916
Heading	95th Brigade 5th Division 12th Battalion Gloucestershire Regiment April 1916		

Heading	From:- O.C. 12th Gloucestershire Regt. To:- Officer, i/c A.G.'s Office Base. Herewith War Diary of This Unit for The month of April 1916,		
War Diary	J. 2 (N.E. of Arras)	31/01/1916	31/01/1916
War Diary	J. 2	01/04/1916	04/04/1916
War Diary	Agnez	05/04/1916	11/04/1916
War Diary	K. I. N.E. Arras	12/04/1916	12/04/1916
War Diary	K. I.	13/04/1916	21/04/1916
War Diary	K. I. Support	22/04/1916	24/04/1916
War Diary	K. I.	25/04/1916	28/04/1916
War Diary	Agnez Les Duisans	29/04/1916	30/04/1916
Heading	95th Brigade 5th Division 12th Battalion Gloucestershire Regiment May 1916		
Miscellaneous	D.A.G. 3rd Echelon	01/06/1916	01/06/1916
War Diary	Agnez	01/05/1916	08/05/1916
War Diary	I. 1 Sector Arras I. right	09/05/1916	09/05/1916
War Diary	Arras I. right	10/05/1916	13/05/1916
War Diary	I. 1 (Right) Arras	14/05/1916	26/05/1916
War Diary	Agnez	27/05/1916	31/05/1916
Heading	95th Brigade 5th Division 12th Battalion Gloucestershire Regiment June 1916		
War Diary	Agnez Les Duisans	01/06/1916	01/06/1916
War Diary	I. Right S. Sector. E. of Arras	02/06/1916	06/06/1916
War Diary	I. Right Arras	07/06/1916	08/06/1916
War Diary	Arras	09/06/1916	14/06/1916
War Diary	I. Right Arras	15/06/1916	19/06/1916
War Diary	Berneville	20/06/1916	30/06/1916
Heading	95th Brigade 5th Division 1/12th Battalion Gloucestershire Regiment July 1916		
War Diary	Berneville	01/07/1916	02/07/1916
War Diary	Oppy	03/07/1916	07/07/1916
War Diary	Berneville	08/07/1916	13/07/1916
War Diary	Ivergny	14/07/1916	14/07/1916
War Diary	Candas	15/07/1916	15/07/1916
War Diary	Puchevillers	16/07/1916	16/07/1916
War Diary	Bresle	17/07/1916	17/07/1916
War Diary	Becordel	18/07/1916	18/07/1916
War Diary	Mametz	19/07/1916	19/07/1916
War Diary	Nr. Montauban	20/07/1916	23/07/1916
War Diary	Longueval	24/07/1916	29/07/1916
War Diary	E. of Mametz	30/07/1916	31/07/1916
Map	Maps		
Miscellaneous	Report On Operation 28th, 29th, 30th July, 1916	30/07/1916	30/07/1916
Miscellaneous	O.C. "B" Company S. 273, 29/7/16		
Miscellaneous	O.C. "C" Company S. 274, 29/7/16		
Miscellaneous	O.C. "C" Coy., 12th G. S. 277, 29/7/16		
Miscellaneous	O.C. "B" Company S. 280 29/7/16		
Miscellaneous	O.C. "B" Coy., 12th G. S. 284 29/7/16		
Heading	95th Brigade 5th Division 12th Battalion Gloucestershire Regiment August 1916		
Miscellaneous	96th Inf. Bde. Herewith War Diary of this Ban for The Month of Aug 1916.		
War Diary	E of Mametz	01/08/1916	05/08/1916
War Diary	Airaines	06/08/1916	06/08/1916
War Diary	Vergies	07/08/1916	24/08/1916
War Diary	W of Dernancourt	25/08/1916	26/08/1916

War Diary	N.W. Carnoy	27/08/1916	31/08/1916
Heading	95th Brigade 5th Division 12th Battalion Gloucestershire Regiment September 1916		
War Diary	Bronfay Farm	01/09/1916	02/09/1916
War Diary	S. of Guillemont	03/09/1916	06/09/1916
War Diary	Happy Valley	07/09/1916	09/09/1916
War Diary	Ville-Sur-Ancre	10/09/1916	18/09/1916
War Diary	N. of Leuze Wood	19/09/1916	20/09/1916
War Diary	S.E. of Ginchy	21/09/1916	22/09/1916
War Diary	S.E. of Guillemont	23/09/1916	24/09/1916
War Diary	S.E. of Ginchy	25/09/1916	25/09/1916
War Diary	Morval	26/09/1916	26/09/1916
War Diary	Oxford Copse	27/09/1916	27/09/1916
War Diary	Citadel	28/09/1916	29/09/1916
War Diary	Sorel	30/09/1916	30/09/1916
Operation(al) Order(s)	12th Bn. Gloucester Regiment-Operation Order No. A.4. 2/9/16	02/09/1916	02/09/1916
Operation(al) Order(s)	Operation Order No. A.3.-2nd September 1916	02/09/1916	02/09/1916
Miscellaneous	Operation Orders	26/09/1916	26/09/1916
Miscellaneous	5th Division	30/09/1916	30/09/1916
Map	Sketch Map		
Map	Maps		
Heading	95th Brigade 5th Division 12th Battalion Gloucestershire Regiment October 1916		
War Diary	Sorel	01/10/1916	01/10/1916
War Diary	Bethune	02/10/1916	05/10/1916
War Diary	Givenchy Sector	06/10/1916	14/10/1916
War Diary	Le Quesnoy	15/10/1916	18/10/1916
War Diary	Givenchy Right S. Section	19/10/1916	21/10/1916
War Diary	Village Line	22/10/1916	26/10/1916
War Diary	Givenchy Right Sub Section	27/10/1916	30/10/1916
War Diary	Le Quesnoy	31/10/1916	31/10/1916
Heading	95th Brigade 5th Division 12th Battalion Gloucestershire Regiment November 1916		
War Diary	Le Quesnoy	01/11/1916	03/11/1916
War Diary	Cuinchy Left S. Section	04/11/1916	07/11/1916
War Diary	Cuinchy Support Line	08/11/1916	11/11/1916
War Diary	Cuinchy Left S. Section	12/11/1916	15/11/1916
War Diary	Le Quesnoy	16/11/1916	19/11/1916
War Diary	Cuinchy Left S. Section	20/11/1916	23/11/1916
War Diary	Cuinchy Village Support Line	24/11/1916	25/11/1916
War Diary	Essars	26/11/1916	30/11/1916
Heading	95th Brigade 5th Division 12th Battalion Gloucestershire Regiment December 1916		
War Diary	Essars	01/12/1916	05/12/1916
War Diary	Ferme Du Bois Left	06/12/1916	09/12/1916
War Diary	Croix Barbee	10/12/1916	13/12/1916
War Diary	Ferme Du Bois Left	14/12/1916	17/12/1916
War Diary	Croix Barbee	18/12/1916	21/12/1916
War Diary	Croix Marmuse.	22/12/1916	22/12/1916
War Diary	Bethune	23/12/1916	28/12/1916
War Diary	Givenchy Left	29/12/1916	31/12/1916
Heading	5th Division 95th Inf Bde 12th Bn Glosters Jan 1917 To 1917 Nov Italy		
War Diary	Givenchy Left	01/01/1917	02/01/1917
War Diary	Gorre	03/01/1917	06/01/1917

War Diary	Givenchy Left	07/01/1917	10/01/1917
War Diary	Givenchy Support	11/01/1917	12/01/1917
War Diary	Givenchy Support Line	13/01/1917	14/01/1917
War Diary	Bethune	15/01/1917	22/01/1917
War Diary	Cuinchy Section	23/01/1917	25/01/1917
War Diary	Cuinchy Right	26/01/1917	26/01/1917
War Diary	Le Quesnoy	27/01/1917	30/01/1917
War Diary	Cuinchy Right	31/01/1917	03/02/1917
War Diary	Cuinchy Support Line	04/02/1917	07/02/1917
War Diary	Cuinchy Right	08/02/1917	11/02/1917
War Diary	Reserve Le Quesnoy	12/02/1917	15/02/1917
War Diary	Cuinchy Right	16/02/1917	27/02/1917
War Diary	Le Quesnoy	28/02/1917	03/03/1917
War Diary	Cuinchy Right	04/03/1917	15/03/1917
War Diary	Le Quesnoy	16/03/1917	17/03/1917
War Diary	Bethune	18/03/1917	18/03/1917
War Diary	Burbure	19/03/1917	31/03/1917
Heading	12th Battalion Gloucestershire Regiment 95th Infantry Brigade 5th Division April 1917		
War Diary	Burbure	01/04/1917	06/04/1917
War Diary	Ruitz	07/04/1917	07/04/1917
War Diary	Bois Des Alleux	08/04/1917	13/04/1917
War Diary	Bois des Alleux-Quarries N. E. of Souchez	14/04/1917	17/04/1917
War Diary	In Trenches Bois De L' Hiron Delle	18/04/1917	24/04/1917
War Diary	Niagara Camp	25/04/1917	30/04/1917
War Diary	Petit Servin	01/05/1917	03/05/1917
War Diary	E. of Fresnoy	04/05/1917	04/05/1917
War Diary	Trenches E. of Fresnoy	05/05/1917	08/05/1917
War Diary	Nine Elms A 17 C 89 51 B N.W.	09/05/1917	10/05/1917
War Diary	Maroeuil	11/05/1917	21/05/1917
War Diary	St. Aubin	22/05/1917	25/05/1917
War Diary	Les Quatre Vents G 610 B.	26/05/1917	29/05/1917
War Diary	Field G. 10 B. S. of Roclincourt	30/05/1917	31/05/1917
Miscellaneous	95th Inf Bde The Following Is My Report on The Enemy Attack on Fresnoy on The 8th inst	10/05/1917	10/05/1917
War Diary	Le Quatre Vents	01/06/1917	01/06/1917
War Diary	Dieval	02/06/1917	09/06/1917
War Diary	Nr Roclincourt	10/06/1917	10/06/1917
War Diary	Camp G.4 D.	11/06/1917	14/06/1917
War Diary	Front Line	15/06/1917	19/06/1917
War Diary	Willerval	19/06/1917	24/06/1917
War Diary	Arleux	25/06/1917	30/06/1917
War Diary	Front Line	01/07/1917	01/07/1917
War Diary	Bde. Reserve W. of Farbus Wood	02/07/1917	04/07/1917
War Diary	St. Aubin	05/07/1917	16/07/1917
War Diary	Front Line Arleux Fresnoy Rd To B 12d 2.8	17/07/1917	17/07/1917
War Diary	Front Line	17/07/1917	20/07/1917
War Diary	Red Line	21/07/1917	26/07/1917
War Diary	Front Line	27/07/1917	29/07/1917
War Diary	B. 23 B. 51 N. of Roclincourt	30/07/1917	31/07/1917
Operation(al) Order(s)	12th Bn. Gloucestershire Regiment-Operation Order No. 5		
Operation(al) Order(s)	Operation Order No. 5 By Lt.-Col. R.I. Rawson Commanding 12th Bn. Gloucestershire Regiment		
War Diary	A. 23 B 5.1 N. of Roclincourt	01/08/1917	03/08/1917
War Diary	Ecurie Wood Huts	04/08/1917	09/08/1917

War Diary	Front Line	10/08/1917	12/08/1917
War Diary	Front Line Arleux	13/08/1917	15/08/1917
War Diary	Bde Reserve	16/08/1917	21/08/1917
War Diary	N of Ecurie	22/08/1917	27/08/1917
War Diary	Ecurie Wood Huts	28/08/1917	31/08/1917
Operation(al) Order(s)	Operation Order No. 10 By Lt. Col. R.I. Rawson Commanding 12th Bn. Gloucestershire Regt.	02/08/1917	02/08/1917
Operation(al) Order(s)	Operation Order No. 11 By Lt. Col. R.I. Rawson Commanding 12th Bn. Gloucestershire Regiment		
Operation(al) Order(s)	Operation Order No. 13 By Lt. Col. R.I. Rawson Commanding 12th Bn. Gloucestershire Regiment		
Operation(al) Order(s)	Operation Order No. 11	14/08/1917	14/08/1917
War Diary	Ecurie Wood Huts	01/09/1917	02/09/1917
War Diary	In Front Line	03/09/1917	07/09/1917
War Diary	Wellington Camp	08/09/1917	08/09/1917
War Diary	A.C.Q.	09/09/1917	09/09/1917
War Diary	Maizieres	10/09/1917	25/09/1917
War Diary	Bayenghem	26/09/1917	27/09/1917
War Diary	Moulle	28/09/1917	28/09/1917
War Diary	Lenieppe	29/09/1917	29/09/1917
War Diary	Meteren	30/09/1917	30/09/1917
Operation(al) Order(s)	Operation Order No. 11 By Lt.-Col. R.I. Rawson Commanding 12th Bn. Gloucestershire Regiments		
Operation(al) Order(s)	Operation Order No. 14 By Lt.-Col. R.I. Rawson Cg. 12th Bn. Gloucestershire Regt.	06/09/1917	06/09/1917
Operation(al) Order(s)	12th Bn. Gloucestershire Regiment Operation Order No. 15.	20/09/1917	20/09/1917
Miscellaneous	Instructions for Attack on 22.9.17	20/09/1917	20/09/1917
Operation(al) Order(s)	Operation Order No. 15 By Lt.-Col. R.I. Rawson Commanding 12th Bn. Gloucestershire Regiments		
Operation(al) Order(s)	12th Bn. Gloucestershire Regiment Operation Order No. 16	23/09/1917	23/09/1917
War Diary	Meteren	01/10/1917	01/10/1917
War Diary	In Reserve	02/10/1917	05/10/1917
War Diary	Sanctuary Wood	06/10/1917	08/10/1917
War Diary	Support	09/10/1917	10/10/1917
War Diary	Sanctuary Wood	11/10/1917	11/10/1917
War Diary	Curragh Camp. Westoutre	12/10/1917	25/10/1917
War Diary	Ridgewood	26/10/1917	28/10/1917
War Diary	Front Line	29/10/1917	01/11/1917
War Diary	Ridgewood	02/11/1917	05/11/1917
War Diary	For Tot 7 Stirling Tunnel	06/11/1917	06/11/1917
War Diary	Front Line	07/11/1917	07/11/1917
War Diary	Bedford House	08/11/1917	09/11/1917
War Diary	Ridgewood	10/11/1917	11/11/1917
War Diary	Arragon Camp	12/11/1917	14/11/1917
War Diary	Quesques	15/11/1917	15/11/1917
War Diary	Henneveux	16/11/1917	25/11/1917
War Diary	Le Parc	26/11/1917	30/11/1917
Heading	WO95/1580/2		
Heading	5th Division 12th Gloucesters-Disbanded 1918 Apr-1918 Oct (Disbanded)		
Heading	95th Brigade 5th Division 51/12th Battalion Gloucestershire Regiment April 1918		
War Diary	Italy Longare	01/04/1918	06/04/1918
War Diary	Ivergny Pas de Calacs	07/04/1918	11/04/1918

War Diary	Pommera	11/04/1918	16/04/1918
War Diary	Le Touquet	17/04/1918	21/04/1918
War Diary	K. 20 B. 7.6 To K. 19 d 9.0.	22/04/1918	27/04/1918
War Diary	Front Line	28/04/1918	28/04/1918
War Diary	Bois Moyen (Foret De Nieppe)	29/04/1918	30/04/1918
Operation(al) Order(s)	Operation Order No. 55 By Lieut.-Colonel H. A. Colt. M.C. Commanding 12th Battalion The Gloucestershire Regiment Appendix 1	08/04/1918	08/04/1918
Operation(al) Order(s)	Operation Order No. 56 By Lieut.-Colonel H. A. Colt. M.C. Commanding 12th Battalion The Gloucestershire Regimen Appendix 2t	09/04/1918	09/04/1918
Operation(al) Order(s)	Operation Order No. 57 By Lieut.-Colonel H. A. Colt. M.C. Commanding 12th Battalion The Gloucestershire Regiment Appendix 3.	11/04/1918	11/04/1918
Diagram etc	Appendix 5		
Heading	War Diary of 12th Battalion Gloucestershire for The Month of May-1918 Vol 31.		
War Diary	In Support Rt. Sub Sector	01/05/1918	03/05/1918
War Diary	In Reserve J. 15 a	04/05/1918	09/05/1918
War Diary	In front Line Left Front	10/05/1918	10/05/1918
War Diary	Left S. Sector	11/05/1918	15/05/1918
War Diary	K. 8 a 25	16/05/1918	21/05/1918
War Diary	In Support	21/05/1918	22/05/1918
War Diary	Steen Becque	23/05/1918	29/05/1918
War Diary	Villorba Camp	30/05/1918	31/05/1918
Miscellaneous	Operation Order No. Lt.-Col. H.A. Colt M.C. Cmdg. Appendix 1	02/05/1918	02/05/1918
Operation(al) Order(s)	Operation Order No. 40 By Lieut.-Colonel H.A. Colt. M.C. Commanding 12th Battalion The Gloucestershire Regt. Appendix 2		
Operation(al) Order(s)	Operation Order No. 40 dated 6/5/18 Appendix 2 A.	06/05/1918	06/05/1918
Operation(al) Order(s)	Operation Order No. 41 By Lieut. Col. H.A. Colt. M.E. Appendix 3.		
Operation(al) Order(s)	Operation Order No. 42 Appendix 4	22/05/1918	22/05/1918
Operation(al) Order(s)	Operation Order No. 43 Appendix 5		
Heading	War Diary of 12th Battalion Gloucestershire Regt. for The Month of June 1918 Vol 32.		
Miscellaneous			
War Diary	Villorba Camp J. 15 c 02 Sheet 36 a	01/06/1918	04/06/1918
War Diary	L 2 S Sector	05/06/1918	12/06/1918
War Diary	Arcade Cap. J. 8 A.	13/06/1918	13/06/1918
War Diary	Arcade Camp	14/06/1918	19/06/1918
War Diary	Support	20/06/1918	20/06/1918
War Diary	Support Line	21/06/1918	23/06/1918
War Diary	Front Line	24/06/1918	25/06/1918
War Diary	Spresiano Camp J. 14 B. (Sheet 36 a)	26/06/1918	27/06/1918
War Diary	Caudescure	28/06/1918	30/06/1918
Operation(al) Order(s)	Operation Order No. 44 By Major W.G. Chapman M.C. Cmdg. 12th Battalion The Gloucestershire Regt. Appendix 1		
Operation(al) Order(s)	Operation Order No. 48 By Major W.G. Chapman M.C. Cmdg. 12th Battalion The Gloucestershire Regt. Appendix 2.		
Operation(al) Order(s)	Operation Order No. 50 Major W.G. Chapman M.C. Commanding 12th Bn. Gloucestershire Regiment Appendix 3.		

Miscellaneous	All Recipients of O.O. No. 50		
Operation(al) Order(s)	Operation Order No. 50 Lieut. Col. H.A. Colt. M.C. Cmdg. 12th Battalion Gloucestershire Regiment Appendix 4.		
Operation(al) Order(s)	Operation Order No. 51 By Lt.-Col. H.A. Colt. M.C. Cmdg. 12th Bn. The Gloucestershire Regiment Appendix 5.		
Operation(al) Order(s)	Operation Order No. 49 By Lt.-Col. H.A. Colt. M.C. Cmdg. 12th Bn. The Gloucestershire Regiment Appendix 6.		
Miscellaneous	Barrage Table		
Operation(al) Order(s)	Administrative Orders Issued With Operation Order No. 49 d. 26/6/18		
Miscellaneous	Major General R.B. Stephens CB., CMG, Commanding 5th Division	01/07/1918	01/07/1918
Map	My Organization		
Heading	War Diary of 12th Bn. Gloucestershire Regiment for The Month of July 1918 Vol 33		
War Diary	Steen Becque	01/07/1918	05/07/1918
War Diary	In Support	06/07/1918	09/07/1918
War Diary	Support Left S. Sector R. Sector	10/07/1918	11/07/1918
War Diary	Front Line Left S/Sector Right Sector	12/07/1918	17/07/1918
War Diary	La Lacque Camp	18/07/1918	19/07/1918
War Diary	La Lacque	19/07/1918	23/07/1918
War Diary	Spresiano Camp J 14 G	24/07/1918	30/07/1918
War Diary	Front Line Left S. Sector	31/07/1918	31/07/1918
Operation(al) Order(s)	Operation Order No. 52 By Lt.-Col. H.A. Colt M.C. Cmdg. 12th Bn. The Gloucestershire Regiment Appendix 1		
Operation(al) Order(s)	Operation Order No. 53 By Lieut.-Col. H.A. Colt N.C. Cmdg. 12th Bn. The Gloucestershire Regiment Appendix 2	10/07/1918	10/07/1918
Operation(al) Order(s)	Operation Order No. 55 Appendix 3 by Lt Col H.A. Colt M.C. Cmdg R E H I		
Operation(al) Order(s)	Operation Order No. 56, By Lt.-Col. H.A. Colt. M.C. Cmdg. 12th Bn. The Gloucestershire Regiment Appendix 4.	23/07/1918	23/07/1918
Miscellaneous	Addition To Para 12 Officers Mess Kit.		
Heading	War Diary of 12th Bn. Gloucestershire Regiment for The Month of August 1918 Vol 34.		
War Diary	Front Line Left S. Sector	01/08/1918	05/08/1918
War Diary	Spresiano Camp	06/08/1918	06/08/1918
War Diary	Orchard Camp	07/08/1918	12/08/1918
War Diary	Racquinghem	13/08/1918	14/08/1918
War Diary	Remaisnil	15/08/1918	16/08/1918
War Diary	Field	17/08/1918	19/08/1918
War Diary	Rossignol Farm	20/08/1918	31/08/1918
Heading	War Diary of 12th Bn. Gloucestershire Regiment for The Month of September 1918 Vol 35.		
War Diary		04/09/1918	04/09/1918
War Diary	Reserve	05/09/1918	14/09/1918
War Diary	Neuville	14/09/1918	20/09/1918
War Diary	Reserve Line	21/09/1918	22/09/1918
War Diary	In Reserve	23/09/1918	25/09/1918
War Diary	Divl Reserve	26/09/1918	30/09/1918

Heading	War Diary of The 12th Bn Gloucestershire Regt. for The Month of October 1918 Vol 36.		
War Diary		01/10/1918	06/10/1918
War Diary	Velu Wood	07/10/1918	19/10/1918
Heading	WO95/1580/3		
Heading	5th Division 95th Inf Bde 95th Mach. Gun Coy. Jan-Dec 1916		
Heading	95th Brigade 5th Division 95th Brigade Machine Gun Company January 1916		
Heading	5th Div Bde 95th M.G. Coy. Vol I		
War Diary	Suzanne	26/12/1915	30/12/1915
War Diary	Maricourt & Suzanne	31/12/1915	08/01/1916
War Diary	Suzanne	09/01/1916	11/01/1916
War Diary	Vaux-Sur-Somme	12/01/1916	12/01/1916
War Diary	Beaucourt	13/01/1916	31/01/1916
Heading	95th Brigade 5th Division 95th Brigade Machine Gun Company 20th February To 30th April 1916		
Heading	War Diary of 95th Brigade Machine Gun Company Period Ending 30-4-16 Vol 4.		
War Diary	Belton Park	20/02/1916	10/03/1916
War Diary	Grantham	10/03/1916	10/03/1916
War Diary	Southampton	10/03/1916	10/03/1916
War Diary	Le. Havre	11/03/1916	14/03/1916
War Diary	Mondicourt	14/03/1916	14/03/1916
War Diary	Le Grand Rullecourt	15/03/1916	15/03/1916
War Diary	Agnez Les Duisans	18/03/1916	22/03/1916
War Diary	Arras	03/04/1916	05/04/1916
War Diary	Arras-Agnez	06/04/1916	06/04/1916
War Diary	Agnez	07/04/1916	07/04/1916
War Diary	Agnez-Arras	13/04/1916	13/04/1916
War Diary	Arras	16/04/1916	30/04/1916
Heading	95th Brigade 5th Division 95th Brigade Machine Gun Company May 1916		
Heading	War Diary of 95th Brigade Machine Gun Company From 1-31 May 1916 Vol 5.		
War Diary	Agnez	01/05/1916	02/05/1916
War Diary	Agnez-Arras	03/05/1916	03/05/1916
War Diary	Arras	04/05/1916	31/05/1916
Heading	95th Brigade 5th Division 95th Brigade Machine Gun Company June 1916		
Heading	War Diary of 95th Brigade Machine Gun Company Period 1-30 June 1916 Vol 4.		
War Diary	Arras	01/06/1916	20/06/1916
War Diary	Simoncourt	21/06/1916	26/06/1916
War Diary	Berneville	27/06/1916	30/06/1916
Heading	95th Brigade 5th Division 95th Brigade Machine Gun Company July 1916		
War Diary	Beaudricourt	01/07/1916	07/07/1916
War Diary	Bernville	07/07/1916	13/07/1916
War Diary	Beaudricourt	14/07/1916	14/07/1916
War Diary	Candas	15/07/1916	15/07/1916
War Diary	Rubempre	16/07/1916	16/07/1916
War Diary	Bresle	17/07/1916	17/07/1916
War Diary	Becourt	17/07/1916	17/07/1916
War Diary	Becordel	18/07/1916	18/07/1916
War Diary	Manetz	19/07/1916	19/07/1916

War Diary	In The Field	20/07/1916	30/07/1916
War Diary	Pommiers Redoubt	31/07/1916	31/07/1916
War Diary	Field	01/08/1916	01/08/1916
Heading	95th Brigade 5th Division 95th Brigade Machine Gun Company August 1916		
War Diary	Pommiers Redoubt	01/08/1916	01/08/1916
War Diary	D 18 D	02/08/1916	04/08/1916
War Diary	Airines	05/08/1916	05/08/1916
War Diary	Vergies	06/08/1916	24/08/1916
War Diary	D 18 D	24/08/1916	24/08/1916
War Diary	Citadel	25/08/1916	25/08/1916
War Diary	In The Field	26/08/1916	31/08/1916
War Diary	Talus Boise	01/09/1916	01/09/1916
Heading	95th Brigade 5th Division 95th Brigade Machine Gun Company September 1916		
War Diary	Talus Bois	01/09/1916	02/09/1916
War Diary	In The Field	03/09/1916	06/09/1916
War Diary	Happy Valley	07/09/1916	09/09/1916
War Diary	Ville-Sur Ancre	10/09/1916	13/09/1916
War Diary	Treux	14/09/1916	16/09/1916
War Diary	Sandpits	17/09/1916	17/09/1916
War Diary	In The Field	18/09/1916	26/09/1916
War Diary	Citadel	27/09/1916	28/09/1916
War Diary	Fontaines	29/09/1916	30/09/1916
Heading	95th Brigade 5th Division 95th Brigade Machine Gun Company October 1916		
War Diary	Bethune	01/10/1916	02/10/1916
War Diary	Gorre	03/10/1918	03/10/1918
War Diary	Le Rreol	10/10/1916	28/10/1916
Heading	95th Brigade 5th Division 95th Brigade Machine Gun Company November 1916		
War Diary	Cuinchy	01/11/1916	28/11/1916
Heading	95th Brigade 5th Division 95th Brigade Machine Gun Company December 1916		
War Diary	Sloane Sqare II B 3.3	01/12/1916	01/12/1916
War Diary	Les 8 Maisons R. 29 d	04/12/1916	04/12/1916
War Diary	R 35 B 4.9	20/12/1916	20/12/1916
War Diary	Beuvry	22/12/1916	22/12/1916
War Diary	Gorre	29/12/1916	31/12/1916
Heading	5th Division 95th Inf Bde 95th Machine Gun Coy. 1917 Jan-1917 Nov To Italy Dec 1917		
Heading	95th Machine Gun Company 95th Brigade 2nd Division April 1917.		
War Diary	Givenchy (Sector)	01/01/1917	14/01/1917
War Diary	Beuvry Sheet 36 B N.E.	14/01/1917	21/01/1917
War Diary	Le Preol	22/01/1917	31/01/1917
War Diary	Cuinchy Sector	01/02/1917	25/02/1917
War Diary	Givenchy	01/03/1917	16/03/1917
War Diary	Bethune	18/03/1917	19/03/1917
War Diary	Burbure	20/03/1917	09/04/1917
War Diary	A. 22 C. 5.6 (57 B)	09/04/1917	10/04/1917
War Diary	Villers-Au Bois	10/04/1917	30/04/1917
War Diary	Chateau De La Haie (W12 Central Sheet 36 B)	01/05/1917	05/05/1917
War Diary	Fresnoy Sector	05/05/1917	10/05/1917
War Diary	Camp Ecurie	14/05/1917	18/05/1917
War Diary	Corps Line	20/05/1917	24/05/1917

War Diary	Ecurie	24/05/1917	24/05/1917
War Diary	Anzin	25/05/1917	31/05/1917
War Diary	Comblain Chatelaine	01/06/1917	16/06/1917
War Diary	Arleux Sector	16/06/1917	26/06/1917
War Diary	Arleux	27/06/1917	30/06/1917
War Diary	Arleux Sector	01/07/1917	18/07/1917
War Diary	Oppy Sector	18/07/1917	29/07/1917
Miscellaneous	Machine Gun Defence		
War Diary	Oppy-Arleux Sector	01/08/1917	31/08/1917
War Diary	Arleux Sec.	01/09/1917	18/09/1917
War Diary	Villers-Sir Simon	18/09/1917	23/09/1917
War Diary	Ligny	24/09/1917	25/09/1917
War Diary	Mentque	25/09/1917	27/09/1917
War Diary	Serques	27/09/1917	28/09/1917
War Diary	Nieppe	28/09/1917	30/09/1917
War Diary	Meteren area	30/09/1917	30/09/1917
Operation(al) Order(s)	95th Machine Gun Company Operation Order No. 15 By Captain Lt R.J. Culters M.C. Commanding	01/09/1917	01/09/1917
Miscellaneous	Time Table of Relief To Accompany O.O. 15		
Operation(al) Order(s)	95th Machine Gun Coy. Operation Order No. 16	02/07/1917	02/07/1917
Miscellaneous	Time Table To Accompany O.O. 16		
Operation(al) Order(s)	95th M.G. Company Operation Order No. 17	05/09/1917	05/09/1917
Miscellaneous	Time Table of Relief To Accompany O.O. No. 17		
Miscellaneous	Training O.O. No. 1		
Miscellaneous	Appendix A		
Miscellaneous	Timing Table		
Miscellaneous	95th M.G. Company Training O.O. 2		
Miscellaneous			
War Diary	Meteren (Sheet 27)	01/10/1917	02/10/1917
War Diary	Reutel Beek Sector.	02/10/1917	15/11/1917
War Diary	Brumemburt	16/11/1917	22/11/1917
Heading	WO95/1580/4		
Heading	5th Division 95th M.G.C. 1918 Apr		
Heading	95th Brigade 5th Division 95th Machine Gun Company April 1918		
Heading	War Diary of 95th Machine Gun Company for The Month of April 1918		
Miscellaneous			
War Diary	Loncare	01/04/1918	06/04/1918
War Diary	Ivergny	07/04/1918	09/04/1918
War Diary	Grincourt	10/04/1918	12/04/1918
War Diary	In The Field	13/04/1918	13/04/1918
War Diary	Foret De Nieppe	13/04/1918	22/04/1918
War Diary	L 1 & L 2 Sub Sectors	23/04/1918	30/04/1918
Heading	WO95/1580/5		
Heading	95 Trench Mortar By 1915 Oct To 1915 Dec		
Heading	3rd Army No. 95 Trench Mortar Batty Vol. I Oct. 15		
Heading	War Diary of 95th Trench Mortar Battery for October 1915		
Miscellaneous	95th Trench Mortar Battery		
War Diary	Valheureux 3rd Army Trench Mortar School	03/10/1915	03/10/1915
War Diary	Harbonniers	05/10/1915	05/10/1915
War Diary	Foucacourt	06/10/1915	12/10/1915
War Diary	Raincourt	13/10/1915	13/10/1915
War Diary	Harbonniers	14/10/1915	14/10/1915
War Diary	Raincourt	16/10/1915	22/10/1915

War Diary	Guellacourt	22/10/1915	22/10/1915
War Diary	Dormart	25/10/1915	28/10/1915
Heading	Trench 95th Mortar Battery Nov 1915 Vol II		
War Diary	Epecamps	01/11/1915	30/11/1915
Heading	95th Trench Mortar Batty. Dec, Vol III, 26 Bde.		
War Diary	St. Riquier	01/12/1915	15/12/1915
War Diary	Forceville	15/12/1915	24/12/1915
Heading	WO95/1580/6		
Heading	B.E.F. 5 Div. 95 Bde. 95 Trench Mortar Bty. 1916 July		
War Diary	Wailly	01/07/1916	02/07/1916
War Diary	Etree Wamin	03/07/1916	06/07/1916
War Diary	Berneville	07/07/1916	13/07/1916
War Diary	Beaudricourt	14/07/1916	14/07/1916
War Diary	Candas	15/07/1916	15/07/1916
War Diary	Herissart	16/07/1916	16/07/1916
War Diary	Bresle	17/07/1916	17/07/1916
War Diary	Becordel	18/07/1916	19/07/1916
War Diary	Longueval	20/07/1916	31/07/1916
Heading	95 Infantry Brigade. 12 Bn. Gloucestershire Regiment. 1915 Nov To 1918 Oct. 95 Brigade Machine Gun Company. 1916 Jan To 1918 Apr. 95th Trench Mortar Bty 1915 Oct To 1915 Dec. and 1916 July.		
Heading	95 Infantry Brigade. 12 Bn. Gloucestershire Regiment. 1915 Nov To 1918 Oct. 95 Brigade Machine Gun Company. 1916 Jan To & 1917 Nov. 1918 Apr. 95th Trench Mortar Bty 1915 Oct To 1915 Dec. and 1916 July.		

No 95/1580/1

5th Division
25. Infy Bde

1/12th Glosters

~~Oct 1918~~

1915 NOV — 1916 DEC

manuscript   K. 1.

95/32   12th P'cullrs
               Photo: 1, 2.   12/
                                   ───
                                   7911

3rd 32 H Strain
Transferred to 5th Div. Dec 26"

Nov 21st – Dec 31st 1915

WAR DIARY or INTELLIGENCE SUMMARY

Army Form C. 2118

Vol I

12th S. Batt. Gloucestershire Battn

Place	Date 1915.	Hour	Summary of Events and Information	Remarks and references to Appendices
Codford	21st Nov	4.5am 4-45	The Battalion entrained at Wylye-(Wilts) Rly Station under the command of Lt. Col. M. Archer-Shee D.S.O., M.P., for Folkestone & crossed to Boulogne. (The transport having preceded on 20th inst. via Southampton & Havre under command of Major Blenkinsopp) Lieut. G.E.R. Geary remained at Havre as Asst. M.L.O. with his servant.	27. Off. 886 O.Ranks 3 - 103 1 - 1 31 990 30.988 30.989
Boulogne.	22nd Nov	11.15am 2o. 0p.m	Arrived at Folkestone and proceeded straight on board transport "Stranrear" Arrived at Boulogne & proceeded to Ostrohove Rest Camp Resting at Ostrohove Rest Camp. The Interpreter - Joseph Storch joined	1 30.989
Boulogne.	23rd Nov	2.0am 7-30am	Marched to Gare Central Rly Station an entrained. Sergt. E.S. Mollin No 14539 & No 16807 Pte T.M. Moorey & were left in hospital. Sergt J Marlow - O.R. Sgt went to Base from Major Blenkinsopp's party. Arrived at LONGPRÉ and detrained - Marched to BUIGNY L'ABBÉ at 2 p.m. no casualties - Found Major Blenkinsopp had arrived by the 22nd instant with his party, baggage & transport & was billeted in the village - Billeted in comfortable billets	30.987 30.986
Buigny l'Abbé	24th Nov 25th Nov 26th Nov		Resting in billets Resting in billets - 1 Corpl. (Cole) & 4 men attached to A.S.C orderns - 1 man attached to Div H.Q.	
Buigny l'Abbé Buigny l'Abbé	27th Nov	8.45am	Resting in billets The Battalion paraded & moved via AILLY LE HUT CLOCHER - LONG - BOUCHON to L'ÉTOILE at about 12.30 p.m. and billeted in close quarters - no casualties - about 10 miles	
L'Étoile -	28th Nov	8.45am	The Battalion paraded moved via FLIXECOURT- St SAUVEU- VAUX- EN. AMIENOIS- to BERTANGLES & billeted - no casualties - about 16 miles	

Army Form C. 2118

WAR DIARY
or
INTELLIGENCE SUMMARY
(Erase heading not required.)

12th Batt. Gloucestershire Regt.

Instructions regarding War Diaries and Intelligence Summaries are contained in F. S. Regs., Part II. and the Staff Manual respectively. Title Pages will be prepared in manuscript.

Place	Date 1915	Hour	Summary of Events and Information	Remarks and references to Appendices
Bertangles	29 Nov		Resting in billets.	1100
Bertangles	30 Nov		Resting in billets — No 13149 Sgt A. E. Rice to No 9 C. C. Station.	

Army Form C. 2118

WAR DIARY
or
INTELLIGENCE SUMMARY
(Erase heading not required.)

Instructions regarding War Diaries and Intelligence Summaries are contained in F.S. Regs., Part II. and the Staff Manual respectively. Title Pages will be prepared in manuscript.

Vol II

1/2th L. Batt. Gloucestershire Regt.

Place	Date	Hour	Summary of Events and Information	Remarks and references to Appendices
Bertangles	1st Dec	9 am	The Battn. moved via COISY - ALLONVILLE - QUERRIEUX into billets at LA HOUSSOYE about 1.15pm. Nos 14,19,0 Pn. & C.J.R. Walker. Nos 3, 24 to C.Y. Johnson. Nos 9, 26 Pn. E. Payne to No 21 C.C. Station.	
La Houssoye	2nd Dec	9 am	The Battn. moved via BONNAY - VAUX SUR SOMME - SAILLY-LE-SEC into billets at SAILLY LORRETTE about 12.30pm. Nos 20 But. Pte. M.H. Green to No 21 C.C. Station.	
Sailly Lorrette	3rd Dec	10.30am	The Batt. less 2 Coys - 2 sections M. Gun + Pte. Mitchell Bearer – in all 17 Offr + 458 others ranks moved via BRAY SUR SOMME into billets at SUZANNE about 4.15pm. The remainder remaining at SAILLY-LORRETTE. No Casualties.	
SUZANNE	4th Dec	9 am	The Offrs of HQ + "A" + "B" Coys (except the QMTO) + the MOO of "A" + "B" Coys went into the trenches in A+ B sector attacked to the 2nd Bn. E. Surrey Regt. for instruction for 24 hours. B.Coy A2 - knocking trench.	
SUZANNE	5th Dec	9 am	The Offrs + MGOs in Trenches came out at 9pm returned to the same trenches with their accoutrements. (Major Blomefield with 15 Offr. + 69 Other ranks arrived from SAILLY LORRETTE at 3pm + billeted.	
MARICOURT	6th Dec	11 am	"A" Coy attacked to 1st E. Surrey in Sector A2 a platoon - at 6pm took over trenches 19, 20, 21 as a Company for 48 hours. B.Coy attacked to 2nd Innisskilling Fus. – Sector A4 as a platoon - at 6pm took over trenches 29-30-31 as a Company for 48 hours.	
MARICOURT	7th Dec		In trenches as on the 6th (the Offr. of "C" Coy + NCOs attached to 1st E. Surrey Regt. for instruction to 24 hrs. (the Offrs. + NCOs. of "D" Coy attached to 2nd D.C.L.I for instruction for 24 hrs.	
MARICOURT	8th Dec		In trenches as on the 7th. At 5pm "A" Coy was relieved by the 1st Manchester Regt. + B.Coy by the 2nd Manchester Regt. + D Coy to D.C.L.I. reliefs all over by 9pm.	ano

1875 Wt. W593/826 1,000,000 4/15 T.B.C. & A. A.D.S.S./Forms/C. 2118.

Army Form C. 2118

WAR DIARY
or
INTELLIGENCE SUMMARY
(Erase heading not required.)

1st/5th Batt. Gloucestershire Regt.

Place	Date 1915	Hour	Summary of Events and Information	Remarks and references to Appendices
MARICOURT	8th Dec.		A & B Coy returned to SUZANNE & billeted independently. H.Q. returned to SUZANNE arriving about 8.30 p.m. No. 16751 Pte YONDLES - F.H. slightly wounded in hand	
SUZANNE	9th Dec.		H.Q. A & B Coys in SUZANNE - At 5 p.m. C Coy took over trenches No. 19.20.21 in Sector A3 from MANCHESTER REGT & D Coy took over trenches 16-17-18 from D.C.L.I. both on Corps fronts. No. 11905 Pte LEWIS. A.S. - C'Coy killed - caused by bullet falling on him	
SUZANNE	10th Dec.		Exactly same distribution as on 9th. No 14861 Pte COLLINS - N.G. - C'Coy killed by rifle bullet	
SUZANNE	11th Dec.		Exactly same distribution as on 10th until 5 p.m. when C & D Coys were relieved by Manchester & DCLI parties respectively & returned to billets at SUZANNE. D. Coy arriving at about 8 p.m. - C Coy in small parties up till about 2 a.m. 12th inst. - Many men exhausted - much equipment lost in leaving trenches which were in dreadful state. No. 16682 Pte COOK. F.E. D. Coy dangerously wounded left side - thigh - some day - No. 14091 Pte DAVIS. N.E. - C. Coy accidentally wounded in the foot by rifle bullet fired by No. 14914 Pte PLACE. J.G. C Coy	
SUZANNE	12th Dec.		Resting in billets - No. 16682 Pte COOK. F.E. was buried at SUZANNE - No. 14905 Pte LEWIS. A.S. No. 14861 Pte COLLINS. N.G. was buried at MARICOURT. C Coy & No. 14861 Pte COLLINS. N.G. At 5 p.m. the Batty. took over Sector A2 - Trenches 13.14.15 being held by I Company of 9th Rl. Scots 5 p.m. the Batty. took over Sector A2 - Trenches 13-15 -18-, 10-11-12 being held by I Company of 9th Rl. Scots. A Coy took over 13.14.15 Trenches - B. Coy 16.17.18. A Coy reported relief complete at 8.45 p.m. & B Coy at 5.40 a.m. 13th Dec. - C & D Coys in reserve. No. 14012 Pte DENNING. H.H. killed by rifle bullet	
Sector A2	13th		Occupying sector of front. No. 14042 Pte DENNING H.H. No. 14058 Pte (Peter) FRIEND. J.E. wounded right cheek. No. 16738 Pte	
Sector A2	14th		Occupying sector of front. COLLIER. G.H. wounded head - died of wounds. - No. 14195 Pte WEEKS. R.W. wounded COLLIER. G.H. shrapnel forearm - No. 14040 S/L/Cpl. DENHAM wounded hand shrapnel. No. 14042 Pte DENNING. H.H. and No. 16738 Pte COLLIER. R.G.H. buried at MARICOURT by Rev. St. SOUTHAM at 2 p.m. - Relieved by 1st D.C.L.I at 6 p.m. relief complete at 9.45 p.m. & returned to billets in SUZANNE.	

Army Form C. 2118

WAR DIARY
or
INTELLIGENCE SUMMARY
(Erase heading not required.)

12" S. Batt" Gloucestershire Regt.

Place	Date Dec	Hour	Summary of Events and Information	Remarks and references to Appendices
SUZANNE	15th		Billeted in Area A.	
SUZANNE	16th		Billeted in Area A. - Nz 16620 Pte JAMES - G.H. A. Coy attacked 6 WEST SPRING.GUN battery in Sect" A2. Killed in action -	
		5.30pm	Took over Sect" A2 from 1st D.C.L.I. relief complete at 7.50 pm. 9th R' Scots on right, Sect" A.1. 2nd Inniskillen Fus" on left Sect" A3.	
Sect" A2	17th		No.16620 Pte JAMES - G.H. - A Coy - buried at MARICOURT. Dispositions as yesterday. - 16th inst.	
Sect" A2	18th		Dispositions as 16th & 17th. Took over MARICOURT defences from Devon Regt. having been relieved in Sect" A2 by 1st D.C.L.I. Relief complete about 9.30 pm.	
MARICOURT	19th		Garrisoning MARICOURT. Took over from Devons	
MARICOURT	20th		Garrisoning MARICOURT. were relieved by MANCHESTER REGT. relief completed about 9.30 pm. Took over Sect" A2 from 1st DCLI relief comp. left 11.10 pm. - Right group trenches 10-11-12. MOULIN de FARGNY. 'C' Coy. - Centre group. 13-14-15 - 'D' Coy. - Left group 16. 17. 18. 'B' Coy - Reserve at RAVINE dugouts & H.Q. dugouts. 'A' Coy - 9th R' Scots in trenches on right. 2 Inniskellen Fus" on left.	

Strength of Bn & Banks & Transports Vol II

WAR DIARY
or
INTELLIGENCE SUMMARY

(Erase heading not required.)

Army Form C. 2118

Instructions regarding War Diaries and Intelligence Summaries are contained in F. S. Regs., Part II. and the Staff Manual respectively. Title Pages will be prepared in manuscript.

12th (S) Batt. Gloucestershire Regt.

Place	Date 1915 Dec	Hour	Summary of Events and Information	Remarks and references to Appendices
Sector A2	21st		Holding sector – disposition as shown on 20th. No casualties.	
Sector A2	22nd		Holding sector – disposition as shown on 21st. No 14636 Pte CRUMPTON. W.V. "D" Coy wounded in No 13. Fire Trench – by splintered bullet ricco off official observation slit. At 5.30 p.m. the Batt: was relieved by 1/D.C.L.I. & moved into billets in SUZANNE.	
SUZANNE	23rd		Billeted in Area B.	
SUZANNE	24th		Billeted in Area B. – At 4.30 p.m. the Batt: took over Sector A2 from 1st D.C.L.I. 9th Rl. SCOTS on right and 1st DEVONS on left. Relief completed at 8.25p.m. No casualties.	
Sector A2	25th		Holding Sector – quiet day. No casualties.	
Sector A2	26th		Holding Sector – No 14191 Pte WAY. R.P. "A" Coy wounded in hand. No 14639 Pte CLARKE. J., "D" Coy wounded in side – both slight – by rifle bullets. at 6.30 p.m. the Batt: was was relieved by 2/MANCHESTER. REGT. & moved into billets in Area B. SUZANNE – Relief completed at 1.25 a.m. 27th. Brig Genl Ballard took over command of 1st Bde from Brig Genl Compton.	
SUZANNE	27th		Billeted in Area B.	
SUZANNE	28th		Billeted in Area B – At 4.30 p.m. the Batt: took over Sector A2 from 2/MANCHESTER. REGT. from No 13 F.18 (7.18 trench inclusive. The 9th Rl. Scots holding the MOULIN de FARGNY & the right & the 1/DEVONS. A.3 on the left. Relief completed at 7.45 p.m. "A" Coy: in front line. "B" in reserve at S. shelters + H.Q. 2 platoons D in RAVINE + 2 in SUZANNE. No casualties. The 8" was officially handed over to 115 Bde – 5th Div.	
Sector A2	29th		Holding sector. 2 Lt. FitzGerald – Sgt Pope + 2 men fired & bomb enemy Sap on PERONNE R. unsuccessfully. No casualties – very heavy bombardment on left.	
Sector A2	30th		Holding sector – Nothing of importance occurred. No casualties.	
Sector A2	31st		Holding sector – at 5.30 pm "D" Coy relieved "C" in 18.17. 16 trenches + "C" went into billets in SUZANNE. "B" Coy relieved "A" in trenches 13-14.15. + "A" held RAVINE with 2 platoons + H.Q. 2 platoon. No casualties.	

95th Brigade.

5th Division.

12th BATTALION

GLOUCESTERSHIRE REGIMENT

JANUARY 1916

K.2

12th Pealers
tot: 3
Tu '16

5th Div

Army Form C. 2118

WAR DIARY or INTELLIGENCE SUMMARY

(Erase heading not required.)

12½ (S) Bn Gloucestershire Regt

Place	Date 1916	Hour	Summary of Events and Information	Remarks and references to Appendices
Sector A2	1st Jan		Holding sector - Only a little shelling - No Casualties	
Sector A2	2nd Jan		Holding sector - Heavier shelling - No Casualties	
Sector A2	3rd Jan		Holding sector - Slight shelling - Casualties No 14997 Pte AMESBURY. R.A.- No 16569 Pte YORK. W. both slightly wounded	
Sector A2	4th Jan		Holding sector - Heavier shelling about 200 shells - Casualties 1 other rank (by shrapnel) wounded	
Sector A2	5th Jan		Holding sector - Nothing of importance -	
Sector A2	6th Jan		Holding sector - A hostile bombing attack was beaten off from No 13 F.T. about 3 AM - no Casualties	
Sector A2	7th Jan		Holding sector - Casualties - 1 other rank wounded by shrapnel	
Sector A2	8th Jan		Holding sector - Heavy shelling - Casualties - 1 other rank killed - 1 other rank wounded at 6.30 p.m. the Battn was relieved by the 2nd Bn R.I.S. Two coys moved into billets in SUZANNE relief complete at about 10-45 p.m.	
SUZANNE	9th Jan		At 3.30 p.m. the Battn moved by platoons at 2½ minute interval via BRAY. sur. SOMME to SAILLY LORETTE + billeted - arriving about 8.30 p.m. - Lt.Col M. ARCHER-SHEE. D.S.O, M.P. proceeded on leave for Parliamentary Business - (Compulsion Bill) - Major. W.A.R. BLENNERHASSETT assumed command of the Battn.	
SAILLY LORETTE	10th Jan		The Battalion moved about 9 a.m. via SAILLY-le-SEC - VAUX.sur.SOMME - CORBIE - NEUVILLE - PONT-NOYELLES. QUERRIEUX to ALLONVILLE into 5th D.W. Rest area arriving at 3.30 p.m. billeted.	
ALLONVILLE	11th Jan		In rest billets	WAR
do	12th "		- do -	
do	13th "		- do -	
do	14th "		- do -	

Army Form C. 2118

WAR DIARY
or
INTELLIGENCE SUMMARY
(Erase heading not required.)

12th (S) Bn Gloucestershire Regt

Instructions regarding War Diaries and Intelligence Summaries are contained in F. S. Regs., Part II. and the Staff Manual respectively. Title Pages will be prepared in manuscript.

Place	Date 1916	Hour	Summary of Events and Information	Remarks and references to Appendices
ALLONVILLE	Jan 15th		Inspect billets - about 6 p.m. a draft of 30 other ranks arrived from the Base.	
- do -	16th		- do -	
- do -	17th		- do -	
- do -	18th		- do - about 10.30 am the Battn was inspected by Major Genl. C.T.McM.KAVANAGH. CVO, CB, DSO, who was pleased with the Battn	
- do -	19th		In rest billets.	
- do -	20th		In rest billets.	
- do -	21st		- do -	
- do -	22nd		- do -	
- do -	23rd		- do - Draft of 20 other ranks arrived from the Base about 5 p.m.	
- do -	24		- do -	
- do -	25		- do -	
- do -	26		- do - Lt Col M. Archer-Shee DSO, M.P. returned from England & assumed command of the Battn	
- do -	27		- do -	
- do -	28		- do -	
- do -	29		- do -	
- do -	30		- do -	
- do -	31		- do -	WP

95th Brigade.
5th Division.

12th GLOUCESTERSHIRE REGIMENT

FEBRUARY 1 9 1 6

12th G'cester
Vol: 4

5½

K.3

Army Form C. 2118

WAR DIARY or INTELLIGENCE SUMMARY

of 12th Bn. Gloster Regt.

(Erase heading not required.)

Instructions regarding War Diaries and Intelligence Summaries are contained in F.S. Regs., Part II. and the Staff Manual respectively. Title Pages will be prepared in manuscript.

Place	Date	Hour	Summary of Events and Information	Remarks and references to Appendices
ALLONVILLE	Feb 1		In rest billets 2/Lt E.L. HILLBORNE joined for duty	
do	2		- do -	
do	3		- do -	
do	4		- do -	
do	5		- do - 2/Lt H.C. RYLAND joined for duty	
do	6		- do -	
do	7		- do -	
do	8		- do - Capt. C.D. FOWLER transfd to England Sick & struck off strength accordingly	
do	9		- do -	
do	10		- do -	
do	11		- do -	
do	12		- do -	
do	13		- do -	
do	14	10 am	Bn moved to COISY - 3 - miles and billets	
COISY	15		Resting in billets	
do	16	10 am	The Battn left COISY and moved via POULAINVILLE - LONGPRE - MONTIERES - AILLY sur SOMME - BREILLY - FOURDRINOY - CAVILLON into billets at RIENCOURT, arriving 5.15 pm. About 15 miles	
RIENCOURT	17		In rest billets	
do	18		- do -	
do	19		- do -	
do	20		- do -	
do	21		- do -	
do	22		- do -	
do	23		- do -	
do	24	11.45am	The Battn left RIENCOURT and moved via LE MESGE - SOUES - HANGEST - FLIXECOURT - BETTENCOURT - ST. OUEN - into billets at BERTEAUCOURT - arriving about 4 pm. about 12 miles. Major WAR. BLENNERHASSETT Capt. H.A. Cole and 10 OR procd to U.K. on leave	

WAR DIARY or INTELLIGENCE SUMMARY

Army Form C. 2118

of the 12th Bn. Gloster Regt

Place	Date	Hour	Summary of Events and Information	Remarks and references to Appendices
BERTEAUCOURT	25	9.40 a	The Battn left BERTEAUCOURT and moved via CAVAPLES - CANDAS - HARDINVAL into billets at HEM - arriving about 5.30 pm. About 12 miles in severe blizzard. Difficulty with transport some of which arrived several hours late. MAJOR F. WILSON FOX transferred to England 'sick' & struck off strength.	
HEM	26		Resting in billets	
Do	27		- Do -	
Do	28		- Do -	
Do	29	11 am	Battalion left HEM and moved via Hte VISEE - BOUQUEMAISON - LE SOUICH - IVERGNY - SUS-St LEGER into billets at GRAND RULLECOURT arriving 4 pm. About 10 miles.	
GRAND RULLECOURT	30			

A. Nicholson Lt Col
O.C. 12 Bn Gloster Regt

95th Brigade.
5th Division.

12th BATTALION

GLOUCESTERSHIRE REGIMENT

MARCH 1916

Army Form C. 2118

WAR DIARY
or
INTELLIGENCE SUMMARY
(Erase heading not required.)

12th Bn Gloucestershire Regt

Place	Date	Hour	Summary of Events and Information	Remarks and references to Appendices
GRAND RULLECOURT	MARCH 1st	—	Resting in billets.	
Do	2nd	1.45 pm	Battn. left GRAND RULLECOURT and moved via SOMBRIN - BARLY - FOSSEUX - WANQUETIN - WARLUS into billets at DAINVILLE. about 11½ miles. Transport left at WARLUS in charge of Quartermaster	
DAINVILLE	3rd	7.40 pm	Battn. moved up through FAUBORG D'AMIENS - ARRAS - into ST NICHOLAS taking over REDOUT LINE from the FRENCH 68/Bde. Bn. disposed of in E Sectr as follows - 'A' Coy in Bosky works. 'B' Coy in OBSERVATOIRE + TYRONE 40 ½ 'C' Coy in 'THELUS' WORK, ½ 'C' Coy in DUGOUTS, ST NICHOLAS and 'D' Coy in billets at ARRAS Holding Redout line - nothing of importance	
E. Sectr	4		-Do-	
-Do-	5		-Do-	
-Do-	6		-Do-	
-Do-	7		-Do-	
-Do-	8		-Do-	
-Do-	9	8 pm	Battn relieved 1/D.C.LI. in front line E Sector. 'A' Coy holding E 2. 'C' Coy E 3. 'D' Coy E.1. 'B' Coy being in support. One platoon of 'B' Coy was left at ST. NICHOLAS under MAJ. C.B. LEE WARNER to act as carrying party. &c	
-Do-	10	·	Holding E. Sector No. 14006 Pte. W.B. BRADFORD shot through head (sniper) + died same night. No 16481 L/Cl R.J. WILTSHIRE + No 16541 Pte. E. TURNER both machine gunners attached to D. Coy slightly wounded by bullet splinters	K.4
-Do-	11	—	Holding E sector. Nothing to report.	

Army Form C. 2118

WAR DIARY
or
INTELLIGENCE SUMMARY
(Erase heading not required.)

Instructions regarding War Diaries and Intelligence Summaries are contained in F.S. Regs., Part II. and the Staff Manual respectively. Title Pages will be prepared in manuscript.

Place	Date	Hour	Summary of Events and Information	Remarks and references to Appendices
E Sector	March 12	-	Holding E Sector. Nothing to report. 'B' Coy relieved 'D' Coy in E.1. Latter Coy sending 1 platoon to St NICHOLAS to replace platoon of 'B' Coy.	
-	13	-	Holding E Sector. No 16725 Pte Woodward A 'C' Coy slightly wounded in arm by shrapnel.	
-	14	-	Holding E Sector. Nothing to report. Lt R.B. JOHN RAMC Med Officer transferred to C.S. sick. Capt. DODGE RAMC temporarily takes charge. CAPT BINGHAM HALL T.B. and 2nd Lt WA. REED join Bn as reinforcement. Capt. BINGHAM HALL from 15th Glouc R. & Lt REED from 11th Glouc Regt. Also No 16766 Pte E MILLS 'C' Coy wounded - rifle bullet.	
-	15	8/m	MAJ. C.B. LEE WARNER proceeded to BEAUQUESNE to take up his duties as COMMANDANT, 3rd Army Troops. No 21633 Cpl Ellis G. 'B' Coy wounded head & wrist by enemy sniper. Bn was relieved by 1/K.O.S.B and marched to rest billets at AGNEZ les DUISANS. March completed independently by Coys. Last arriving at 3.40 am on 16th	
AGNEZ les DUISANS	16	-	In rest billets. Nothing to report	
-Do-	17	-	-Do-	
-Do-	18	-	Draft of 9 O.R. joined	
-Do-	19	-	Nothing to report	

WAR DIARY
or
INTELLIGENCE SUMMARY

Army Form C. 2118

(Erase heading not required.)

Place	Date	Hour	Summary of Events and Information	Remarks and references to Appendices
AGNEZ les DUISANS	20	—	In rest billets. Nothing to report.	
	21	7.8pm	Bn marched via ARRAS - ST NICHOLAS and relieved 1/NORFOLKS in Reserve line J.2 sector. Relief complete about 10.15 pm. 'A' Coy being in reserve at ARRAS. B Coy NICHOL WORK 'C' Coy Dugouts at ST NICHOLAS + 'D' Coy in "BRITANNIA" WORK	
J.2	22	—	Holding reserve line. Nothing to report.	
J.2	23	—	Holding reserve line. No 14131 Pte A.T. PARK 'A' Coy killed whilst on R.E Fatigue about 3 a.m. No. 14551 Shoemaker - Sergt & W PYMAN killed - and No 20088 Pte W. WILSON and No 14577 Pte H.M WESTLAKE wounded — by bullet from rifle being cleaned by Arm's Corpl. No 14251 Pte. A.B. COTTERELL.	
J.2	24	—	Holding reserve line — nothing to report	
J.2	25	—	Bn. relieved 1/D.L.I. in front line. Relief complete 10.20 pm No 20298 L/C. S. HOOK wounded by shell whilst on duty with 95/2 T.M Batty.	
J.2	26	—	Holding. sector. No 14312 Pte S. Hathaway + No 16526 Pte A. Ingwell both of B Coy wounded	
J.2	27	—	Holding sector. Nothing to report	

WAR DIARY or INTELLIGENCE SUMMARY

Army Form C. 2118

(Erase heading not required.)

Place	Date	Hour	Summary of Events and Information	Remarks and references to Appendices
J.2	28	7 p.m.	Bn. were relieved by 1/9.C.L.I and took over support line from latter. 'B' Coy going into billets at ARRAS. 'A' Coy holding 'NICOLL' 'BOSKY' works. 'C' Coy 'BRITTANIA' work and 'D' Coy going into CANDLEWORKS Dugouts. - No Casualties.	
J.2 (S/1)	29		Holding support line - Nothing to report	
J.2 (S/1)	30		- Do - - Do - Draft of 24 O.R. arrived	
J.2 (S/1)	31		- Do - - Do - Maj Genl. KAVANAGH, C.V.O C.B. D.S.O. called at Bn. H.Q. to say good-bye to all ranks on giving up command of 5/Divn.	

G. IV/Glouc. Regt.
Lt. Col.

95th Brigade.

5th Division.

12th BATTALION

GLOUCESTERSHIRE REGIMENT

APRIL 1916

From:- O.C.
         12th Gloucestershire Regt.

To :- The Officer,
         i/c A.G's Office
              Base.

                    Herewith War Diary of this
Unit for the month of April 1916,

                              [signature]
                                    Lieut. Col.
                         Cmg 12th Gloucestershire Regt.

1/5/1916.

Army Form C. 2118

WAR DIARY
or
INTELLIGENCE SUMMARY
(Erase heading not required.)

1/7 Gloucester Regt.

Instructions regarding War Diaries and Intelligence Summaries are contained in F.S. Regs., Part II. and the Staff Manual respectively. Title Pages will be prepared in manuscript.

Place	Date	Hour	Summary of Events and Information	Remarks and references to Appendices
T.2 (N.E of ARRAS)	31/1	7pm	Bn relieved 1/D.C.L.I in T2 Front Line A Coy trenches 101-99 B Coy 98-96. C Coy 95-93, D Coy 92-90.	
T.2.	1		Holding Front line, usual amount of Artillery, Trench Mortar activity.	
T.2	2		do do do No.16505 Pte. J.H. Barnes "B" Coy and No.14553 Pte W. Roper "C" Coy wounded. Trench Mortar Bomb.	
T.2	3		Holding front line No: 22716 Pte. F. Maggs A. Coy seriously wounded Bn relieved by 1/R.W.KENTS and proceeded to rest Billets at AGNEZ L3 - DUISANS, rest billets reached at 1-30 a.m. 4th inst.	
AGNEZ	4		Resting in billets	
	5		-do-	Baths at Company & Platoon Drill
	6		-do-	Bayonet fighting, Gas Helmet Drill
	7		-do-	Physical Training, Grenade & Signalling
	8		-do-	Classes. Bathing, Arms Equipment & Clothing
	9		-do-	Inspections.
	10		-do-	Flammenwerfer Demonstration.

1875   Wt. W593/826   1,000,000   4/16   T.B.C. & A.   A.D.S.S./Forms/C. 2118.

Army Form C. 2118

WAR DIARY
or
INTELLIGENCE SUMMARY
(Erase heading not required.)

Instructions regarding War Diaries and Intelligence Summaries are contained in F. S. Regs, Part II. and the Staff Manual respectively. Title Pages will be prepared in manuscript.

Place	Date	Hour	Summary of Events and Information	Remarks and references to Appendices
AGNEZ	11		Resting in billets. LEWIS GUN detachment relieve L.G. detachment 1/NORFOLKS in K.1. Support line	
K.1. NR ARRAS	12	7pm	Bn. left AGNEZ and relieved 1/NORFOLKS in K.1. Support line. 'C' Coy billeted in ARRAS. 'D' in Dugouts ST. NICOLAS. 'A' 'B' Coy in THELUS + BOSKY REDOUBTS, TRENCH 40. OBSERVATORY + CHALK FARM. WORKS.	
K.1.	13		Holding support line. No casualties } Bn. working on communication trenches and supplying fatigue parties to TUNNELING Coy R.E.	
"	14		Do Do Do	
"	15		Do Do Do	
"	16		Bn. relieved 1/D.C.L.I. in front line. 'A' Coy Trenches 102, 103, 104. 'C' Coy Trenches 105, 106, 107. B Coy 108, 109, 110. D Coy 111, 112, 113. + G. WORK + E WORK + F WORK	
"	17		Holding K.1. front. No casualties } Situation normal. Usual activity on part of Enemy snipers. Trench mortars and artillery.	
"	18		Do	
"	19		Do	
K.	20		Holding front line. No 16511 9te. R.E. Cross killed. Bn relieved by 1/D.C.L.I. and retired to support line. 'A' Coy going into billets at ARRAS. 'B' Coy ST. NICOLAS dugouts. C. D Coys into Stokes in Redoubt line. Draft of 40 O.R. arrived.	
K.1.	21		Holding support line. Enemy artillery very active. 2 O.R. wounded. Draft of 16 O.R. arrived.	

1875 Wt. W593/826 1,000,000 4/15 T.R.C. & A. A.D.S.S./Forms/C. 2118.

WAR DIARY
or
INTELLIGENCE SUMMARY
(Erase heading not required.)

Army Form C. 2118

Instructions regarding War Diaries and Intelligence Summaries are contained in F. S. Regs., Part II. and the Staff Manual respectively. Title Pages will be prepared in manuscript.

Place	Date	Hour	Summary of Events and Information	Remarks and references to Appendices
K.I. Support	22		Holding support line. No casualties. Enemy artillery and Trench mortars very active	
	23		Do Do	
	24		Do Do	
	24	8/-	Bn. relieved 1/D.C.L.I. in K.I. front. Same disposition as on 16th inst. Lt. A.L. HALE & Lt. S. WILKINS joined as reinforcements. No casualties.	
K.I.	25		Holding front line. 4 O.R. wounded. Enemy Trench Mortar and Artillery very active. Our heavy artillery retaliated on enemy front line, right of K.I. sector.	
	26		Holding K.I. front. 1 O.R. wounded. Artillery active on both sides. Weather fine & warm.	
	27		" " " No casualties	
	28	9/-	Bn. was relieved by 1/K.O.S.B. and marched back to rest billets at AGNEZ lès DUISANS. No casualties.	
AGNEZ lès DUISANS	29		Resting in billets. Bn. at Company & drill. Bombing, Bayonet practice and wiring drill.	
"	30		Do	

M. Mud Ohee Lt. Col
G. 17 Glouc R

1875 Wt. W593/826 1,000,000 4/17 T.R.C. & A. A.D.S.S./Forms/C. 2118.

95th Brigade.

5th Division.

12th BATTALION

GLOUCESTERSHIRE REGIMENT

M A Y 1 9 1 6

D.A.G.,
3rd Echelon,

I enclose herewith, duly signed, A.F.C.2118 (War Diary) of the 12th Bn., Gloucestershire Regiment, for the month of May, 1916, in accordance with Field Service Regulations, Part II.

A. Onslow Lieut.Col.
Cmdg., 12th Bn., Glouc. Regt.

1st June, 1916.

Army Form C. 2118

WAR DIARY
INTELLIGENCE SUMMARY of 12th Gloucestershire Regt Vol 7
May 1916
(Erase heading not required.)

Instructions regarding War Diaries and Intelligence Summaries are contained in F.S. Regs., Part II. and the Staff Manual respectively. Title Pages will be prepared in manuscript.

Place	Date	Hour	Summary of Events and Information	Remarks and references to Appendices
AGNEZ	May 1st	—	Resting in Billets	
"	2nd	—	Do. Bn. at Company and Platoon Drill, practising Wiring, Gas helmet drill &c	
"	3		Do.	
"	4		Do.	his West
"	5		Do.	
"	6		Do.	
"	7		Do.	
	8	8 p.m.	Bn. relieved 1/D.C.L.I. in I.1. Sector	
I.1. Sector ARRAS I right	9		Holding I Sector. Situation quiet. Weather fine. No casualties	
	10		Do. Enemy shelled neighbourhood of Station near Bn. HQrs, at intervals. No casualties. Weather fine	
Do.	11		Do. Situation normal. No casualties. Weather fine	
Do.	12		Do. Enemy artillery active. Weather fine. No 16532 Pte E. Curtis 'C' Coy wounded slightly.	
Do.	13		Do. Situation normal. No casualties. Weather fine	K.6

Army Form C. 2118

WAR DIARY
INTELLIGENCE SUMMARY of 12th Gloucestershire Regt
MAY. 1916

(Erase heading not required.)

Place	Date	Hour	Summary of Events and Information	Remarks and references to Appendices
L.I.(Right) ARRAS	14	7.30 p.m	Bn was relieved in T. right by 1/9CLI and went into reserve in ARRAS. "A + D" Coys occupying billets in ARRAS. "B" Coy in St. SAUVEUR Defences and "C" Coy in "Cemetery." Weather dull. No Casualties.	
Do	15	—	Holding reserve line. No casualties. Weather dull.	
Do	16		In reserve ARRAS. No 7076 Pte W. Cotton "B" Coy seriously wounded G.S. Enemy artillery active, especially towards dusk. Weather fine.	
Do	17		In reserve ARRAS. Enemy artillery bombarded ARRAS at intervals all day. Weather fine. No 4447 Pte H. Thompson wounded.	
Do	18		In reserve ARRAS. Artillery on both sides active. Weather fine. No Casualties.	
Do	19		In reserve ARRAS. Situation quiet. Weather fine. No. 14005 L/Cpl A.J. Bradford wounded and No. 2767 Pte G.R. King killed by accidental explosion of bomb.	
Do	20		In reserve. ARRAS. Weather fine. No. 1474 Pte Marsh. D. wounded, shell fire. Milne and No. 1471 Pte Enemy artillery active between Pt J. Bn. relieved 1/9CLI in front line I. right. 1 O.R. slightly wounded	

1875 Wt. W593/826 1,000,000 4/15 T.R.C. & A. A.D.S.S./Forms/C. 2118.

WAR DIARY
or
INTELLIGENCE SUMMARY

(Erase heading not required.)

Army Form C. 2118

Instructions regarding War Diaries and Intelligence Summaries are contained in F.S. Regs., Part II. and the Staff Manual respectively. Title Pages will be prepared in manuscript.

Place	Date	Hour	Summary of Events and Information	Remarks and references to Appendices
I Right ARRAS	21/5/16		Holding front line. Enemy quiet. Artillery activity normal on both sides. No casualties. Weather fine.	
Do	22/5/16		Holding front line. Weather fine. Little artillery activity. No casualties.	
Do	23/5/16		Do. Enemy shelling support trenches of Bn HQs and support billets with 77 M.M. guns. No damage. Casualties: Cpl 10 p.m. all Lewis Guns fired on enemy parapet and Vimy Ridge. No 6729 Pte J.Edmonds killed. Weather dull — not persistent quiet.	
Do	24/5/16		Do. Considerable artillery activity, both sides. ARRAS and neighbourhood heavily shelled. Bombardment continuing at 6 a.m. Our guns replied and duel continued at intervals all day. No casualties. No damage. Weather dull.	
Do	25/5/16			
Do	26/5/16	9.30 p.m.	Bn. was relieved by 1/9 C.R.I and marched to rest billets at AGNEZ les DUISANS. No casualties. Weather fine. Usual amount of Artillery activity.	
AGNEZ	27		Resting in billets. Bn. practicing Company Drill, Musketry, wearing Drill and Gas helmets &c.	
	28		Resting in billets. Programme as for 27th. Draft of 55 O.R. joined.	

WAR DIARY
or
INTELLIGENCE SUMMARY
(Erase heading not required.)

Army Form C. 2118

Instructions regarding War Diaries and Intelligence Summaries are contained in F. S. Regs., Part II. and the Staff Manual respectively. Title Pages will be prepared in manuscript.

Place	Date	Hour	Summary of Events and Information	Remarks and references to Appendices
AGNEZ	29		Resting in billets. Bn. at Physical & Bayonet Training, Musketry & Gas Helmet drill. 2/Lt. A W Ellison joined from 11th Glosters Regt.	
	30		Resting in billets. Gas demonstration for all drafts. Bn. at Wiring drill, Company drill, Physical Training & Bayonet fighting.	
	31		Resting in billets. Usual Programme.	

A. Archer-Shee
Lt. Col.
Comg. 12th Bn. Gloucestershire Regt.

95th Brigade.
5th Division.

12th BATTALION

GLOUCESTERSHIRE REGIMENT

JUNE 1916

Vol 8

Army Form C. 2118

12th GLOUC. REGT.
NO. ....
DATE ....
TIME ....

12th GLOUCESTERSHIRE REGT.

WAR DIARY or INTELLIGENCE SUMMARY
(Erase heading not required.)

JUNE

Place	Date	Hour	Summary of Events and Information	Remarks and references to Appendices
AGNEZ to DUISANS I Right S.Sector E. of ARRAS	1st	8 p.m.	Bn. marched from AGNEZ to relieve 1/D.C.L.I. in I Right front line E. of ARRAS. No Casualties. Weather stormy	
	2nd		Holding front line and ST. SAUVEUR DEFENCES. Enemy artillery active. No Casualties. Weather stormy	
Do	3rd		Holding front line. Situation quiet. No Casualties. Draft of 8 O.R. arrived	
Do	4th		Holding front line and ST SAUVEUR trench, shelled with 5.9 from 3.30 to 4.30 p.m. B.S.M. HEALY wounded - splinter. Weather fine.	
Do	5		In front line. Situation normal. Enemy artillery active. No Casualties.	
Do	6th		On the night of 4/5th the enemy blew 4 mines on left of J.2. and night of K.1. S. Sectors causing large craters which he immediately endeavoured to occupy. The 1st Norfolk Regt. (J.2) and 15 R. Warwick Regt (K.1) seized the near lip and prevented the enemy taking possession. Holding front line. No Casualties. Less artillery activity. Weather fine.	K.7

1875 Wt. W593/826 1,000,000 4/15 T.B.C. & A. A.D.S.S./Forms/C. 2118.

Army Form C. 2118

WAR DIARY
or
INTELLIGENCE SUMMARY
(Erase heading not required.)

Instructions regarding War Diaries and Intelligence Summaries are contained in F.S. Regs., Part II. and the Staff Manual respectively. Title Pages will be prepared in manuscript.

Place	Date	Hour	Summary of Events and Information	Remarks and references to Appendices
I. Right ARRAS	7		Holding front line. Enemy activity normal. Weather dull. No casualties. Relief postponed until night of 8th.	
"	8	7.45	Bn relieved by 1/D.C.L.I and retired to ARRAS and CEMETERY Defences. 2 O.R. Killed + 2 O.R. wounded during relief (all of 'C'Coy). Enemy shelled ARRAS + ST.SAUVEUR at intervals throughout the day. Weather cold and dull.	
ARRAS	9		In reserve ARRAS. Nothing to report. Artillery activity nil. No casualties. 1 Company working in J2 + K1. Consolidating craters.	
"	10		In reserve ARRAS. No casualties. Do. Do. Do.	
"	11		Do. Do. Do. Do.	
"	12		Do. Do. Do. Do.	
"	13		In reserve ARRAS. 1 O.R. 'B'Coy wounded. Weather dull. On June 10th, 11th, 12th, 13th and 14th the enemy artillery was noticeably inactive, scarcely a shot being fired.	
"	14	7.45	Bn relieved 1/D.C.L.I in front line I. Right. No casualties. Relief complete 10.30 p.m. Situation quiet.	

Army Form C. 2118

WAR DIARY
or
INTELLIGENCE SUMMARY 12th Gloucester Regt.
(Erase heading not required.)

Place	Date	Hour	Summary of Events and Information	Remarks and references to Appendices
I. Right ARRAS	15th		Holding front line. Situation quiet. Nothing of any note to report.	
...	16		Holding front line. Weather fine. Situation quiet. No casualties. No Artillery activity on both sides. No casualties.	
...	17		Do Do	
...	18		Holding front line. Weather fine. Enemy shelled neighbourhood of Bn. H.Q. and ARRAS with shrapnel – 18 fuzed 9.30 to 7.30 pm. No casualties.	
...	19		Situation quiet. Bn was relieved in I Right by 5/K.S.L.I. and marched to BERNEVILLE. No casualties.	
BERNEVILLE	20		Bn. in Army reserve. Physical Drill + Bayonet Training. Bombing and route marching.	
Do	21		In reserve. Continuing training.	
Do	22		Do	
Do	23		Do	
Do	24		Do	

Army Form C. 2118

WAR DIARY

or

INTELLIGENCE SUMMARY

(Erase heading not required.)

Instructions regarding War Diaries and Intelligence Summaries are contained in F.S. Regs., Part II. and the Staff Manual respectively. Title Pages will be prepared in manuscript.

Place	Date	Hour	Summary of Events and Information	Remarks and references to Appendices
BERNEVILLE	25		In III Army Reserve. Route marching, Physical Training, Bayonet Drill, Signallers, Lewis Gunners ie under special instruction	
Do	26		In reserve. Training continued	
Do	27		Do. Do.	
Do	28		Do. Do.	
Do	29		Do. Do.	
Do	30		Do. Do.	

M. McAlice
Lt. Col.
Cg. 12th Bn. Glouc. Regt.

95thv Brigade.

5th Division.

1/12th BATTALION

GLOUCESTERSHIRE REGIMENT

JULY 1 9 1 6

Report on Operations 28th-30th July attached.

Army Form C. 2118

95/1

12th Bn Gloucestershire Regt
July 1st

WAR DIARY
INTELLIGENCE SUMMARY
(Erase heading not required.)

Instructions regarding War Diaries and Intelligence Summaries are contained in F.S. Regs., Part II. and the Staff Manual respectively. Title Pages will be prepared in manuscript.

Vol 9

K.8

Place	Date	Hour	Summary of Events and Information	Remarks and references to Appendices
	1916			
BERNEVILLE	July 1st	—	In Army Reserve. Battalion practicing Bayonet fighting, musketry, Physical Drill &c	
OPPY	July 2nd	5 pm	Bn marched to OPPY via SIMENCORT, FOSSEUX, BARLY, SOMBRIN, SUS ST LEGER and BEAUDRICOURT. 14½ miles. Under orders to move at short notice.	
"	July 3	—	In reserve. Awaiting orders. Practice in advancing and attacking carried out	
"	July 4		In reserve. III Army. Under orders to move at short notice. Practice in attack, musketry, Bayonet fighting and Physical Drill	
"	July 5			
"	July 6			
"	July 7	3 pm	Bn marched to BERNEVILLE following same route as on 2nd	
BERNEVILLE	July 8		In Army reserve. Awaiting orders to move at short notice. Company drill. Physical training, Bayonet Exercises, musketry &c practised	
"	9			
"	10			
"	11			
"	12			
	13	4.45 p	Bn marched to WANQUETIN (via WARLUS) and moved thence by bus to IVERGNY. Transport moving by road	
IVERGNY	14	10 am	Bn marched via LE SOUICH, HR VISEE, HEM, HARDINVAL to CANDAS. about 13 miles	

1875 Wt. W593/826 1,000,000 4/15 J.B.C. & A. A.D.S.S./Forms/C. 2118.

Army Form C. 2118

1/4 Glouc/Regt

WAR DIARY or INTELLIGENCE SUMMARY

July 1916

(Erase heading not required.)

Instructions regarding War Diaries and Intelligence Summaries are contained in F.S. Regs, Part II. and the Staff Manual respectively. Title Pages will be prepared in manuscript.

Place	Date	Hour	Summary of Events and Information	Remarks and references to Appendices
CANDAS	July 15	9.40 a.m	Bn. marched via VAL de MAISON to PUCHEVILLERS. About 11 miles. Gas broke out in billet 44, PUCHEVILLERS, occupied by Bn., causing considerable damage.	
PUCHEVILLERS	16	10 am	Bn. marched via CONTAY to BRESLE. About 10 miles	
BRESLE	17	10 Jan	Bn. marched via ALBERT to BECORDEL and bivouacked	
BECORDEL	18		In Bivouacs BECORDEL. No casualties	
MAMETZ	19	9 p	Bn. proceeded to Bivouac. E. of MAMETZ. Transport remained BECORDEL	
M. MONTAUBAN	20		Bn. proceeded to trenches in CATERPILLAR VALLEY. 1 O.R. killed and 1 O.R wounded. Bng. Genl. C.R. BALLARD, Comdg. 95th Bde wounded. LT. COL. M. ARCHER SHEE. D.S.O. assumed command of 95th Bde	
Do	21st		In support trenches CATERPILLAR WOOD VALLEY. Heavily shelled with 5.9 and lachrymatory shells from 5 pm to 10 pm. 5 O.R. killed 11 O.R. wounded. LT. COL. M. ARCHER. SHEE returned to Bn. 2/LT E.L. HILBORNE and Bns. [crossed out] Brig. Genl. LORD E. GORDON-LENNOX assumed command of 95th Bde. Bn. ordered to LONGUEVAL for counter attack but were not required and returned to trenches in CATERPILLAR WOOD VALLEY	
Do	22		In support trenches CATERPILLAR WOOD VALLEY (on hill S. of) 2/LT S REYNOLDS 2/LT A BARNES joined on reinforcements. Heavily shelled all day. No casualties	
Do	23	8/pm	Bn. relieved 'E SURREYS in front line at LONGUEVAL. Heavily shelled 7 O.R. wounded	

WAR DIARY or INTELLIGENCE SUMMARY

Army Form C. 2118

1/5 Glouc Regt
July

Place	Date	Hour	Summary of Events and Information	Remarks and references to Appendices
LONGUEVAL	24		In front line LONGUEVAL. Also took over 1 Coy front on S. side of DELVILLE Wood. 2/Lt N.F.K. RICHARDS 1 O.R. killed. 18 O.R. wounded.	
Do	25		In front line LONGUEVAL and DELVILLE WOOD. CAPT E.H. BURRIS and 2/Lt A.W. ELLISON wounded. 2/Lts D. KINS. HIGGS, H.S. PAINTER, F.C. HOWARD, S.G. BENNETT joined as reinforcements. 68 O.R. wounded. 1 O.R. killed. 2/Lt E.L. HILBORNE rejoined from Hospital.	
Do	26		In front line LONGUEVAL and DELVILLE WOOD. 4 O.R. killed. 34 O.R. wounded. Relieved by 1/NORFOLKS night of 26/27 July and marched to POMMIERS Redoubt E of MAMETZ and bivouacked. 13 O.R. wounded during relief.	
	27		POMMIERS REDOUBT. No casualties. Lt. R. FEDDEN joined as reinforcement.	
	28		Bn. relieved 1/CHESHIRES in front line W of LONGUEVAL. 2/Lt L.C. EVANS joined.	
LONGUEVAL	29		In front line. B+C Coys attacked at 3.30 p.m. and gained objective. 'E Sunop' attacked on our right. 2/Lt H.S.PAINTER, 2/Lt. E. HUDDY and 8 O.R. killed. 23 O.R. wounded. 7 O.R. missing. The following men commanded by B.G.C. 9th/Bde (on their action in holding on to advanced post (until relieved by 14/Warwicks on 30th July) and preventing its occupation by enemy. No. 9405 Sgt J. HARRIS No 14435 Cpl E.J WARREN. 16805 4/Cpl H. WEATHERHEAD. 14398 Pte E. STREETS. 26134 Pte R. GRAY. 20184 Pte F.J. DYMOCK. 14416 Pte C.H. TAYLOR 20023 Pte A.H. ROBIN 20284 Pte H. CLARKE. 14339 Pte A.F. LEWTAS. 14331 Pte S. KEELER 16635 Pte W. THYER. 25302 Pte A. SCRIBBENS all of "D" Coy. Bn. relieved by 14/R. War. Regt. and proceeded to bivouac in POMMIERS redoubt.	

Army Form C. 2118

WAR DIARY
or
INTELLIGENCE SUMMARY

1/5 Glouc Reg
July

(Erase heading not required.)

Instructions regarding War Diaries and Intelligence Summaries are contained in F. S. Regs., Part II. and the Staff Manual respectively. Title Pages will be prepared in manuscript.

Place	Date	Hour	Summary of Events and Information	Remarks and references to Appendices
E of MAMETZ	30	—	Batn in reserve POMMIERS REDOUBT. H. O R killed. 7/Lt Q.H THOMAS 7/Lt H.C. RYLAND 32 O R wounded 6 O R missing	
	31		In reserve POMMIERS REDOUBT. CAPT. T BIRNSHAM-HALL joined.	

A. Archer Shee
Lt. Col
Comdg 1/5 Bn Glouc Reg

REPORT ON OPERATIONS 28th, 29th, 30th July, 1916.

95th Infantry Brigade,

The Battn. under my command received orders at 9.45-p.m., 28th July, to relieve 1st Cheshire Regt., in action to N.E. of LONGEUVAL and by 4.0.a.m. relief was complete, disposition of Battn. being as under:-

1 Coy., S.10.d.8.8 to S.11.c.1.4., in trench facing N.E.E.

1 Coy., from S.11.c.1.4., to Road Junction at S.17.a.4.6.

1 Coy., supposed to be consolidating road running from S.17.a.4.6, to left of E.SURREY REGT. at S.17.b.1.9.

Owing to heavy and continuous shelling it was impossible to work on this line, and this Company was withdrawn into trenches from S.17.a.4.0 to S.17.a.44.

1 Coy., in reserve about S.16.a.central.

Battn. H.Q., at S.16.c.08.

Soon after 6.0.a.m. I visited all trenches and found them being shelled with 5.9, H.E., and Shrapnel.

Left Coy's trenches were very shallow, and I ordered them to be deepened about 2' immediately. We were not holding point "A" on subsequent sketch and it was at the time of relief held by the Germans.

During the forenoon the bombardment became more intense especially on the Right Coy's Line and as they were very crowded and being shelled with accuracy by 11 inch and 8 inch Howitzers, I ordered them to move further North into the next Coy's trench which was not being as badly damaged and to move 2 platoons into trench running along N. side of valley in S.10.d.

About 1.30.p.m. I received orders that the 95th Bde. would attack after half-an-hour's preliminary bombardment to establish themselves, on a line running E. & W. approximately through the centre of S.11.c. and S.11.d. EAST SURREYS on the Right GLOUCESTERS on the Left with orders to establish strong points, Gloucesters at about S.11.c.3.5., S.11.c.8.5., & S.11.d.05., and Surreys at S.11.d.4.6., and S.11.d.4½.6½., these posts being named in rotation from West to East "A" "B" "C" "D" "E". Orders were, therefore, issued for the Left Coy. to send a patrol forward along the old trench towards point "A" and to establish itself there; for the centre Coy., ("B" Coy.,) to send 2 platoons with bombs along the dip below hedge shown in map running from S.17.a.3.8. to S.11.c.60., and from there to work forward one platoon to point "C" the other to point "B" and that a party with material for consolidation should follow. In accordance with above orders the Left Coy., sent a patrol under 2nd Lieut. H.C.Ryland to establish themselves at point "A". During consolidation 2nd Lieut. Ryland was wounded as well as some of his party. The other 2 parties sent forward by the Centre Coy., and led respectively by 2nd Lieut. R.J. Fitzgerald on the Right and 2nd Lieut. E.L.Hilborne on the Left dashed forward under cover of the barrage and established themselves at points "B" and "C", the leading men getting in without casualties, most of the casualties occurring in the succeeding three waves.

On the Right at point "C" 2nd Lieut. Fitzgerald's Party established themselves at point "C" by 3.31-p.m. and found it to be an old trench which had been obliterated by shell fire. They were fired on by a M.G. approximately at S.11.b.4.2. and were able to dig themselves in. The party consisted of 17 men, the remainder about 15 could not reach point "C" and dug themselves in (those that were left) about S.11.a.9+3. The point reached by the Right party was slightly North of point "C".

The Left party of SURREYS advanced also but could not be seen from point "C" once they got down. About 4.0.p.m. 1 Officer and 3 men of Surreys joined 2nd Lieut. Fitzgerald. Point "C" was not shelled or fired on heavily until after 9.0.p.m., but the party carrying consolidating material were reached as it lost about 50%, including 2nd Lieut. E.Huddy, killed.

(2) The Left party under 2nd Lieut. E.L.Hilborne established themselves at point "B" about 3.32.p.m. and found the trench had been hastily abandoned by Germans, with some loaded rifles, bombs ready to use, etc., and some bodies lying about, apparently killed by our artillery fire. The trench was fairly deep. 2nd Lieut. Hilborne's 2nd line carrying party were able to reach trench and he was consequently able to consolidate his position fairly well.

Enemy put down a heavy barrage behind points "B" & "C" about 4.30.p.m. As 2nd Lieut. Hilborne's Party reached trench it was fired on by M.G. on slope to North. They returned the fire of some Germans they saw and hit a number of them as they showed themselves getting into trenches to avoid our barrage.   2nd Lieut. Hilborne took over 33 and lost 9. The platoon which was carrying consolidating material did not reach and lost 18 out of 36.

Orders were issued that the whole of the Right Coy. were to go out directly it was dark to consolidate.   This they were unable to do owing to the heavy barrage put down at dusk by the enemy. The party which went out to help Point "C" Party in did not reach them owing to heavy barrage and No. 9509.Sergeant J.Harris and 10 men remained and dug themselves in with 4 shovels and entrenching tools. They were very heavily shelled but remained there.

About 4.0.a.m. today (30th) a party of 14th WARWICKS came to occupy post and told Sergeant Harris to bring message to me.   The remainder cannot come back until tonight.

The E.Surreys 1 Officer and 3 had orders to retire but Sergt.Harris not having received orders to retire remained.

He has had 18 months service, was with 1st & 2nd Gloucesters, has been twice wounded, and had done splendid work during his service with this Battalion since November, 1915, and I recommend him for immediate reward of D.C.M.

I have the honour to forward also the names of other officers and N.C.Os. and men who I recommend for an immediate reward for good service under heavy fire.

A list of casualties as far as they can be ascertained will follow a great many of which were caused by the extremely violent bombardment of our main trenches by 8 and 11 inch Howitzers.

(Signed) M.ARCHER-SHEE, Lieut.Col.,
Cmdg., 12th Bn., Gloucester Regiment.

In the Field,
    30th July, 1916.

O.C.   "B" Company,   S.273,   29/7/16,   11.30.a.m.

Expect that we are to be ordered to take posts "B" & "C" this afternoon at 3.30.   "B" is S.11.c.8.5½ "C" at corner of ORCHARD at S.11.d.05½.   If we have to do it in day-time will detail your Coy. to do it. Suggest that you send two platoons via bank running along hedge on map S.17.a.2½.8 to S.17.a.5.9½ and advance from there.   There are two old German trenches running from S.11.a.9.3. to "B" & "C" respectively.   Do not expect opposition until we come under view of GERMAN POSTS at S.11.d.0-8. and S.11.c.6.8. AAA   "C" Coy. will go forward and occupy point "A".
It is proposed to do this under cover of heavy artillery fire.
I have suggested that it would be easier to do it by night, and matter is not finally settled.
I have ordered "D" Coy. to withdraw 2 platoons if possible in daylight to trench running along N. side of DEAD HORSE VALLEY in order to relieve congestion and they will also be ready to act in support from there.

(Signed) M.ARCHER-SHEE, Lt.Col.,
        Cmdg., BINDER.

Surreys are to take the
posts on Right.

O.C., "C" Company,   S.27½,   29/7/16,   11.25.a.m.
___

It is possible that we may be ordered to take posts "A" "B" & "C" this afternoon.   Please reconnoitre post "A" with a view to occupying it if ordered.   Further orders later.

      (Signed) M.ARCHER-SHEE, Lt.Col.,
        Cmdg., BINDER.

O.C., "C" Coy., 12th G.   S.277.   29/7/16.

The Bde. has been ordered to attack and take the line shown in red on enclosed plan.   Enclosed is a copy of orders. Your work is to take point "A" and consolidate.   It is understood that a trench already exists to this point which only requires deepening, but if not, occupy the post and consolidate if possible. Send by return your requirements in sandbags, wire, bombs (if necessary

O.C. BINDER does not consider that you should use more than a platoon at the outside to carry out this work,   If you cannot quite attain point "A" then dig in in the nearest point which you can obtain.

Please be careful to send forward first line before Artillery Barrage *lifts* to see whether any portion of your advance is threatened by M.G. FIRE.

(Signed) M. ARCHER-SHEE, Lt.Col.

O. C. "B" Company,   S.280.   29/7/16,   2.12.p.m.

Further order received that at 5.0.p.m. the guns will lift off S.11.d.08, and fire to the EAST and WEST of it. when if possible a patrol will be pushed forward to ascertain whether it is held or not.   If not held it will also be occupied and consolidated. You may call on "D" Coy. to furnish another platoon if required.

(Signed) M.ARCHER-SHEE,   Lieut.Col.,
                     BINDER.

O.C. "B" Coy.,   12th G.   S.294.   29/7/16. 9.48.p.m.

Your message reference withdrawal of E. SURREYS from point "B" Do not withdraw but establish another post if necessary to right rear of "C"

```
A _____ B _____ C
                         \
                          \
                           D.
```

to form defensive flank.

(I stated in former message that I wished line drawn slightly in rear of Pts. "B" & "C" using them as Adv. Posts) but do not alter position of trench if already begun.

(2) Send patrol out to find E.SURREYS line, stakes and sandbags have gone out to you.

                                BINDER.
                (Signed) M.ARCHER-SHEE, Lt.Col.

95th Brigade.
5th Division.

12th BATTALION

GLOUCESTERSHIRE REGIMENT

AUGUST 1916

95th Inf. Bde.

Herewith War Diary of this Bn. for the month of Aug 16.

MHR Blennerhassett
Major
O.C. Details
4.9.16.   12th Bn. G. loue R.

WAR DIARY or INTELLIGENCE SUMMARY

Army Form C. 2118

12th Bn. Gloucestershire Regt.
August 1916

Vol 16

Mrs Brown (1)   K.9

Place	Date	Hour	Summary of Events and Information	Remarks and references to Appendices
E of MAMETZ	1st		In reserve POMMIERS REDOUBT. About 11 p.m. Bn. was relieved by 7th BORDER REGT. and marched via MEAULTE to camp N. of DERNANCOURT.	
	2		In rest camp W. of DERNANCOURT	
	3		Do Do	
	4		Do Do	
	5		Bn. left camp at DERNANCOURT and marched to MERICOURT. Entrained about 10 p.m. for AIRAINES which was reached about 3 a.m. on 6th	
AIRAINES	6		At 10 a.m. Bn. marched to VERGIES, about 6 miles, and billeted	
VERGIES	7		In rest billets. VERGIES. Bn. practicing the attack, digging, musketry, Gas helmet Drill. Route marching & Contact schemes with Aeroplane carried out. Drafts # amounting to 187 OR received.	
	8			
	9			
	10			
	11			
	12			
	13			
	14			
	15			
	16			
	17			
	18			
	19			
	20			

WAR DIARY or INTELLIGENCE SUMMARY

Army Form C. 2118

August 1916

Place	Date	Hour	Summary of Events and Information	Remarks and references to Appendices
VERGIES	21		In rest billets, continuing training	
	22			
VERGIES	23		At 11.30 p.m Bn left VERGIES and marched via AIRAINES and BETTENCOURT to LONGPRE. Entrained at LONGPRE at 8.45 a.m on	
	24		24th. In MERICOURT to camp N of DERNANCOURT. Marched from MERICOURT to camp N of DERNANCOURT.	
N of DERNANCOURT	25	11 a	Bn left Camp and marched via E. end of MEAULTE to camp at CITADEL F72a	
	26		Bn left camp 10 a.m. and relieved 17th Royal Scots in reserve trenches, SILESIA TRENCHES, A 9 & N.W. of CARNOY	
N.W. CARNOY	27		In SILESIA TRENCHES In reserve	12 casualties
Do	28		Do Do Do	8 casualties
Do	29		Do Do Do	1/Lt DRING-HISS and T.M.Batt. and 4 O.R wounded. Bn supplied digging parties for assembly trenches in front line
Do	30		Do Do Do	4 casualties
Do	31		Bn were relieved on night of 31st by BEDFORDS. and marched to rest camp at BRONFAY FARM. 4 casualties.	

M.R.Bleucknsett Major I/c Bn

17/Bn Glouc Regt

95th Brigade.
5th Division.

12th BATTALION

GLOUCESTERSHIRE REGIMENT

SEPTEMBER 1916

Army Form C. 2118

12 Bn Gloucester Regt.

Vol XI

K.10

WAR DIARY
or
INTELLIGENCE SUMMARY
(Erase heading not required.)

1916

Place	Date	Hour	Summary of Events and Information	Remarks and references to Appendices
BRONFAY FARM	Sept. 1		Resting in camp near BRONFAY FARM.	
"	2		Do. Do. On evening of 2nd Bn. marched to trenches about T 25 C 4.3 & B 1 A 5.7 (Reference Trench Map - GUILLEMONT - 1/20,000) and relieved 1/E. SURREY REGT.	
S. of GUILLEMONT	3	12 noon	Bn. took part in general attack on German Trenches carried out by XIV th and XV th Corps and the French. Final Objective taken. Bn. moving to own Artillery [line] forced to retire to rest [creation.] 2nd Lt. L.CH. VINCENT and Lt. EL. HILLBORNE - 2nd Lt. E.H. HALL - Capt. BA. ROBINSON - 2nd Lt. S. REYNOLDS - 2nd Lt. A. LAIRD - 2nd Lt. L.C. EVANS - CAPT. T.M. MLISON - Lt. C. BARRINGTON - 2nd Lt. F.C. HOWARD and 225 o.R. wounded. 48 o.R. Lt. P. BEN-GEDDGE - 9 captured German trenches. Lt. W.W. PARR & missing. up in front of Bn. to 3rd Objective. 11 DEVON REGT. moved capturing German trenches and carried out attack.	
"	4		9 captured German trenches in LEUZE WOOD from LEUZE WOOD.	
"	5		9 DEVON REGT. captured German trenches. 2 Coys. moved up to 3rd Objective. Bn. was relieved in LEUZE WOOD in evening by 6th Bn. LONDON REGT. and marched to camp at HAPPY VALLEY.	
HAPPY VALLEY	6		Resting in camp at HAPPY VALLEY.	
"	7		Do. Do. 95th Bde. Paraded and was addressed and	
"	8		congratulated by G.O.C. 5th Divn.	
"	9		In camp at HAPPY VALLEY. On afternoon of 9th. Bn. marched to	

WAR DIARY
or
INTELLIGENCE SUMMARY

(Erase heading not required.)

Army Form C. 2118

Place	Date	Hour	Summary of Events and Information	Remarks and references to Appendices
VILLE-SUR-ANCRE	10		Units at VILLE-SUR-ANCRE.	
	11		Resting at VILLE-SUR-ANCRE. Capt. Bt. ROBINSON died of wounds.	
	12		Drafts amounting to 112 O.R. joined as reinforcements.	
	13			
	14		2/Lt. L.C. ROBINSON	
	15		2/Lt. C.S. PETINGRAM joined Bn. 17/9/16.	
	16		2/Lt. G.F. TICEHURST	
	17		2/Lt. R.C. COX	
VILLE-SUR-ANCRE	18		Bn. marched in morning to camp at SAND PITS. In afternoon Bn. marched via MAMETZ and MONTAUBAN and at night relieved 1/YORK and LANCS. REGT. in front line trenches N. of BOULEAUX WOOD.	
In front of LEUZE WOOD	19		In front line trenches.	
N. of LEUZE WOOD	20		Do. On evening of 20th Bn. was relieved by 12th LONDON REGT. and marched to trenches in T.20.A and dug in.	
S.E. of GINCHY	21		In support trenches.	
	22		Do. On evening of 22nd Bn. withdrew to old German trenches in T.25.B (N.W. of WEDGE WOOD)	
S.E. of GUILLEMONT	23		In reserve trenches near WEDGE WOOD.	
	24		Do.	
S.E. of GINCHY	25	12.35pm	Trenches in T.20.A vacated on night of 24th. Bn. moved up to Assembly Trenches in T.20.A. 95th Bde. extended left in XIVth Corps attack. Casualties since 18th = 2 O.R. killed 11 O.R. wounded. 1/DEVON REGT. and 1/E. SURREY REGT.	

WAR DIARY or INTELLIGENCE SUMMARY

Army Form C. 2118

Place	Date	Hour	Summary of Events and Information	Remarks and references to Appendices
MORVAL	26		Assaulted and took 1st and 2nd objectives (German trenches in front of MORVAL). 2nd KOSB and 12th GLOSTERS then captured village of MORVAL. 2nd Lt. R.C. Cox and 2nd Lt. L.C. ROBINSON wounded. 4 O.R. killed – 59 O.R. wounded – 13 O.R. missing. Bn. dug and occupied line of strong points on S. side of village.	
OXFORD COPSE	27		In trenches S. of MORVAL. On evening of 26th Bn. was relieved by 12th RIFLE BRIGADE and marched to bivouacs near OXFORD COPSE. In bivouacs at OXFORD COPSE. In evening Bn. marched to camp at CITADEL. Lt. G.R.A. BECKETT rejoined Bn from hospital. 2/Lt Dn. LEICESTER joined on reinforcement.	
CITADEL	28		In camp at CITADEL. 2/Lt L.C. ROBINSON rejoined. 2/Lt A.E. HICKS joined as reinforcement. Drafts amounting to 10 O.R. joined between 24th and 26th.	
"	29		In camp at CITADEL resting. In afternoon Bn. marched to GROVETOWN Station and entrained at 4.2 p.m. Detrained at LONGPRÉ at 11.0 p.m. and marched via FONTAINE to billets at SOREL.	
SOREL	30		In Resting in billets at SOREL.	

M. Muter Mee
Lt. Col.
Comdg. 12th Glo'ster Regt.

12th Bn. Gloucester Regiment - Operation Order No. A.4.2/9/16.

The Battalion will relieve the 1st East Surreys in the line tonight, marxhing via MARICOURT AND MARICOURT-BRICQUERTERIE ROAD, thence via road about A.4.d.3.4. leading eastwards into MALTZHORN VALLEY, thence via EXETER TRENCH.

Order of march C. A. B. D.   Platoons at 199 yards distance.

Time of parade - 6.45 p.m.

Dress - Fighting order, haversack with 2 days rations as well as iron rations.   4 Sandbags per man and two Mills Bombs to be carried.   Companies will arrange to have these Bombs detonated ready for issue by 4.0 p.m. this afternoon.

Order of relief - "C" Coy marching via EXETER AND BAMTAM TRENCH will relieve the 1st East Surreys with 2 platoons in front line, taking half of DEVON TRENCH and part of LONELY TRECSHh as indicated to Coy Commander.
This latter part as a temporary measure until relieved by D.C.L.I.   Supporting platoons of "C" Coy will march via LONELY TRENCH and occupy BODMIN SOUTH TRENCH.

"A" Coy will be disposed in BANTAM and DEVON TRENCHES with an overflow, if necessary, in LONELY TRENCH.

N.B   It is to be noted that the limit allotted to the Battalion on the left is the junction of DEVON and LONELY TRENCH except for the temporary occupation of LONELY TRENCH North of that junction alluded to above.

"B" Coy on arrival at GLOUCESTER TRENCH will file into that and occupy it from the extreme right nearly as far as CHUTE TRENCH.

"D" Coy will occupy GLOUCESTER TRENCH from the left of "B" with any overflow in ASSEMBLY TRENCH, leaving EXETER TRENCH clear as far as possible.

H.Q. of the Battalion will be in ASSEMBLY TRENCH where old Devon H.Q. where and in accordance with orders received will not move from that point until the 3rd Objective has been captured.

All ranks are warned to be as economical with water as it may be difficult to get fresh supplies.   All water-bottles will be filled before starting.

Officers Kits and packs will be stacked ready for loading at 5.0 p.m. at this bivouac, but will not be removed by transport until after 6 p.m.

A guard of 1 N.C.O. left behind with transport will be detailed by Major Blennerhassett to remain in charge of kits etc until removal by transport tonight is completed.

(Sd) J. P. Webb.
Lieut & A/Adjt.
12th Bn. Gloucester Regt.

1 P.M.
2/9/16.

OPERATION ORDER No. A.3. - 2nd September 1916.

1. The 95th Bde will take part in the General attack upon the German position south of GUILLEMONT tomorrow 3rd inst and will advance on the left of the 13th Inf. Bde.
   The left of the 5th divn runs through the line from T25.a.35 25 and T26.a1.2.
   The right of the 95th Bde will run through the line from GORDON TRENCH B1.d.9.7.B.1.b.30.50. inclusive to Northern Corner of WEDGE WOOD.
   The D.C.L.I. will be on the left of the 12th Glosters and their right will run from junction of LONELY and DEVON TRENCH through and including cross roads about T.25.c.6.4. point about T.25d.7.9.
   1/Devons will support Glosters the 1/E.Surreys the D.C.L.I.

2. A. and C. Coys will form first two waves of the assault, A. Coy on the right and C. on the left, and will devide the area allotted to 12th Glosters.

3. Objectives. The first objective will be the German trench running S.E. from Cross Roads about T.25c.6.4. on the left. This is expected to be only lightly held and the first wave will pass over this as soon as possible, and reach and deal with dugouts about T.25.c.9.4. indicated to Coy Commanders.
   On right "A" Coy will endeavour to capture M.Gun position about B.1.b.3.7.

4. Barrage for first objective. The baggage will lift off the line of the first German trench at O.3 and will lift off the dugouts and M.Gun position at O plus 10. The barrage will then be maintained in front of captured positions until o plus 50 when it will lift on to second objective.

5. Consolidation. After capture of First Objective, first and second waves will consolidate, assisted by 3rd wave (leading platoons of "B" and "D" Coys) whilst 4th wave (rear platoons of "B" and "D" Coys) occupy Assembly Trenches in font of LONELY TRENCH.

6. Second Objective. The German Trenches from N.E. corner of WEDGE WOOD to point about T.25.d.6.8. - inclusive. The first and second waves will advance on second objective at 9 plus 50 if necessary reinforced by 3rd wave. The bombardment of the 2nd objective will be from O plus 50 to O plus 60 and every endeavour will be made to advance as close to the barrage as possible. A creeping barrage will also be kept up in front of our advance. On arrival at second objective the left Coy will bomb up the "Y" shaped trench running back from the German line and establish a block. The right will get touch with the 13th Brigade on our right. The Barrage will remain in front of second objective from O plus 60 to O plus 120 which time is to be spent in consolidating as far as possible.

7. Third objective. At O plus 120 an advance will be made to the third objective, which is N. corner of Wedge Wood to point where Y trench joins GINCHY ROAD. In order to avoid a wheel, the Artillery have arranged to lift off the GINCHY ROAD gradually from the south, timing the lifts in accordance with the distance troops will have to cover.

8. On arrival at 3rd Objective, patrols will be pushed forward and under cover of these patrols, the line will be established as close to next German Position as possible, this line to be in touch with BDES, on flanks and should run through T.26.c. central to T.20.d.

9. Flares — Flares will be lit

        1. On attaining each objective.
        2. at 7 p.m.
        3. at 6 a.m. next morning.

10. <u>Grenades.</u>   24 Bombers per Coy will each carry 10 Bombs before leaving Bivouacs.   2 Mills Bombs per man will be carried on the man.   "P" Bombs will be issued on the 3rd inst to "B" and "D" Coys for use with dugouts on first objective.   A proportion of Smoke Bombs will also be issued on 3rd inst.

11. <u>Prisoners.</u>   Prisoners will all be sent to Brigade H.Q.s – not more than 10% escort.

12. All Coys will arrange to cut steps in trenches in order to get out of them quickly.

13. Watches will be synchronised tonight and at 11 p.m. tomorrow.

14. BRIGADE headquarters will be in MALTZ HORN TRENCH.

15. BATTALION HEADQUARTERS will be in Assembly Trench near Daniel Alley.

                J.P. Webb.
                  Lt & A/Adjt.
                      12th Glouc. Regt.

2nd September 1916.

OPERATION ORDERS.

24/9/16.

The Battalion will move into Assembly Trenches starting at 6.30 p.m. passing Battalion H.Q.s in the following order:-

        B. D. A. C.

All Companies by platoons at 100 yards distance.

Before moving off Company Commanders will see that each man is equipped with

    (1) Pick and shovel.

    (2) Four Sandbags.

Packs will be carried and will be dumped tomorrow in Assembly Trenches on moving foward.

Each Company will arrange to carry sufficient Mills Bombs in boxes to equip each man with two, with the exception of Bombers who will carry ten in buckets where possible.

Orders for the attack have been given to Company Commanders. The Battalion is in Brigade reserve and will follow and support the D.C.L.I. in their attack on the 3rd objective, the village of MORVAL, and will form a defensive right or southern flank of that village.

The Corp Commander has notified the Divisional Commander that the 5th Division will be the first to be relieved and that at the earliest possible moment after the action tomorrow the 25th inst.

It is notified for information that one Zeppelin Airship was brought down over London yesterday and another is reported to have fallen into the sea near Dover.

Water Bottles will be filled. Waterproof sheets will be carried and 120 S.AA. Unexpired rations for the 25th as well as rations for the 26th will be carried in adition to Iron Rtion.

It is notified for information that the following have been awarded the Military Medal for their conduct during the recent operations in the taking of WEDGE WOOD.

    Sgt A. Hammond.   Sgt L. Hughes.
    L/Sgt W.L. Gage.   L/C Boobyer.
    L/C W. Yacomini.   Pte W.E. Dunsford.
        Pte F.G. Taylor.

            (Sd) J. P Webb.
                Lt & A/Adjt.
                  12th Bn. Glouc. Regt.

Gloucesters.   3/9/16

Following from General Rawlinson begins.

Please convey to 5th Division my congratulations and thanks on their success today against FALFEMONT FARM AND LEUZE WOOD. They deserve very great credit for the energy and vigour they have shewn especially after the wi failure of their first attack at FALFEMONT.

5th Division.

G.B.978.

The G.O.C. wishes to thanks all ranks in the Division for their magnificent ^conduct yesterday.

In spite of their heavy losses in previous actions and the hardships which they have endured during the recent bad weather they have shown that their spirit is as good as ever.

No task is too hard for the 5th Division.

R. A. Currir
Lt-Col.
General Staff, 5th Division.

5th Division.
26th September.

Fourth Army No.359(G).

5th Division.

The conspicuous part that has been taken by the 5th Division in the Battle of the SOMME reflects the highest credit on the Division as a whole, and I desire to express to every Officer, N.C.O. and man my congratulations and warmest thanks.

The heavy fighting in DELVILLE WOOD and LONGUEVAL, the attack and capture of the FALFEMONT FARM line and LEUZE WOOD, and finally the storming of MORVAL, are feats of arms seldom equalled in the annals of the British Army. They constitute a record of unvarying success which it has been the lot of few Divisions to attain, and the gallantry, valour, and endurance of all ranks have been wholly admirable.

The work of the Divisional Artillery in establishing the barrages and supporting the Infantry attacks is deserving of the highest praise and proves that a very high standard of training has been reached.

It is a matter of great regret to me that the Division is leaving the Fourth Army, but after three strenuous periods in the battle front they have more than earned a rest.

In wishing all ranks good fortune for the future, I trust I may one day have this fine Division again under my command.

Rawlinson

H.Q., Fourth Army,
30th September, 1916.

General,
Commanding Fourth Army.

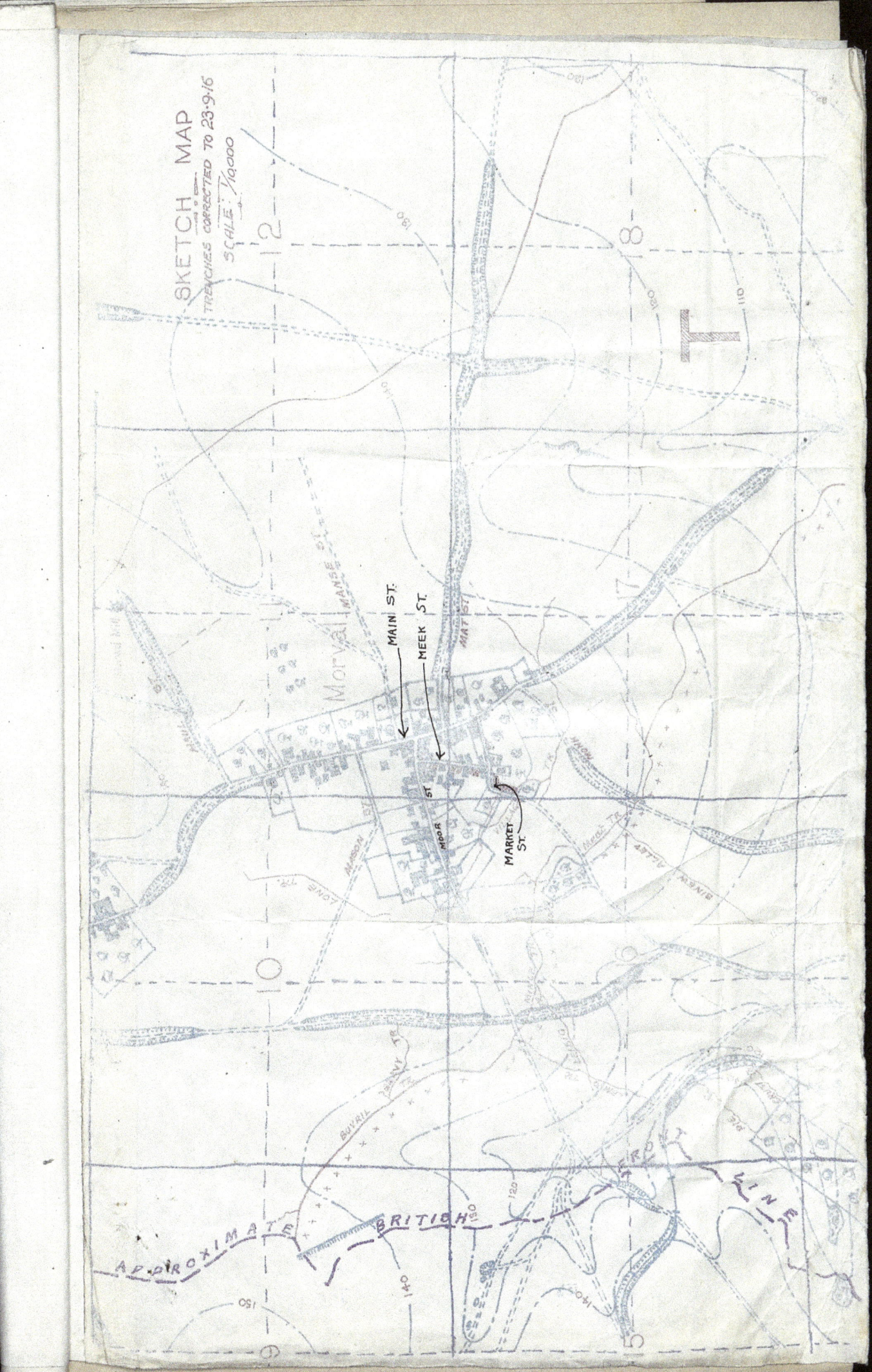

95th Brigade.
5th Division.

12th BATTALION

GLOUCESTERSHIRE REGIMENT

OCTOBER 1916

WAR DIARY
INTELLIGENCE SUMMARY
(Erase heading not required.)

Army Form C. 2118

1/12/ Gloucester Regt

October 1916

Vol 12

K.11

Place	Date	Hour	Summary of Events and Information	Remarks and references to Appendices
SOREL	1st		In rest billets. At 10.30 pm Bn marched to Pont Remy and entrained	
BETHUNE	2nd	7 am	Bn detrained at Chocques and marched into Billets at BETHUNE. 3½ miles	
Do	3rd		In rest Billets	
Do	4th		In rest Billets	
Do	5th	11 am	Bn marched via La Bassée Canal Banks to relieve 18th DLI in Givenchy Village line. 6 miles. No casualties. Weather fine	
GIVENCHY Section	6		In Village line	
Do	7		In Village line	
Do	8		In Village line } Casualties nil - weather fine	
Do	9		In Village line	
Do	10		In Village line	
			On 10th Bn relieved 1st Devons in Givenchy Right Sub Section N. Bank of Canal. Lt. Col. Archer Shee DSO took over command of 95th Inf Bde. during absence on leave of B.G.C.	
Do	11		In front line } No casualties	
Do	12		In front line } No casualties	
Do	13		In front line } No casualties	
Do	14		Bn was relieved by 1/DCLI and marched to reserve billets in Le Quesnoy.	

Army Form C. 2118

WAR DIARY
or
INTELLIGENCE SUMMARY
(Erase heading not required.)

12 Glouc R. October 1916

Place	Date	Hour	Summary of Events and Information	Remarks and references to Appendices
Le Quesnoy	15		In reserve Billets. Bombers Lewis Gunners	
Do	16		Do Snipers &c under training	
Do	17		Do	
Do	18		Bn. relieved 1/D.C.L.I. in Givenchy Right Sub Section. No casualties	
Givenchy Right S. Section	19		Holding front line. No casualties	
	20		Do Do 1 O.R. Killed. Lt. Col. Archer Shee returned to Bn.	
	21		Do Do No casualties	
Village Line	22		Bn. was relieved by 1/DCLI and moved into support in Village Line.	
	23		In support Line. No casualties	
	24		Do	
	25		Do	
	26		Bn. after relief by 1/Devons in Village line relieved 1/DCLI in front line. Givenchy Right Subsection. No casualties	
Givenchy Right Sub Section	27		In front line. No casualties	
	28		Do	
	29		Do	
	30		Bn. was relieved by 1/D.C.LI. and marched to reserve Billets at Le Quesnoy. 1. O.R. Killed	

WAR DIARY
or
INTELLIGENCE SUMMARY

Army Form C. 2118

1/5 Glouc Regt   October 1916

Place	Date	Hour	Summary of Events and Information	Remarks and references to Appendices
LE QUESNOY	31		In same billets. Specialist training. Bn. at fatigues and Coy drill.	

W.R.Flewenkeket
Major
5/12 Glouc/Regt

95th Brigade.
5th Division.

12th BATTALION

GLOUCESTERSHIRE REGIMENT

NOVEMBER 1 9 1 6

Army Form C. 2118.

WAR DIARY
INTELLIGENCE SUMMARY.
(Erase heading not required.)

12th Bn GLOUCESTERSHIRE REGT

Vol 13

K.12

Place	Date	Hour	Summary of Events and Information	Remarks and references to Appendices
Le Quesnoy	1st	—	In Reserve } Bn. at Company Drill, musketry and General Training	
D^o	2nd	—	In Reserve }	
D^o	3rd	8.30 am	Bn marched via S. bank of LA BASSEE CANAL and relieved 1/ D.C.L.I. in CUINCHY LEFT (formerly GIVENCHY RIGHT) sub-section. No casualties.	
Cuinchy Left S. Section	4th	2 am	An enemy raiding party entered our trenches between the two left posts of our left Coy (C. Coy) and surprised a party working there. Before our men could use their rifles they were clubbed and the enemy then proceeded to bomb along the trench towards a post on the right. The man who was working the Lewis Gun on this post was killed by a bomb but the gun was saved. The enemy retired immediately our supports came up and were fired on by our Lewis Guns as they crossed No Mans Land. Our casualties 1 killed 3 missing believed prisoners and 4 wounded. Enemy casualties unknown.	

Army Form C. 2118.

WAR DIARY
INTELLIGENCE SUMMARY.
(Erase heading not required.)

/12 Gloucestershire Regt
November 1916

Place	Date	Hour	Summary of Events and Information	Remarks and references to Appendices
CUINCHY Left S. Section	5th	—	In front line. Weather wet. Casualties nil. Nothing of importance to report	
	6th	—	Do Do Do	
	7th	—	Do Do Do	
CUINCHY Outpost Line	8th	—	was relieved by 1/9 C.L.I. and moved into Village Support line.	
	9th	—	In village line. Bn. holding keeps of CUINCHY VILLAGE LINE	
	10	—	Do Do Do	
	11	2 pm	Bn. relieved 1/9.C.L.I. in front line. CUINCHY LEFT S SECTION	
			At 2 pm Bn. no casualties	
CUINCHY LEFT S SECTION	12	—	In front line. Trenches required a considerable amount of attention owing to wet weather	
	13	—	Do Do Situation normal	
	14	—	Do Do No casualties	
	15	9 am	Bn. was relieved by 1/8.O.L.I. and marched via S. Bank of LA BASSEE CANAL to reserve billets at LE QUESNOY	
			No casualties	

Army Form C. 2118.

WAR DIARY
INTELLIGENCE SUMMARY.
(Erase heading not required.)

1/2th Bn GLOUCESTERSHIRE REGT.
NOVEMBER 1916

Place	Date	Hour	Summary of Events and Information	Remarks and references to Appendices
LE QUESNOY	16		In reserve billets } Bn. engaged in training. Company drill	
"	17		In reserve billets } musketry and Anti-Gas measures practised	
"	18		In reserve billets	
"	19	8.30a	Bn. marched via LA BASSEE CANAL and relieved 1/D.C.L.I in CUINCHY LEFT S.Section. No casualties	
CUINCHY LEFT S.SECTION	20		In front line. Lt.Col. R.I. RAWSON attached from 1/6 A. and S. Highlanders to command Battn. No casualties	
"	21		In front line. Weather dull. No casualties. Enemy artillery	
"	22		– do – and Trench mortar activity less than usual. No casualties	
"	23		Bn. was relieved by 1/D.C.L.I and moved into CUINCHY village outpost line. No casualties	
CUINCHY VILLAGE SUPPORT LINE	24		In village line. No casualties. Nothing to report	
"	25	2/pm	Bn. was relieved by 2/Sherwood Foresters (8 DIV N) and marched to rest billets at ESSARS	
ESSARS	26		In rest billets. Classes formed, inspections carried out and training commenced.	

Army Form C. 2118.

WAR DIARY
~~INTELLIGENCE SUMMARY~~
(Erase heading not required.)

12th Bn GLOUCESTERSHIRE REGT

NOVEMBER 1916

Instructions regarding War Diaries and Intelligence Summaries are contained in F. S. Regs., Part II. and the Staff Manual respectively. Title pages will be prepared in manuscript.

Place	Date	Hour	Summary of Events and Information	Remarks and references to Appendices
ESSARS	27	—	Resting in billets, musketry instruction classes	
Do	28	—	and classes for N.C.Os formed. Specialist classes	
Do	29	—	in ~~gas~~ anti-gas measures, musketry &c. Training continued	
ESSARS	30	—	Do	

W Miurn Lt. Col.
Cg 12th Bn Gloucestershire Regt

95th Brigade.
5th Division.

12th BATTALION

GLOUCESTERSHIRE REGIMENT

DECEMBER 1 9 1 6

Army Form C. 2118

WAR DIARY
INTELLIGENCE SUMMARY
(Erase heading not required.)

12th Gloucestershire Regt.
December 1916

K.13

Place	Date	Hour	Summary of Events and Information	Remarks and references to Appendices
ESSARS	1st	—	Bn. in reserve Billets (95th Bde being in S/Div. Reserve).	
	2		Platoon & Coy. Drill musketry. Gas Helmet drill carried	
	3		on. Specialists at training under specialist officers	
	4			
	5	10 am	Bn. relieved 1st Bedfords (6th Bde) in FERME du BOIS Left S Section	
Ferme du Bois Left.	6		Weather dull. no casualties	
	7		In front line. No casualties. Nothing of importance to report	
"	8		In front line. Weather dull. no casualties	
"	9	9 am	In front line. Nothing to report.	
			Bn. was relieved by 1/D.C.L.I. and moved into support Billets	
CROIX BARBEE	10		at CROIX BARBEE. No casualties	
	11		In Support. No casualties	
	12		In Support. Nothing to report	
	13	9 am	In support. No casualties. Nothing to report.	
			Bn. relieved 1/D.C.L.I. in Ferme du Bois Left S Section. Relief	
Ferme du Bois Left.	14		carried out smoothly. No casualties. Nothing to report	
			At 4·40 am a heavy minenwerfer burst on our parapet and killed or wounded 5 men of a Lewis Gun Team (continued)	

Army Form C. 2118

WAR DIARY
—or—
INTELLIGENCE SUMMARY

(Erase heading not required.)

1/2 Gloucestershire Regt
December 1916

Place	Date	Hour	Summary of Events and Information	Remarks and references to Appendices
Ferme du Bois	14		Two men were blown completely out of the trench and bodies were recovered by Coy. Mikens.	
"	15		In front line. Nothing of importance to report	
"	16		In front line. No casualties	
"	17		Bn. was relieved by 1/D.C.L.I. and moved into Bde Support Billets at CROIX BARBEE. No casualties. Lt Col RAWSON took command of 95 Bde during absence of Brigadier on leave. MAJOR NAR BLENNERHASSETT assumed command of Bn.	
CROIX BARBEE	18		In support billets. Training continued as far as possible	
"	19		Specialists under respective Coy. Officers and remainder of	
"	20		Bn. under respective Coy. Officers. Nothing of importance to report. No casualties	
"	21	11 am	Bn. was relieved by 13th K.R.R. (37 Divn) and marched to CROIX MARMUSE. about 5 miles. No casualties	
CROIX MARMUSE	22		Bn. marched via LOCON to BETHUNE and billeted in ECOLE des JEUNES FILLES. 95th Bde in 5/Divl. reserve.	

Army Form C. 2118

WAR DIARY
INTELLIGENCE SUMMARY
(Erase heading not required.)

12 Bn. Gloucestershire Regt

December 1916

Place	Date	Hour	Summary of Events and Information	Remarks and references to Appendices
BETHUNE	23		In reserve Billets. Musketry, Bayonet fighting and training generally continued except on Xmas day. Draft of 51 O.R. joined 26th Decr. all trained men. 2/Lts. BRADBURY, IRELAND and CULPIN joined 23rd	
"	24			
"	25			
"	26			
"	27			
"	28			
GIVENCHY LEFT.	29	1 pm	Bn relieved 14 R. War. Regt (13 Bde) in GIVENCHY left sector. Weather dull. No casualties.	
	30		In front line. Nothing to report. No casualties.	
	31		In front line.	

W. M. Wheeuhurst
Major
Cg. 12/Glouc. Regt.

5th Division
95th Infy Bde

12th Bn Glosters
Jan ~~Dec 1917~~
JAN 1917 to 1917 NOV

(ITALY)

Army Form C. 2118

WAR DIARY
INTELLIGENCE SUMMARY
(Erase heading not required.)

1/3th Bn. Gloucestershire Regt. January 1915 Vol 1.

Place	Date	Hour	Summary of Events and Information	Remarks and references to Appendices
GIVENCHY LEFT	1		In front line Gv. LEFT Sub sector. No casualties. Weather dull.	
" "	2		Bn. was relieved in front line by 1/ D.C.L.I. and moved into reserve billets at GORRE. No casualties	
GORRE	3		In reserve billets - GORRE. Weather fine. No casualties	
" "	4		Do - Do - Do - Do	
" "	5		In reserve billets. Nothing to report. No casualties	
" "	6		Bn. handed over billets at GORRE to 1/Devons and marched to relieve 1/D.C.L.I. in GIVENCHY LEFT Front line. No casualties	
GIVENCHY LEFT	7		In front line. Weather dull. Nothing to report	
	8		In front line. Enemy artillery active. No casualties. Weather dull and wet.	
	9		In front line. Nothing to report. No casualties	
	10		Bn. was relieved by 1/D.C.L.I. and moved into GIVENCHY support line. One O.R. wounded.	
GIVENCHY SUPPORT	11		In support line. Weather dull. No casualties. Nothing to report.	
	12		In support line. Nothing to report.	

Army Form C. 2118

WAR DIARY

12th Bn. Gloucester Regt. January 1917

INTELLIGENCE SUMMARY

(Erase heading not required.)

Instructions regarding War Diaries and Intelligence Summaries are contained in F. S. Regs., Part II. and the Staff Manual respectively. Title Pages will be prepared in manuscript.

Place	Date	Hour	Summary of Events and Information	Remarks and references to Appendices
GIVENCHY SUPPORT LINE	13	-	In village (Support) line. No casualties. Nothing to report.	
	14	-	Bn. was relieved by 2/KOSB and marched to BETHUNE. Brigade in reserve. No casualties.	
BETHUNE	15		19th Brigade in Divl. Reserve. Bn. at Platoon & drill, musketry, Physical training etc. Specialists being trained under out Officers. Lectures and Recreational training generally.	
-"-	16			
-"-	17			
-"-	18			
-"-	19			
-"-	20			
-"-	21			
-"-	22		Bn. marched from BETHUNE and relieves 1/NORFOLKS (15th Bde) in CUINCHY RIGHT SECTOR. S. of LA BASSÉE CANAL. No casualties. Enemy	
CUINCHY RIGHT S. SECTOR	23		artillery and T.M's. fairly active. Weather cold. In front line. Nothing to report. No casualties	
-Do-	24		In front line. Enemy artillery active. One heavy shell near Bn. H.Q. No casualties.	
-D°-	25		In front line. No casualties. Enemy quiet. Nothing to report.	

WAR DIARY

INTELLIGENCE SUMMARY

1/2 Glouc. Regt No.

January 1917

Army Form C. 2118

Place	Date	Hour	Summary of Events and Information	Remarks and references to Appendices
CUINCHY RIGHT.	26		Bn. relieved by 1/D.C.L.I and marched to reserve billets at LE QUESNOY. No casualties. Relief completed about 2 pm except 1 "B" Coy which could not be relieved until after dark. No casualties.	
LE QUESNOY	27		In Brigade Reserve. Training to report. No casualties.	
— —	28		In Brigade Reserve. Training continued as/as as	
— —	29		In Brigade Reserve Training. Nothing of importance to report	
— —	30		Bn. handed over reserve billets to 1/DEVONS and marched to relieve 1/D.C.L.I in CUINCHY RIGHT SECTOR. Weather cold and fine. 2nd Lt. L. MILTON and 1 O.R. wounded by "MINNENWERFER". Enemy quiet.	
CUINCHY RIGHT	31		In front line. 1 O.R. wounded. Enemy quiet. Snowing.	

M. Arthur

Lt Colonel
Comg 1/2th Gloucester Regt.

Army Form C. 2118.

WAR DIARY

INTELLIGENCE SUMMARY. 12th Bn. GLOUCESTER Regt.

(Erase heading not required.) FEBRUARY, 1917.

Vol 16

Place	Date	Hour	Summary of Events and Information	Remarks and references to Appendices
CUINCHY RIGHT	1		In front line. No casualties. Weather cold and fine. Nothing to report.	
"	2		In front line. 1 O.R. Wounded. Weather cold. Situation quiet.	
"	3		1 O.R. Wounded. Weather cold. Bn. was relieved by 1/D.C.L.I. and were into Village Outpost line.	
CUINCHY SUPPORT LINE	4		In support. 'C' Coy remained in CUINCHY. Keep in support to 1/DCLI. No casualties. Nothing to report.	
"	5		In support. Situation quiet. No casualties.	
"	6		In support. Situation quiet during day. Some enemy artillery activity during night on account of raid by 1/D.C.L.I. No casualties.	K.15
"	7		Bn. relieved 1/D.C.L.I. in CUINCHY RIGHT, FRONT LINE. No casualties. Nothing to report.	
CUINCHY RIGHT	8		In CUINCHY RIGHT FRONT. Enemy artillery active at dusk. Weather cold and fine.	1 O.R. killed 2 O.R. wounded

2353 Wt. W3514/1454 700,000 5/15 D. D. & L. A.D.S.S./Forms/C. 2118.

Army Form C. 2118.

WAR DIARY
or
INTELLIGENCE SUMMARY.
(Erase heading not required.)

12th Bn Gloucestershire Regt February 1917 (contd)

Place	Date	Hour	Summary of Events and Information	Remarks and references to Appendices
CUINCHY RIGHT	9		In front line. No casualties. Nothing to report	
"	10		In front line. 1 O.R. killed. 2 O.R. wounded. Enemy artillery active. Weather cold fine	
	11		Bn. was relieved by 1/D.C.L.I. and marched to reserve billets at LE QUESNOY. No casualties. Nothing to report.	
Reserve LE QUESNOY	12		In reserve billets. Bn cleaning up, bathing and training	
Do	13		Do No casualties. Nothing to report.	
Do	14		Do	
	15		Bn relieved 1/D.C.L.I. in CUINCHY RIGHT SECTOR FRONT LINE. Situation quiet. No casualties.	
CUINCHY RIGHT	16		In front line. Enemy artillery + T.M.S. active. 1 O.R. killed and 1 O.R. wounded by Rifle Grenade. Weather cold	
	17		In front line. Situation quiet. Nothing to report	
	18		In front line. No casualties. Situation normal. Nothing to report	

Army Form C. 2118.

1st Bn Gloucester Regt

February 1917

WAR DIARY
or
INTELLIGENCE SUMMARY.
(Erase heading not required.)

Instructions regarding War Diaries and Intelligence Summaries are contained in F.S. Regs., Part II. and the Staff Manual respectively. Title pages will be prepared in manuscript.

Place	Date	Hour	Summary of Events and Information	Remarks and references to Appendices
CUINCHY RIGHT	19		Bn. was relieved by 1/D.C.L.I. in front line and moved into Village Support line. No casualties. Nothing to report. 'A' Co proceeded to OBLINGHEM	Draft 101 joined
"	20		In Village Support line. No casualties. Weather warmer. Nothing to report	
"	21		Do Do No casualties. Nothing to report	
"	22		Do Do 1 O.R. wounded by M.O. fire. Situation normal	
"	23		Weather dull & wet	
"			Bn relieved 1/D.C.L.I. in front line. Trenches in very bad state owing to thaw & wet. No casualties. Situation quiet	
"	24		In front line. 1 O.R. wounded. Nothing to report	
"	25		In front line. 2 O.R. wounded (T.M.) Enemy artillery active otherwise situation normal. LT. COL. M. ARCHER SHEE. D.S.O. proceeded on leave prior to relinquishing command of the Battn	
"	26		In front line. Situation quiet. No casualties	
"	27		Bn. was relieved in front line by 1/D.C.L.I. and marched to reserve billets at LE QUESNOY. 1 O.R. wounded. A Coy still at OBLINGHEM. No casualties. Nothing to report	1 Officer 55 O.R. joined
LE QUESNOY	28		In reserve. Training continued. No casualties. Nothing to report	

J.H. Major
O.C. 1st Bn 1st Regt

Army Form C. 2118

98

12th Bn Gloucestershire Regt
March 1917

WAR DIARY
of
INTELLIGENCE SUMMARY
(Erase heading not required.)

Instructions regarding War Diaries and Intelligence Summaries are contained in F.S. Regs., Part II. and the Staff Manual respectively. Title Pages will be prepared in manuscript.

Vol 17

K.16

Place	Date	Hour	Summary of Events and Information	Remarks and references to Appendices
LE QUESNOY	1		In reserve. No casualties. Nothing to report.	
"	2		In reserve. No casualties. Weather fine. Nothing to report.	
"	3	8.30 am	Bn. marched via LA BASSEE CANAL and relieved 1/D.C.L.I. in CUINCHY RIGHT SECTOR - front line. No casualties. Weather fine.	
CUINCHY RIGHT	4		In front line. 2 O.R. wounded (1 at duty). Enemy T.M's active. Situation otherwise normal.	
"	5		'A' Coy carried out a successful raid on enemy trenches between A.22.A.0 and A.22.a.10.40. The raiding party entered enemy trenches at 5 a.m. and remained there until 5.20 a.m. Two prisoners were captured and 6 were known to have been killed whilst it is estimated that about 50 others were killed in the dugouts, which were blown in by means of mobile charges. Our casualties were 1/Lt. E.A. BRADBURY and 3 O.R. slightly wounded, 1 O.R. wounded and 2 O.R. wounded at duty. Enemy retaliation feeble. During the day enemy T.M's were active and 1 O.R. was killed and 1 O.R. wounded.	

Army Form C. 2118.

WAR DIARY
or
INTELLIGENCE SUMMARY.
(Erase heading not required.)

12th Gloucester Regt
March 1917

Place	Date	Hour	Summary of Events and Information	Remarks and references to Appendices
CUINCHY	6th		In front line. Situation normal. Nothing to report	
RIGHT	7		Bn was relieved by 1/1 D.C.L.I. and moved into CUINCHY VILLAGE. Support line. Nothing to report. Weather fine	
-"-	8		In support line. Situation normal. Nothing to report	
-"-	9		In support line.	
-"-	10		In support line	
-"-	11		Bn relieved 1/D.C.L.I. in front line. Weather wet and trenches in bad condition. 2 O.R. killed and 2 O.R. wounded by minenwerfers which were active on this day	
-"-	12		In front line. Situation quiet. Party of 4/E LANCS (T.F.) 198th Bde. attached for 24 hrs instruction. 1 O.R. slightly wounded by Rifle Grenade. Nothing to report. Party of 9/Manchesters, T.F. 198th Bde. attached	
-"-	13		In front line. Party of 9/Manchesters attached for 24 hrs instruction	
-"-	14		In front line. Guarded party of 9/Manchesters attached for 24 hrs instruction. Situation quiet. Nothing to report.	

WAR DIARY
or
INTELLIGENCE SUMMARY.
(Erase heading not required.)

Army Form C. 2118.

March 1917
12th Gloster Regt

Place	Date	Hour	Summary of Events and Information	Remarks and references to Appendices
CUINCHY RIGHT	15	10 am	Bn. was relieved in front line by 1/DCLI and marched via LA BASSEE CANAL to LE QUESNOY. 1 O.R.(W.O) wounded by rifle fire. Weather fine. Nothing to report.	
LE QUESNOY	16		In reserve. Weather fine. Nothing to report.	
"	17	4 pm	Bn. was relieved by 2/10 Manchesters 198th Bde. and marched to BETHUNE en route for Training Area. Remained one night at BETHUNE	
BETHUNE	18	7 am	Bn. marched via CHOCQUES, ALLOUAGNE to Billets at BORBURE. Weather fine. Lt. Col. R.I. RAWSON assumed Command of Battn. vice Lt. Col. M. ARCHER-SHEE, whose resignation has been accepted (A.S.2 No >3135 of 10/3/17) Casualties NIL	
BORBURE	19		Bn. resting and cleaning up prior to commencing training. Nothing to report	
"	20		Bn. at Training. Practising attack in new formation.	
"	21		Musketry, Physical Training and Bayonet fighting	
"	22		Lewis Gunners, Bombers and other specialists under respective officers.	

Army Form C. 2118.

WAR DIARY
or
INTELLIGENCE SUMMARY.
(Erase heading not required.)

March 1917. 12 Glouc.r Regt

Place	Date	Hour	Summary of Events and Information	Remarks and references to Appendices
BURBURE	23		Battalion in rest billets. Training continued.	
-"-	24		Attack in new formation. Grenade practice (especially	
-"-	25		with Rifle Grenades) Bayonet training. Physical	
-"-	26		Training and Musketry on range	
-"-	27			
-"-	28			
-"-	29		Training continued. 7/Lt. E.M.T BURGES and 1 O.R. accidentally	
			wounded by premature explosion of bomb. 2/Lt. W.T MERRELL	
			and 93 O.R. joined as reinforcements	
-"-	30		Training continued. Weather dull. Nothing to report	
-"-	31		do. do.	

31/3/17

R.Y. Harman Lt. Col.
C.g. 12/ Glouc Regt

12th BATTN GLOUCESTERSHIRE REGIMENT

95th INFANTRY BRIGADE

5th DIVISION

APRIL 1917

Army Form C. 2118.

WAR DIARY of 12th Bn. GLOUCESTERSHIRE REGT.
INTELLIGENCE SUMMARY.
(Erase heading not required.)

April 1917 Vol 18

K.17

Place	Date	Hour	Summary of Events and Information	Remarks and references to Appendices
BURBURE	1st		In rest billets - training.	
Do	2		Do	
Do	3		Do	
Do	4		Do	
Do	5		Do	
Do	6		Do — Battalion practising attack. Rifle Grenadiers and Bombers, Lewis Gunners and other specialists in training under respective Specialist Officers. No casualties. Nothing to report.	
RUITZ	7	8am	Bn marched via LOZINGHEM, MARLES les MINES and HAILLICOURT to RUITZ en-route for forward area. Weather fine. No casualties. 8 miles	
BOIS des ALLEUX	8	4.30/-	Bn. marched to Bois des ALLEUX. W. of MONT St ELOY and billeted in huts. 15 miles. No casualties.	
Do	9		In huts. Brigade in Reserve to Canadian Corps. No casualties. Weather cold with frequent rain and snow storms. Nothing to report	
Do	10			
Do	11			
Do	12			
Do	13			

Army Form C. 2118.

WAR DIARY of the 12th Bn Gloucestershire
— or —
INTELLIGENCE SUMMARY. 12th Bn Gloucestershire Regt.

(Erase heading not required.)

Page 2   April 1917

Place	Date	Hour	Summary of Events and Information	Remarks and references to Appendices
Bois de ALLEUX — QUARRIES N.E. of SOUCHEZ	14th		At midnight 13th/14th Battalion marched via MONT ST ELOY and CABARET ROUGE to QUARRIES (S&u 3.7) relieving Support Battn of 10th Canadian Bde. Enemy shelled track during relief. 1 O.R. being killed. Bn in Support. Parties found for carrying water &c. to front line to Devons and 1/D.C.L.I. 1 O.R. killed, 3 O.R. wounded. 34 O.R. joined as reinforcements. Weather fine.	
Do	15		In support. Enemy artillery fairly quiet. 3 O.R. wounded. Weather wet. Carrying parties as on 14th.	
Do	16		In support. Little activity. No casualties. Weather fairly fine. Carrying parties found as on 14th.	
Do	17		Battn marched forward in afternoon and took up positions in the old German trenches running through S.E. Corner of BOIS de l'HIRONDELLE + VIMY – ANGRES LINE, being still Battn in Support. Enemy shelled heavily with shrapnel. No casualties.	

Army Form C. 2118.

WAR DIARY 1st Gloucestershire Regt.
or
INTELLIGENCE SUMMARY.
(Erase heading not required.)

April 1917

Place	Date	Hour	Summary of Events and Information	Remarks and references to Appendices
In Trenches Bois de L'Hirondelle	18		Bn still in support. Large working parties found. Forbidon heavily shelled with H.E. and shrapnel. 10 O.R. Wounded. Weather dull and wet	
Do	19		In support until dusk when Battn relieved 1/D.C.L.I. in front line. Bn not heavily shelled during relief. 4 O.R. wounded. Outpost line running from SOUCHEZ RIVER S.E. through CITE des PETITS BOIS, with strong points in front held by 'A' and 'B' Coy: C & D Coy held main line of resistance about 300 yards in rear of A + B Coy	
Do	20		In front line. Heavy enemy shelling. 7 O.R. killed. 15 O.R. wounded. 5 O.R. joined as reinforcements	
Do	21		In front line shelling continued. 5 O.R. killed. 13 O.R. wounded	
Do	22		D Coy relieved A Coy on night of 21st. A Coy relieving to main line Forbidon wreckled by D Coy. Heavy enemy shelling. 2/Lt C.J. RUTLAND wounded. 5 O.R. killed. 13 O.R. wounded. (continued next page)	

WAR DIARY
INTELLIGENCE SUMMARY.
(Erase heading not required.)

Army Form C. 2118.

1/2th Gloucester Regt. April

Place	Date	Hour	Summary of Events and Information	Remarks and references to Appendices
In trenches Bois de L'HIRONDELLE	22		During night of 22 and 23rd D.C.L.I. and Devons took up positions in front of our line.	
Do	23		At 4:45 am D.C.L.I. and Devons attacked - this Bn being in support. Our front heavily shelled during day. Casualties 4 O.R. killed, 12 O.R. wounded. Night of 23rd - "C" Coy. relieved "B" Coy in Quarry. "B" Coy retiring to positions vacated by "D" Coy. D.C.L.I. were relieved by 1/4 R Warkgt and 1Devons by 1/E Devons.	
Do	24		Enemy was active until dusk when "C" Coy was heavily shelled. 1 O.R. wounded. Batn was relieved by 47 Bn Canadian and marched to huts at NIAGARA CAMP, BOIS de la HAIE, arriving 3 am 25th.	
NIAGARA CAMP BOIS	25		Battalion resting, bathing & report	
	26		Baths and inspections. Cleaning up general, bathing & report	
	27		Baths in morning. Parade and address by O.C. in afternoon.	
	28		Training continued. Musketry, bombing and B. fighting	

2/Lt. R.C. Cox joined Battn.

Army Form C. 2118.

WAR DIARY
or
INTELLIGENCE SUMMARY.

12th Gloucester Regt April 1917

(Erase heading not required.)

Place	Date	Hour	Summary of Events and Information	Remarks and references to Appendices
NIAGARA CAMP	29		Church Parade in morning remainder of day for recreation. Battalion training continued. Nothing to report. In afternoon Bn. marched to PETIT SERVINS and billeted. Weather fine.	
	30			

R. Rawson Lt Col
O/C 12th Bn Glou Regt

WAR DIARY

12th Bn Gloucestershire Regt.

INTELLIGENCE SUMMARY

Army Form C. 2118.

Place	Date	Hour	Summary of Events and Information	Remarks and references to Appendices
PETIT SERVIN	1/5/17		Battalion in billets. Training. 2/Lieut Bradbury wounded while instructing in bombing together with 4 other ranks.	
"	2/5/17		In billets. Training. Open warfare scheme. Boussey Woods. 2 OR joined as reinforcement	
"	3/5/17		Battalion marched at 12 noon to Kivsac near MAISON BLANCHE. 9 miles. Hutchest. Transport marched to camp in X Road F.23.a.5.5. about square 52 NE	
E. of FRESNOY	4/5/17		Battalion relieved 1st Canadian Batt. after dark in the lines East of FRESNOY which the latter captured the day before. A difficult relief as he could not be reached in daylight. Approached by way of Railway. Relief complete at 1.30am on 5th. B Coy on right, D Coy on left, A Coy in Support North of FRESNOY Park & C Coy in reserve with Batt H.Q. in ARLEUX LOOP. 1E SURREYS on the right & 19th Canadian Batt. on left. Heavy shelling all night. Transport Camp shelled with H.V. shells. 2 OR Transport moved to ECURIE. wounded	K.18

12th Batt. Gloucestershire Regt.
Army Form C. 2118.

WAR DIARY
INTELLIGENCE SUMMARY.
(Erase heading not required.)

MAY 1917

Place	Date	Hour	Summary of Events and Information	Remarks and references to Appendices
Trenches E. of FRESNOY	5.5.17		Enemy continued to shell on the keyboards during the day & put down a heavy barrage on the front & support lines at 8 p.m. B Co seeing large numbers of enemy preparing to attack sent up the S.O.S signal. Our artillery were effective & thinned & never developed. Much work was done improving the line during the night & a push was effected by the leaders & no left with on front line which had been in the air. Lieut IRELAND killed by shell fire during S.O.S. 10 O.R. killed 3 O.R. missing 9 wounded. Shelling continued all night.	
Trenches E of FRESNOY	6.5.17		Enemy shelling although quieter was still continuous. Enemy aeroplanes were very busy. Two machines with photographs & reconnaissance on line which a quarter of an hour up to party of the enemy put down a heavy barrage at 6 p.m. & later. JEUNE was wounded by a sniper (and 3 Co) 2 O.R. killed 1 Germ. N.C.O. was captured by D Co this morning. 2 O.R. killed 2 O.R. wounded	

WAR DIARY 12th Bn Gloucestershire Regt   MAY 1917

Army Form C. 2118.

INTELLIGENCE SUMMARY.
(Erase heading not required.)

Place	Date	Hour	Summary of Events and Information	Remarks and references to Appendices
Trenches E. of FRESNOY	7.5.17		Enemy shelled all lines heavily from 3 a.m. onwards & allotted B.H.Q., both judging from heavy trench barrages several times. His aeroplanes also flew over B.H.Q. & the lines between every trench. A.Cy. which was officered by 2 men only, & the men brought into shelters in rear of it. Lieut. FitzGerald went up to take charge of B.Cy., & Captn. W.W. Parr came up from transport lines to take command of A.Cy. A.Cy. relieved B.Cy. during the night & C.Cy. relieved D.Cy. Brigad. H.Qrs were warned that an attack was expected & all artillery were warned to stand by. The enemy relief complete 1.30 a.m. & D.Cy. arrived at B.H.Q. 3.30 a.m. & 2/Lieut Digby (killed) by a shell & wounded & 2/Lt Connell slightly wounded during evening	
Trenches E. of FRESNOY	8.5.17		Rain fell all about midnight. At 3.45 a.m. a very heavy barrage started on all lines & Batt.H.Q. There was a thick mist making observation at 50 yards difficult. S.O.S. was repeated at once by H.Qrs. & observers as long there was an on front & S.O.S. was	

WAR DIARY 12th Bn. GLOUCESTERSHIRE REGT.

INTELLIGENCE SUMMARY. MAY 1917

Place	Date	Hour	Summary of Events and Information	Remarks and references to Appendices
Trenches E. FRESNOY			Sent through to Brigade & Wilking by telephone. The enemy attacked in force, & they afterwards had to hand through the 5th Gloucesters sent in that quarter. When darkness had first arrived, the remnants of our front line held. Order, whether men made up mainly of B Co, D Co, 1/D E 11 and remains of C Co & B Coy, had been re-covered, but were out to the hotel over to the enemy, having already sent in a large party on both flanks. D Co. men who were found to establish a line & join up with Canadians on left & troops on right in front of Oppy drive & attacked. Eventually the Battalion was relieved by 1/Devons at 10.p.m. The following details marched out of the line with the Battalion. 5 officers & 177 other Ranks. The Battalion went into Huts at NINE ELMS at 1.30 a.m. 9/A. 2/Lt D.N. LEICESTER killed. 2/Lt C.J. HOULSTON, 2/Lt A. METCALF, 2/Lt R.C. COX, 2/Lt C.H. CULPIN, 2/Lt D.D. HERRING MAJOR T.M. ALLISON and 2/Lt J.T. RYDE and 2/Lt G.F. TICEHURST wounded. LT. R.J. FITZGERALD 2/Lt J.T. RYDE wounded and missing. 2/Lt N.T. BURGE, 2/Lt A.W. MERRELL and CAPT. I.V. PARK M.C. missing. 288 O.R. killed wounded & missing. 2/Lt S. REYNOLDS and 2/Lt M.K. MILLARD joined as reinforcements.	

WAR DIARY 12th Bn. GLOUCESTERSHIRE REGT.
INTELLIGENCE SUMMARY.
MAY 1917

Army Form C. 2118.

(Erase heading not required.)

Place	Date	Hour	Summary of Events and Information	Remarks and references to Appendices
NINE ELMS A17c & 9 51 B N.W.	9th		2/Lt. G.B. HALL joined as reinforcement. Battn left NINE ELMS and marched to camp at A28a 9.9	
	10th		Cleaning up and resting. In the afternoon Battn marched to MARŒUIL and billeted. Weather fine, no casualties. About 4 miles.	
MARŒUIL	11		In billets. Repeating cleaning up on first day. Remainder of time occupied in training, Musketry, Bayonet training and specialist work.	
	12			
	13			
	14			
	15			
	16			
	17		One draft of 5 O.R. joined 19th	
	18			
	19			
	20			

WAR DIARY 12th Bn GLOUCESTERSHIRE Regt

INTELLIGENCE SUMMARY.

MAY 1917

Place	Date	Hour	Summary of Events and Information	Remarks and references to Appendices
MARŒUIL	21		Battalion marched to ST AUBIN and billeted. Draft 1 O.R. arrived. Lt MAYNOOD /D.C.L.I. attached for duty as Adjutant. Weather fine.	
ST AUBIN	22		Nothing to report. Battn training carried on. 7 men sent to Army Gas School. Weather wet.	
ST AUBIN	23		Battalion training continued for Mr W REED admitted hospital sick.	
ST AUBIN	24		Battalion training continued. Nothing to report.	
ST AUBIN	25		Training in morning. At 1.30 p.m. Bn marched to camp at LES QUATRE VENTS. L 10 B. Very hot and dusty. Nothing to report.	

WAR DIARY
or
INTELLIGENCE SUMMARY

Army Form C. 2118.

12th Bn Gloucestershire Regt

May 1917

Place	Date	Hour	Summary of Events and Information	Remarks and references to Appendices
LES QUATRE VENTS Glo. B.	26		Training continued in the morning. In the evening working party of 2 Officers and 60 O.R. was found for work under 76 Survey Coy. R.E.	
Do	27		Training continued with all available men. Party of 2 Officers and 100 O.R. found for work this evening.	
Do	28		Training continued as far as possible. Working party of 200 O.R. under 2 Officers sent to R.E. Working park. 2/Lt. C.S. PETHERAM and 4 instructors sent to XIII Corps draft Training depot FLORINGHEM for training duties. Draft 10 O.R. joined Training depot.	
Do	29		Nothing of importance to report. Working party of 2 Officers and 177 O.R. found for work under 176th R.E. in the evening.	

WAR DIARY 12th Bn GLOUCESTERSHIRE REGT

Army Form C. 2118.

INTELLIGENCE SUMMARY

MAY 1917

(Erase heading not required.)

Instructions regarding War Diaries and Intelligence Summaries are contained in F.S. Regs., Part II. and the Staff Manual respectively. Title pages will be prepared in manuscript.

Place	Date	Hour	Summary of Events and Information	Remarks and references to Appendices
Field G.10.b. S. of ROCLINCOURT	30/5/17		Major G.G.H. READE left Bn. for training duties at ROUEN. No casualties. Weather fine except for thunderstorm about 4 p.m. Working party of 2 Off. + 200 O.R. found for work under 176 Coy. R.E.	
Field G.10.b S. of ROCLINCOURT	31/5/17		Weather fine. No casualties. Battalion training continued as for as possible. Working party of 2 Off. + 200 O.R./noon for work under 176 Coy. R.E.	

M Mourron Lt. Col.
Cg 12th Gloucest/Regt

95th Inf Bde.

The following is my report on the enemy's attack on FRESNOY on the 8th inst.

1. During the whole of the 7th inst he had barraged our lines very heavily all day, during which time I constantly called for Artillery Support but got practically none.

2. During the previous day enemy aeroplanes had been all over our lines at a height of 200 feet as reported previously; our aeroplanes did nothing to prevent this.

3. During afternoon of the 7th enemy laid down a practice barrage on front close support Support & 4th & 9th lines which practically obliterated our trenches, especially the front line & support lines. The men were put into shell hole during the day.

4. During the night 7th – 8th I relieved my two front line companies & my dispositions then were A Coy on right, C Coy on left, B Company in Support; D Coy 1/DCLI in reserve in T.30C C Coy 1/DCLI in ARLEUX LOOP in T.29d, both about 60 strong. D Company of this Battn. arrived in ARLEUX LOOP & Sunken Road at Batt. H.Qrs at 3.30 a.m. on relief, having been in 3 nights in front line previously.

5. On evening of 7th I had asked Brigade to warn Corps & Divisional Artillery to be ready from 2 a.m. & was assured by Brigadier that this had been done & we would get every support.

6. About 3.6 a.m. a very heavy barrage was laid on Battalion Hd Qrs & at same moment the Battalion however reported one red rocket but that smoke, dust & mist made it impossible to see lights or anything.
 I myself at once sent through the S.O.S on all lines & on Artillery Line by the Liaison officer.

7. The barrage put up by us was practically NIL. No heavy shells were heard passing over & the Field Artillery barrage was very thin & slow. I called on the Brigade for more but was told they could do no more & the Artillery were not responding.

8. We could hear Lewis Gun & Rifle fire continuously up in front but could see nothing owing to fog & dust etc. It was also raining hard & the ground very muddy.

9. Scouts were sent up to try & get information. The two Companies of D.C.L.I. & D.C.L.I. in Shore shoved two & Bn M.Gs fired a barrage times

10. About 4 a.m. or a little after, having a report from a wounded Sergeant that the enemy were attacking our front line in force & that my support company had moved up under Captain PARR & was holding them, I ordered D Co. /DCLI under Capt. KENDAL to move up in support & if necessary counter attack.

I also ordered C Co. /DCLI to move to the position vacated by DCo. & to be ready to support my left flank.

11. About 4:30 a.m. Capt. Kendal reported to me in person that C. O. 1st Gloucs & a mixed crowd of Canadians were back on top of him & he had formed them in the SUNKEN road running North from 29 b.9.0. to 29 b.9.5. I ordered him to counter attack with his company (D) & my own C. Co. & regain the front line.

2 Wounded Officers of my C Co came in & reported the Canadians on their left had fallen back carrying some of C.Co. with them & gradually the whole Co. had come back. Casualties were heavy.

I could get no information about my right
except that when last seen by wounded men
the O.C. XCo. had been seen but very badly
wounded & had asked how the fourth going
& that Captain Carr was up to fighting on
the front line.

I moved a Platoon of C Co. 1/DCLI into
the Sunken road left empty by Capt Kendal
Many Canadians were passing through Battn
H.Qtrs saying they had been relieved & were
going out. My Adjutant held them up
with a revolver & eventually they went back
towards their own front.

My own DCLI under Major Alison was now
refreshed & I warned it to get ready.

12/ At 6.35 a.m. I received a message from
Captain Kendal saying that front line was
retaken (message in hand) & we were holding
situation on left clear & Canadians holding
on left situation on right not clear. The
counter attack had been held up for a time
by machine gun fire from FRESNOY PARK
which I could not understand as no Germans
were reported to me by Col Gargus as still
holding the front line. I thought it likely
that the enemy had got through the gaps left

by E.Cs. Just Lieut Leicester, Batt. Intelligence Officer with two runners to report situation of Capt Parr.

12. About 7 a.m. rec'd message from Capt. Kendall "Our line is now roughly from T.30.c.8½ running North. We have been forced out of the trenches we occupied. Parties of Canadians keep coming through, but stopping our men. Casualties are getting heavy. Germans appear to be rifling in from FRESNOY wood about T.30.c.9.8 There do not appear to be many Germans in front of us but artillery fire is very heavy. There are plenty of men for immediate action."

Almost on top of this message Capt Kendall himself came in & reported all his people back in the SUNKEN Road he started from. He had enough men to carry on with & it was hopeless counter-attacking without a barrage which we could not get.

14. Capt Kendall reported about 7.30 a.m. that casualties were very heavy & his men shaken & asked for a 2nd company. I ordered Major Allison with D Coy 12/York to advance to SUNKEN Road & make good to the front, & join himself

on the left to Canadians at T 30 b 95
and I now took the Canadian dispositions
from their C.O.

This was done, & at 9.45 Major Allison
reported his Company held up by Machine
Gun fire on line N & South through T 30 Cenhal
& heavily barraged.

15/ At 8 a.m. all wires were cut &
position seemed very serious as I was
informed the E Surreys had fallen back
on APRICOX, I had no news of my own
right except that they had been
surrounded when they stood by both flanks.

I sent a runner message to Col Furgens
asking for all possible assistance &
the heaviest possible barrage on
FRESNOY WOOD & North of it.

I also sent off a Pigeon message which
unfortunately was not addressed, but undersher
it got through in 40 minutes.

It had no result as regards any
artillery fire.

16/ I received a reply from Col Furgens timed
8.20 a.m. to say my message recd & 1 Co
of Devons were behind me in APRICOX
LOOP & request for barrage had been given

17. At this time there were about 130 wounded in the Regt'l 1st Aid Post at Batt. H.Q. including 30 stretcher cases.

18. About 11.30 Major Allison having been previously wounded, my D Company began to fall back & arrived mixed up with OC 4 Canadians in the SUNKEN Road running through T.29.d central in at T.29.d.9.0 west.

I had now no one in front. I rallied Capt. Kendal & his company who had rested while my D Co. were in front to hold the SUNKEN Road from T.29.b.9.5 to b.9.0 40 strong now & C Co. DCLI from there to T.29.d. central will show point on at the little places, while I re-organized the remains of 12 Glos. & got their rifles clean as they were all clogged with mud & men very shaken.

One company of DEVONS in ARLEUX LOOP behind Batt'n H.Q. & 8 Bd'n M. G's along the ARLEUX LOOP.

Shelling was now quieter though it never stopped. By 2 P.M. we had about 150 of 12 Glos. re-organized in 6 Platoons with 3 Lewis guns, my line was firmly established & my left flank joined up & right flank well guarded provided

the heads of D Coy. A Coy was not
attacked from JAGER X.

There was not a single Company Officer
left in 12/Glos. & the Senior S. Officer
was also killed about 11.6 a.

Major Colt arrived up to assist me &
we were able to rest a little.

The position remained thus until evening
when Colonel Blunt of 1/DEVONS arrived to
take over.

An S.O.S. was sent up by Canadians on
our left who reported to have enemy N of
FREZENBERG WOOD. This time we got a
good barrage which broke up any attack.
Barrage was discontinued at 9.15
& at 10 pm the remains of 12/Glos were
relieved by 1/Devons.

19. Before the enemy's infantry attack,
most of the Lewis guns in front line had
been blown up, but two were kept going, in
each case the No. 1 being the only one remaining
of the team. 1 gun claims to have wiped
out 4 waves of Germans with 15 drums
firing point blank at 50 yards.

The German losses as stated by our men
who have been over begins + they been pulled
in numbers on the ground.

Our men after being clogged with
mud from being buried, they pulled the
pins out of their rifle grenades + used
them as hand grenades, doing much
damage.

There is no doubt that A + B Coy on
the right were surrounded, stood their
ground + fought to the last.

Taking known casualties + men returned
+ allowing for a large number of killed
from shell fire, there could not have been
more than an odd unwounded prisoner.
A Coy had practically ceased to exist before
the Infantry attack began + the brunt was
borne by B Coy.

Capt Parr was never heard of again but
was last seen surrounded + fighting with a shovel.

20. This disaster is due to the following
(1) Attempting to hold an impossible salient
as a defensive position.
(2) Lack of aeroplanes

(3) Lack of Artillery support on our side.

(4) Was largely contributed to by the bad weather, the thick dust turning into mud at once & visibility being NIL.

10-5-17

R J Rawson Lt Col
Comg 12/ Glos Rgt

WAR DIARY or INTELLIGENCE=SUMMARY.

Army Form C. 2118.

12th Battalion Gloucestershire Regt
June 1917

Vol 20

K.19

Place	Date	Hour	Summary of Events and Information	Remarks and references to Appendices
Aux Quatre Vents	1st	11.50	Battn. marched to x rds above ROCLINCOURT and boarded buses. Moved by bus to DIEVAL and billeted. No casualties. Weather very hot.	
DIEVAL	2		Cleaning up and refitting. Draft 20 O.R. arrived. Bn v 22 joined 7g Septr	
Do	3		Training commenced. Attack in new formation, musketry, &c	
Do	4		Do Do Do 1 Officer 7 O R joined	
Do	5		Usual Training in morning. 95/Bde Horse show in afternoon. 1st 6/ Rutland joined as reinforcement	
Do	6		Training continued. Firing completion arranged and carried out	
Do	7		Battn. was inspected by G.O.C. XIII Corps on training ground. 1st O R joined	
Do	8			
Do	9	7 am	Bn moved by bus from DIEVAL to G.4.d in ROCLINCOURT. No casualties, nothing to report	
nr ROCLINCOURT	10		In camp at G.4.d. Bn. training continued. Working party of 100 O.R. found for work on range and another of 46 O.R. for work on defences in + near front line	

Army Form C. 2118.

WAR DIARY
INTELLIGENCE SUMMARY.
(Erase heading not required.)

13th Gloucester Regt

JUNE 1917

Place	Date	Hour	Summary of Events and Information	Remarks and references to Appendices
Camp G4D	11		Training continued. Weather fine. Working parties amounting to 1 & 40 OR found as on 10th	
"	12		Nothing to report. Training continued and party of 1 & 40 OR for work found as before	
"	13		Working parties of 1 & 40 OR found. Training continued. No casualties	
B''	14		Training continued in morning starting at 8.35 pm Bn moved into front line and relieved 9 kings in front of ARLEUX. No casualties	
Front line	15		In front line. Weather fine. 1 OR killed by shell fire. Hqrs at B.30.79. 150am on left. otherwise situation quiet	
"	16		In front line. No casualties - nothing to report	
"	17		In front line. Weather fine. Enemy artillery fairly active thro' morn. OR	
"	18		In front line. No casualties. Nothing to report. We were relieved	
"	19		In front line. Bn. was relieved by 1/9 G.L.I. relief commencing at 11.30 pm. and moved into support at VILLERVAL	

WAR DIARY 12th Bn Gloucestershire Regt

Army Form C. 2118.

June 1917

INTELLIGENCE SUMMARY.

(Erase heading not required.)

Place	Date	Hour	Summary of Events and Information	Remarks and references to Appendices
MILLERVAL	19	(cont)	No casualties. Enemy quiet. Nothing to report.	
"	20		In Bde support. No casualties. Enemy averry shelled MILLERVAL frequently during day, apparently counter battery work	
"	21		In support in MILLERVAL. No casualties. Nothing to report	
"	22		In support. Nothing to report	
"	23		In support. Enemy again shelled village heavily. 3 O.R. buried and slightly wounded	
"	24		In support during the day. At 10.45 pm Bn moved up to front line and relieved 1/D.C.L.I. Headquarters at B 50. 7.9. No casualties	
ARLEUX	25		In front line. No casualties. Nothing to report. Draft of 5 O.R. joined. 2/Lt INGRAM + 2/Lt SMITH joined	
"	26		In front line. Situation normal. No casualties	
"	27		In front line. Weather stormy. No casualties	
"	"		In front line. Weather dull with heavy storm in the evening. 2/Lt N.O. BLOODWORTH + 7 O.R. joined 1 O.R. killed and 1 O.R. wounded	

Army Form C. 2118.

WAR DIARY
or
INTELLIGENCE SUMMARY.
(Erase heading not required.)

Instructions regarding War Diaries and Intelligence Summaries are contained in F. S. Regs., Part II. and the Staff Manual respectively. Title pages will be prepared in manuscript.

Place	Date	Hour	Summary of Events and Information	Remarks and references to Appendices
ARLEUX	28	Contd.	Brigade on our right carried out successful operation on their front gaining all objectives & capturing 240 prisoners.	
Do	29		In front line. Weather fine. Some enemy artillery activity on our front line. 1 O.R killed + 1 O.R wounded	
Do	30		In front line. Weather dull & wet. Lt Col RAWSON proceeded to 9th Bde in temporary Command and Major H.A. COLT M.C. assumed command of the Battalion	

H.A. Colt
Major
O.C 12th Gloucester Regt

Army Form C. 2118.

WAR DIARY
12th Bn. Gloucestershire Regiment
INTELLIGENCE SUMMARY
(Erase heading not required.)

JULY 1917   Vol 21

K.20

Place	Date	Hour	Summary of Events and Information	Remarks and references to Appendices
Front line	1st	—	On night 30th June/1st July - Bn. was relieved in front line by 1/DCLI and moved into Bde. Reserve in trenches W of FARBUS WOOD. No casualties. Weather fine.	
Bde. Reserve N of Farbus Wood	2nd	—	Heavy shelling of FARBUS WOOD by enemy. 1/Lt A.H. INGRAM wounded by shell splinter. No other casualties.	
"	3rd		Enemy shelled FARBUS WOOD & vicinity with H.E. apparently counter battery shoots. No casualties caused to us	
"	4		Situation normal. No casualties. Night of 4/5 July 90th Bde was relieved by 15th Bde and this Bn. marched to reserve Billets at ST AUBIN	
ST AUBIN	5		In Devl Reserve. Bn bathing and cleaning up generally.	
"	6		1/Lt W.J. HALE 1/Lt H. WOOD 1/Lt N.D. DAVIDSON joined as reinforcements	
"	7		In reserve billets. Training continued, musketry, bayonet fighting + attack in new formation.	
"	8			
"	9		Firing on MARIEUIL RANGE	
"	10		1/Lt F. WILLIAMS joined	

WAR DIARY
or
INTELLIGENCE SUMMARY

Army Form C. 2118.

12th Bn. Gloucestershire Regt

July 1917

Place	Date	Hour	Summary of Events and Information	Remarks and references to Appendices
ST. AUBIN	11		10 A.m. The King visited the area and the Bn. was formed up on ARRAS-SOUCHEZ Road from S.9.a.4.5. to S.9.c.3.0. to see him pass.	
"	12		2/Lt H. MC SHANE joined.	
"	13		In reserve training continued. 2/Lt J.F. MAINSTONE joined.	
"	14			
"	15			
"	16		Bn. preparing for march to trenches. At 3 p.m. Bn. left ST AUBIN & marched via ECURIE to relieve troops in trench B.12.d.2.8. to ARLEUX CRUCIFIX - FRESNOY RD., a halt being made on W. slope of ridge near ROCLINCOURT for teas. Bn. being left Bn. of Right Bde with 1/Somer on right. C Coy on left A on Right B in Centre and D in Reserve.	
Front line ARLEUX FRESNOY Rd. 17 to B.12.d.2.8	17		In front line. Weather fine. The enemy shelled our trenches heavily on night of 17th during and after	

WAR DIARY 12th Gloucester Regt

INTELLIGENCE SUMMARY July 1917

Army Form C. 2118.

Place	Date	Hour	Summary of Events and Information	Remarks and references to Appendices
Front line	17		a bombing raid by 1/E SURREYS on enemy trenches opposite our left. Our casualties 3 O.R. killed 5 O.R. wounded	
"	18		In front line. Situation normal. Enemy M.G. fire on our support lines + tracks. 1 O.R. wounded. 2/Lt Barley joined	
"	19		Situation quiet. Weather stormy. No casualties	
"	20		1/9.C.L.I. relieved Bn on night of 20th and we retired into support in Red Line – B.10.d – B.16.b. B.16.d Sugar Factory trops to casualties. Weather fine	
Red line	21		In support in Red Line. No casualties. Nothing to report	
"	22		In support. Working party found for work in front line. nothing unusual to report	
"	23		} No casualties during this period. Trenches in Red line cleared + improved + shelters built. Working parties found for work in front line. 2/Lt. L.C. MAY and 2/Lt R.A. BEER joined 23/7/17	
"	24			
"	25			

WAR DIARY
or
INTELLIGENCE SUMMARY

12th Gloucester Regt. July 1917

Army Form C. 2118

(Erase heading not required.)

Place	Date	Hour	Summary of Events and Information	Remarks and references to Appendices
Red Line	26		Nothing to report during day. Starting from Red Line at 5pm Bn. moved up into Front line and relieved 1/9.C.L.I. 1 O.R. wounded by indirect M.G. fire. Situation quiet.	
Front Line	27		At 3 a.m. Gas + Oil were projected on enemy trenches opposite our front by Special Coy. R.E. Enemy retaliated limply and our casualties were 6 O.R. wounded - 2 of whom remained at duty. During remainder of day there was nothing unusual to report.	
	28		In front line. Situation normal. No casualties. On night 28/29 Bn. was relieved by 1/Bedfords 15th Bde. and went into reserve C + D Coys + HQrs being in KITCHENER CAMP B.23 b.5/1. N. of ROCLINCOURT and A + D Coys in Trenches at WILLERVAL NORTH + SOUTH the last 2 Coys being employed on trench work &c in RED LINE.	
	29		In reserve. No casualties. Weather wet. Nothing to report	

Army Form C. 2118.

WAR DIARY
or
INTELLIGENCE SUMMARY.   July 1917

(Erase heading not required.)

Place	Date	Hour	Summary of Events and Information	Remarks and references to Appendices
B 23 b 5 1 N of ROCLINCOURT	30		In reserve HQ C + D Coys in Kitchener Camp and A + B Coys in trenches at MILLERVAL N + South. C + D Coys mostly working parties for work on roads + tracks and A + B Coys working on trenches in RED LINE.	
- " -	31		At 5 pm C + D commenced to relieve A + B in MILLERVAL N + South. Weather fine. Working parties as usual.	
			31/7/7	

R. McLaren Lt. Col.
Cg D/ Glouc. Regt

12th Bn. GLOUCESTERSHIRE REGIMENT - OPERATION ORDER No. 5.

1. **Intention.** The Battalion will move to ST. AUBIN after dark tomorrow night 4/5th.

2. **Instructions.**

   Order of March;: "B" - "A" - "C" - "D" and H.Q. at ten minutes interval by half Coys at 200 yards interval.

   Time;- 10.15 p.m.

   Route;- Track by Ration Dump towards ROCLINCOURT - turn to right by watering trough just North of ROCLINCOURT to ECURIE - MADAGASCAR CORNER, ANZIN - ST. AUBIN.

   Galts;- For ten minutes at every hour.

3. **Advance Party.** 1 N.C.O. per Coy (including H.Q.) under 2nd Lt. E.G. Wills will leave B.H.Q. at 9.15 p.m. picking up C.Q.M.S's at ECURIE and will report to Staff Captain at Town Major's Office at ST. AUBIN.

4. **Transport.** Mess Stores, Valises, Lewis Guns and Petrol Tins to be at Battalion Dump by 10 p.m.

5. **Officers Chargers.** To be at Battalion Dump by 10.15 p.m.

6. **Trenches.** and Dugouts must be left clean.

7. **Reports.** O.C. Coys will report to B.H.Q. on arrival of their Coy at ST. AUBIN.

8. **Tea.** Hot tea will be ready for men on reaching ST. AUBIN.

AT ARRIVAL AT ST. AUBIN.

To O.C. All Coys.

1. **Reveille.** At 8 a.m.   ?

2. **Breakfasts.** At 9.45 a.m.   ?

3. **Bathing.** If fine, Coys will arrange for all men to bathe in river and put on clean underclothing (an Officer must be present with each Coy) before dinners.

4. **Dinners.** 1.30 p.m.

5. **Afternoon.** Coys at disposal of Coy Commanders for cleaning of kit, arms and S.A.A.   Inspection of kit and regimental equipment. Pay.

6. **SICK PARADE.** 10.30 a.m.   ?

(Sd) G.R.A. Beckett.   Capt.
Og. 12th Bn. Gloucester Regiment.

SECRET.   Copy No. 9

OPERATION ORDERS No. 5

by

Lt-Col. R.I. RAWSON,
Commanding 12th Bn. GLOUCESTERSHIRE REGIMENT.

Ref Map: 1/10,000 SUGAR FACTORY.
1/10,000 THE QUARRY.

1. The Battalion will relieve the front line trenches on the night 16th/17th July from B.12.d.2.8. (L Post exclusive) to the Northern Boundary of the Brigade ARLEUX CRUCIFIX - FRESNOY ROAD exclusive. Boundary between Battalions B.12.d.2.8. - B.11.d.82.52, thence along TOMMY ALLEY inclusive to left Battalion. Battalion H.Q. will be just North of junction of W. Trench with the ARLEUX LOOP.

2. The 1st DEVON Regiment will relieve the line on the right from L. Post inclusive simultaneously.
The 13th Brigade will remain in position on the left.

3. Dinners tomorrow will be at 12 noon.
The Battalion will parade for the trenches at 2 p.m. in the following order:-

    H.Q. - "D" Coy - "C" Coy - "A" Coy - "B" Coy.

Head of the column on the road at entrance to "C" Coys billets, and will march to ground on the VIMY RIDGE, West of the entrance to TOMMY TRENCH, where it will have teas and rest.

4. At dusk "D" Coy will proceed via TIRED TRENCH and will relieve the 15th ROYAL WARWICKS in the ARLEUX LOOP in B.6.d. and will be in Battalion Reserve.
This ~~party~~ Coy will send parties for its Lewis Guns to ORCHARD DUMP.

5. "C" Coy will follow "D" Coy via TIRED TRENCH - Transport track to ORCHARD DUMP and thence to 15th ROYAL WARWICK H.Q. at B.5.c.8.9. where guides will meet it.
The Company must be told off by posts from left to right and will relieve "A" Coy 15TH ROYAL WARWICKS from the NORTHERN Boundary to Z Post inclusive about B.6.d.4.0. All posts must know their number or letter.
"C" Coy will pick up its Lewis Guns en route at ORCHARD DUMP. "D" Coy will attach one Lewis Gun and team to "C" Coy.

6. "A" Coy will proceed after dusk via TOMMY ALLEY and Z Trench and KING STREET to relieve a platoon of "D" Coy NELSON Battalion in ALBERT TRENCH from S Post inclusive to L Post exclusive, and one platoon of "C" Coy NELSON Battalion in support in KING STREET. Company H.Q. will be in KING STREET.
Lewis Guns will be picked up at B.11.d.2.6. en route. Guides from NELSON Battalion will meet it at junction of OLD KENT ROAD and TOMMY ALLEY.

7. "B" Company will move via TOMMY ALLEY in rear of "A" Coy and will relieve the Company of 15th ROYAL WARWICKS with one platoon in ALBERT TRENCH from S Post exclusive to Z Post exclusive, and one platoon in Support in BARON TRENCH.

8. The Sergeant Cook will arrange for teas at 5 p.m.

Rations for the 17th will be cooked under arrangements detailed and will be carried up to the Trenches on the men.
Officers Rations will be taken up on Lewis Gun Limbers.

9. O.C. Coys will detail one Officer, one N.C.O. and one runner per Coy will proceed ahead in daylight and take over all Stores from their opposite number.
The Battalion Bombing Officer, Bombing Sergeant and the Sergeant Major will also move forward after teas for the same purpose.

10. The Signalling Sergeant will arrange for all Companies to be connected up to the new Battalion H.Q. by telephone during the day of 18th.

11. All kits to be left with Transport to be dumped at Quartermasters' Stores by 10 a.m.
All trench kits to be ready at H.Q. Mess by 12 noon.

12. The Transport Officer will arrange for carriage of kits, Lewis Guns and Water as detailed to him.

13. The Battalion Aid Post will be in KENT ROAD at B.11.d.8.8.

14. Companies will take over trench Stores, Aeroplane Photos if any, and Defence Schemes. Complete lists to be forwarded to Battalion H.Q. on completion of relief.

15. O.C. Coys will see that they are provided with S.O.S. Signals. For S.O.S. purposes, the Battalion Sub-Sector will be known as C.2. S.O.S. is three green rockets or lights.

16. Completion of relief to be reported to Battalion H.Q. by runner and by B.A.B. Code message.

(Sd) J.H. Maywood. Lieut.
Adjt., 12th Bn. Gloucestershire Regiment.

WAR DIARY

INTELLIGENCE SUMMARY

Army Form C. 2118

12th Bn Gloucestershire Regt

August 1917

Place	Date	Hour	Summary of Events and Information	Remarks and references to Appendices
A 23 B.5.1. N of ROCLINCOURT	1/8	—	In KITCHENER CAMP. Weather wet. Usual Working Parties found for work behind lines. No casualties	
	2/8	—	In KITCHENER CAMP. No casualties, weather wet. Usual Working Parties found. Nothing to report.	
	3/8	—	At 3pm Bn left camp at A 23 B.5.1 and moved into camp at ECURIE WOOD HUTS (A 27.d.1.9) taking over from 1/E. SURREYS who moved into camp at A 23.a.5.1. vacated by us and assumed all working parties.	
ECURIE WOOD HUTS	4/8	—	Bn cleaning up and bathing + disinfecting clothing as hitherto of importance to report. Showery	
	5/8	—	In camp at ECURIE WOOD HUTS. Commemoration Service of 3rd Anniversary of War held under 1st Army arrangements at RANCHICOURT CHATEAU. 12 O.R. attended from this Battn. Weather fine. 2/Lt T.A. WILMOT, 4/Lt M.G.H. SMITH, 2/Lt R.G. ROBERTS and S.O.R. joined as reinforcements.	

Army Form C. 2118.

WAR DIARY of the 12th Bn Gloucestershire Regt
INTELLIGENCE SUMMARY.

(Erase heading not required.)

August 1917

Place	Date	Hour	Summary of Events and Information	Remarks and references to Appendices
ECURIE WOOD HUTS	6		In Camp at ECURIE WOOD. 2 Coys Firing and 2 Coys general training. Fine morning, wet evening 2 O.R joined as reinforcements. Nothing of importance to report.	
Do	7		Training continued with night operations on Zero track 8.30pm to 10.30pm. Weather fine. 2/Lt G.O. PAGETT, 2/Lt W.H. MILLS + 2/Lt G.E. FOWLER joined as reinforcements.	
Do	8		Training continued. Lecture on musketry by Capt A.V. MURRAY. 10 Offrs and 500 O.R attended. Weather fine.	
Do	9		Bn relieved 7th Khans (5th Bde) in Front line, finding one Company leaving camp at 2.40 pm same sector as before i.e. B.D.d 20/15 to FRESNOY - ARLEUX GAVREY Rd. Weather dull + showery. No casualties.	
Front line	10		In Front line. No casualties.	
Do	11		In Front line. 1 O.R missing.	
Do	12		In Front line. 1 O.R wounded. Wet.	

Army Form C. 2118.

WAR DIARY 12th Gloucestershire Regt
or
INTELLIGENCE SUMMARY. August 1917
(Erase heading not required.)

Instructions regarding War Diaries and Intelligence Summaries are contained in F. S. Regs., Part II. and the Staff Manual respectively. Title pages will be prepared in manuscript.

Place	Date	Hour	Summary of Events and Information	Remarks and references to Appendices
Front line Colonce	13		In front line. Enemy carried out hurricane bombardment on our front line at 7 am lasting for 2 minutes. 1 O.R. killed 1 O.R. wounded. Otherwise situation normal. Weather dull.	
Do	14		In front line. Situation quiet and nothing of importance to report. No casualties. Weather wet.	
Do	15		Bn was relieved by 1/D.C.L.I. in afternoon of 15th and went into Bde Reserve on "Brown line". Headquarters at Jungle Dump B.15.c.6.3. No casualties. Situation quiet.	
Bde. Reserve	16		In reserve. Working parties found for work under R.E. improving trenches. Weather wet. No casualties.	
	17		In Brigade Reserve. Weather fine. No casualties. Usual working parties found.	
	18		In Brigade Reserve. No casualties. Nothing to report. Usual working parties found.	

Army Form C. 2118.

WAR DIARY
or
INTELLIGENCE SUMMARY.

12th Bn Gloucestershire Regt

August 1917

(Erase heading not required.)

Instructions regarding War Diaries and Intelligence Summaries are contained in F. S. Regs., Part II. and the Staff Manual respectively. Title pages will be prepared in manuscript.

Place	Date	Hour	Summary of Events and Information	Remarks and references to Appendices
Bde Reserve	19		In Brigade reserve at Tunnel Camp. Weather fine. Working parties found. Nothing to report.	
Do	20		In Reserve. Weather fine. Working parties. Nothing to report.	
Do	21	4.20	Bn. was relieved by 1st Cheshires (15 Bde) and moved from JORDAN ALLEY to ROBERTS CAMP A + C Coys of the Bn of ECURIE, 9th Bde being in Div. Reserve, 2 Coys of the Bn remained in WILLERVAL NORTH + SOUTH for work under R.E.	
N. of ECURIE	22		In Reserve. Bn cleaning up and refitting. Nothing of importance to report.	
Do	23		In Brigade Reserve. A Party of 1 Officer + 20 O.R. at work on Transport Lines — 1 Officer 40 O.R. at work on shelters in REDLINE (B.19.A.15/60.) — 2 Coys at work under R.E. in WILLERVAL NORTH — Remainder at Coy. Commanders disposal for training.	
Do	24		In Brigade Reserve — 2 Coys at work in Redline WILLERVAL N. and 1 Officer and 40 O.R. at work in RED LINE — 1 Officer 20 O.R. at work	

WAR DIARY
INTELLIGENCE SUMMARY
(Erase heading not required.)

12th Bn. Worcestershire Regt.

August 1917

Place	Date	Hour	Summary of Events and Information	Remarks and references to Appendices
N. of FOSUIÉ	24th		On transport lines, remainder of Coy at disposal of Coy Commander. 1 Coy at work on "Demolition of gun-pits and salvaging of material" commencing at 6.30 A.M. (rendezvous F.24.C.)	
Do	25		In Brigade Reserve - 1 Company having finished work in WILLERVAL N. arrived in ROBERTS CAMP at 12 noon - 1 Company remaining in WILLERVAL N. Party of 1 Officer + 40 O.R. continuing work in RED LINE. 2 Companies at disposal of Bn Commander for training, less 1 Officer and 20 O.R. continuing work at Transport Lines.	
Do	26		In Brigade Reserve - Last Company arrived in ROBERTS CAMP from WILLERVAL N. at 8.30 A.M. 1 Officer + O.R. continuing work on shelters in RED LINE - 1 Company on work "Demolition of gun-pits and salvaging of material" commencing at 6.30 A.M. to 2.4th inst., remainder of Bn. Church Parade in the morning, remainder of day "Yoto". - A carrying party consisting of 1 Officer + 30 O.R. was provided for work under "E" Special Coy. R.E. Party left camp at 7 P.m. proceeded to B.S.C. 9/8 + commenced work at 9.30 p.m. which lasted until 1 A.M. (27th) and party arrived in camp at 4.15 A.M. (27th)	

WAR DIARY 12th Bn. Gloucestershire Regiment

INTELLIGENCE SUMMARY

Aug 1917

Place	Date	Hour	Summary of Events and Information	Remarks and references to Appendices
N. of ECURIE	27th		Bn Brigade Reserve. 2 Coys mustered & clean up under Coy arrangements remainder of Bn training under Coy arrangements. Afternoon - Bn relieved in ROBERTS CAMP by 1/E. SURREY REST and moved to ECURIE WOOD HUTS vacated by 1/E. SURREYS. The Party of 1 Officer 40 O.R. who had been working on shelters in RED LINE (B.19.b.15/60) joined Bn at ECURIE WOOD HUTS.	
ECURIE WOOD HUTS	28th		2 Coys Musketry range at BRAY. 2 Companies general training and classes under Lewis Gun & Bombing Officers.	
"	29th		Bn parade at 8.45 AM in musketry order for march to trench attack. Bn returned to camp about 1 P.M. Afternoon & evening "games".	
"	30		2 Coys on range until 12 noon. 1 Coy using #1 Coy general training. 2 Coys bathing in afternoon.	

WAR DIARY 12th Bn. Gloucestershire Regt.
INTELLIGENCE SUMMARY
AUGUST 1917

Army Form C. 2118.

Place	Date	Hour	Summary of Events and Information	Remarks and references to Appendices
ECURIE WOOD HUTS	31		Bn. bathing during day. Coys not bathing will be at the disposal of Coy. Commanders for training & musketry drill. The Bn. will parade at 9 p.m. for night march in gas helmets - Drew fighting order.	

M Morrison
Lt. Col.
Cmdg. 12th Bn. Glouc. Regt.

OPERATION ORDERS No. 10.

by

Lt. Col. R. I. RAWSON
Commanding 12th Bn. GLOUCESTERSHIRE REGT.
....

In the Field.   2nd August 1917.

      Ref. Map:- Sheet 51 B. N. W. 1/20000.

1. **RELIEF.** The Battalion will be relieved tomorrow afternoon the 3rd inst., and will withdraw to ECURIE WOOD Huts at A.27.b., vacated by 1/E. Surrey Regt.

2. **ADVANCE PARTY.** Company Commanders will detail 1 Officer and 1 N.C.O. Headquarters, 1 Officer and 1 O.R. to report at Battn. Headquarters at 1.30 p.m. for instruction. C.Q.M.Ss. will report to Major COLT M.C. in the new Camp at 2.30 p.m.

3. **PARADE.** Companies will parade under Coy. arrangements in time to move off - H.Q. at 3 p.m., A Coy at 3.10 p.m., B Coy at 3.20 p.m., C Coy at 3.30 p.m. and D Coy at 3.40 p.m.

4. **CLEANLINESS OF CAMP.** All tents etc. must be left clean. Weather permitting, tent flies will be rolled up.

5. **TRANSPORT.** The Transport Officer will arrange for all Stores etc. to be moved to the new Camp. Officers' Valises - Signals' Stores - Tools etc., will be dumped near Hd. Qrs. by 10 a.m. Lewis Guns and Mess Kit at 2 p.m.

6. **MEALS.** Tea will be served on arrival in new Camp.

7. **HANDING OVER.** The Orderly Officer will make a complete list in duplicate, of all tents, shelters and other material to hand over to incoming Unit. A receipt for same must be obtained.

8. **REPORTS.** Coy Commanders will report to the C.O. when their Companies are settled in the new Camp.

                              (Sd) J. H. Maywood, Lieut.
                        Adjt., 12th Bn. Gloucestershire Regiment

SECRET.

OPERATION ORDERS No. 11
by
Lt-Col. R.I. RAWSON,
Commanding 12th Bn. GLOUCESTERSHIRE REGIMENT.

Ref. Map. 1/10,000 SUGAR FACTORY.
1/10,000 THE QUARRY.

1. **Relief.** The Battalion will relieve the 1st CHESHIRES in the front line trenches on the afternoon of the 9th instant, in the same Sector as when last in the front line.

2. **Dinners.** 11.30 a.m.

3. **Parade.** Coys will parade in time to move off at -

    "C" Coy 12.40 p.m. to relieve left front.
    "D" Coy 12.50 p.m. to relieve left support.
    "A" Coy 1 p.m. to relieve right front.
    "B" Coy 1.10 p.m. to relieve right support.
    Headquarters will parade under Lieut A.K. Hicks and move off at 1.20 p.m.

    "A" and "B" Coy will move via TOMMY TRENCH and will be at junction of OLD KENT ROAD and TOMMY at 3.45 p.m. where guides will meet them.

    "C" and "D" Coys will move via TIRED ALLEY and ARLEUX LOOP and will be at junction of SEVERN ALLEY and ARLEUX LOOP at 3.30 p.m. where guides will meet them.

4. **Attached.**

    "D" Coy will detail two Lewis Gun teams to be attached to "C" Coy.

5. **Advance Party.**

    O.C. Coys and one N.C.O. per platoon, Signallers and Observers, Regimental Sergeant Major, one runner, Bombing Officer and Bombing Sergeant will parade at 12 noon to go forward to take over Stores, etc.

6. **Taking Over.**

    O.C. Coys will pay particular attention to taking over Defence Schemes, Aeroplane Photographs and Log Books, etc.

7. **Officers Trench Kits, Mess Stores, etc.**

    To be dumped outside Guard Room at 12 noon. Officers Valises to be dumped in a separate pile near Orderly Room by 12 noon.

8. **Transport - Lewis Guns.**

    One Limber will march with each Company to entrances of TOMMY and TIRED ALLEY. Lewis Guns with Buckets must be carried forward from these points.
    Lewis Gun Officer will arrange with Coys for the dumping of Battalion Reserve Buckets.

9. **Rations & Water.**

    Rations and water will be drawn from the same place as when last in the front line. Quartermaster will arrange to bring rations to this Dump on night of 9th.

10. **Officers Rations.**

　　　　The Transport Officer will detail one half limber for H.Q. Rations.　Coy Officers Rations will be taken up by Lewis Gun Limbers.　These rations will have to be carried forward by Servants from TOMMY or TIRED Trenches.

11. **Reports.** Completion of relief will be reported to B.H.Q. by Runner.

12. **Note.** Attention of Company Commanders is drawn to the correct way in which to send S.O.S.

　　　　Troops coming out of the trenches will give way to troops coming in.

　　　　　　　　　　　　　　　(Sd' J.H. Maywood.　Lieut.
　　　　　　　　　　　　　Adjt., 12th Bn. Gloucester Regiment.

SECRET

OPERATION ORDERS No. 13
by
Lt-Col. R.I. RAWSON,
Commanding 12th Bn. GLOUCESTERSHIRE REGIMENT.

Map Ref:- SUGAR FACTORY 51b N.W. 1/10000.

1. **Relief.** The Battalion will be relieved by the 1st CHESHIRES tomorrow at 4.30 p.m. the 21st instant and immediately after relief the Battalion will withdraw via TOMMY ALLEY into Brigade Reserve at ROBERTS CAMP at A.22.c., with the exception of the following:-

   O.C. "A" Coy will detail one Officer and one platoon made up of 40 Other Ranks for work on the RED LINE to commence at 9 a.m. 22nd instant, rendezvous B.19.b.15/6. The party will be accommodated by the 491st R.E's and will billet at A.18.d.8/3. *& will proceed there via TIRED ALLEY*

   "B" and "C" Coys, less the Nos 1 of Lewis Guns and Company Signallers, will proceed to WILLERVAL NORTH where they will be billeted. "B" Coy will work under the C.R.E. and "C" Coy will work under 5th Divisional Signal Company. O.C's "B" and "C" Coys will meet representatives of the Divisional Signals and C.R.E. at junction of CLYDE TRENCH and WILLERVAL NORTH at 10 a.m. tomorrow 21st when work will be pointed out to them. Company Commanders may take with them any Officer or N.C.O. they think necessary.

   RED LINE

2. **Meals.** The Master Cook will arrange for the necessary cooking material to go with "B" and "C" Coys and one platoon of "A" Coy. The Quartermaster will arrange for rations and water - dump WILLERVAL NORTH as before.

3. **Advance Party.**

   C.Q.M.S's, one Officer and one O.R. from B.H.Q., and one Officer from "D" Coy will report to Major H.A. Colt. M.C. in ROBERTS CAMP at 3 p.m.

4. **Teas.** The Battalion will have tea at 4 p.m. and the Master Cook will arrange for hot teas on arrival at ROBERTS CAMP.

4. **Officers Valises**, Mess Kits, Trench Kits, etc.

   The Q.M. will arrange for Officers Valises to be in new camp at 6 p.m. Officers Trench kit and Mess Stores, etc. will be dumped at the West end of TOMMY ALLEY by 2 p.m. O.C's "B" and "C" Coys will arrange for the carrying of their own trench kits, etc. The Officer i/c of "A" Coys working party will send for his kit on arrival of the Battalion in the new area.

6. **Lewis Guns.**

   The Lewis Guns of "B" and "C" Coys and the platoon of "A" Coy will be dumped at the West end of TOMMY ALLEY by 2 p.m. The Nos 1 will remain with the guns and proceed to ROBERTS Camp with them. Lewis Guns of "A" and "D" Coys will be taken down with them and placed on limbers at end of TOMMY. All Nos 1 will march with the limbers. The Transport Officer will arrange for Limbers to be at TOMMY ALLEY by 4.30 p.m., also Limbers for cooks material, Officers kits, etc.

(Sd) J.H. Maywood. Lieut.
Adjt., 12th Bn. Gloucester Regiment.

SECRET.

Operation Order No 11

1. The Battalion will be relieved by 1/D.C.L.I. tomorrow about 3.45 p.m. and will withdraw to trenches at present occupied by 1/E. SURREYS in Brigade Reserve with B.H.Q. at TUNNEL Dugout.

2. Details of relief will be sent to Companies later.
   TOMMY ALLEY will be used by all Companies for withdrawal.

3. 1 Officer and 1 N.C.O. per Coy will report at B.H.Q. at 10 am and proceed to take over trenches occupied by their opposite letter in new area.
   1 Officer, 1 N.C.O. and 1 Runner from B.H.Q. will report at same time and place and take over H.Q.

4. All Maps, plans etc which were taken over, and all Trench Stores and explosives will be carefully checked and handed over, and receipts taken and given as usual and rendered to HQ by 10 am on 16th inst.

5. All Trench Kits, Men Kits, Regimental Equipment, Lewis Guns and Magazines, empty water tins over and above those on Trench Store List will be carried down to new area.

6. The Quartermaster will arrange for sufficient cooking pots for the Battalion to be taken to N.E. SURREY cookhouse at the TUNNEL tonight with coke and charcoal and a guard of two men left in charge.
Cooks to be there on 15th in time to have tea ready for the Battalion at 8.p.m.

7. X Working parties on arrival in new area to be detailed to O.C. Companies.

8. The 2 Sappers attached to each Coy will report at B.H.Q. at 2 p.m. ready to rejoin their own Unit.

9. Coys will report completion of relief by runner.

14/8/17

J. M. Haywood Lt, Adjt
1/5 Gloucester Regiment

Army Form C. 2118.

12th Bn Hampshire
12 Gloucester Regt
SEPTEMBER 1916

WAR DIARY
or
INTELLIGENCE SUMMARY.
(Erase heading not required.)

Instructions regarding War Diaries and Intelligence Summaries are contained in F.S. Regs., Part II. and the Staff Manual respectively. Title pages will be prepared in manuscript.

K.22

Place	Date	Hour	Summary of Events and Information	Remarks and references to Appendices
EBURIE WOOD HUTS	1		Bn. paraded at 8.30 a.m. to march to French trenches. Ones. — Fighting O.A.C.	
"	2		Bn. Paraded for Dinner Parade at 9.30 a.m. Afternoon- Bn relieved the 16 Machine Regt (15 Bde.) in front line trenches, first Company leaving camp at 1 p.m. Same pace as when last in front line. i.e. B.17.d. 70/75 to FRESNOY-ARLEUX CRUCIFIX RD. - b. acreatic N.L.	
In front line	3		In front line - casualties nil weather fine. Draft ot. 29 D.R. taken on strength of Battn. 66 O.R. joined Battn. remainder to base trenches and reinforcement camp.	
D.O.	4		In front line - casualties 1 O.R. wounded. weather fine 2/Lt. T. J. BENJAMIN joined Bn. as reinforcement.	

2353 Wt. W2544/1454 700,000 5/15 D.D.&L. A.D.S.S./Forms/C.2118.

Army Form C. 2118.

WAR DIARY
or
INTELLIGENCE SUMMARY.

12th Bn. L. Lincolnshire Regt.

SEPTEMBER 1917

Place	Date	Hour	Summary of Events and Information	Remarks and references to Appendices
In front line.	5		In front line. Casualties Nil. Weather fine. Situation quiet.	
Do	6		In front line. Casualties Nil. Weather fine. Situation quiet.	
Do	7		Battalion relieved by 10th E. YORKS Regt in afternoon & in relief Battalion marched to WELLINGTON Camp ROCLINCOURT. Arrived in camp at 6.30 pm.	
WELLINGTON CAMP	8		Battalion marched to ACQ leaving camp at 9 am. Arrived and billeted in ACQ at 12 noon. Rest and clean up in afternoon.	
ACQ.	9		Battalion paraded at 6.35 am. and marched to training area at MAIZIERES. Route taken HAUTE-AVESNES - HERMAVILLE -	

WAR DIARY
12th Bn. A. Leicestershire Regt.
INTELLIGENCE SUMMARY

SEPTEMBER 1917

Army Form C. 2118.

Place	Date	Hour	Summary of Events and Information	Remarks and references to Appendices
	(continued)		IZEL-LEZ-HAMEAU - VILLERS-Sur-SIMON - PENIN. Bn. arrived and billeted in MAIZIERES at 11 A.M.	
MAIZIERES	10		Battalion cleaning up, inspection of kit etc, and Company arrangements. Draft of 223 O.R. joined Battn. from Corps Reinforcement and Musketry Camp.	
Do	11			
Do	12	}	Battalion training - Instruction in Bombing, Lewis Gunnery, Physical training and Musketry under Coy. arrangements.	
Do	13		Two Coys. allotted range on Brigade training ground, remainder of Battn. Physical training, Musketry, Bombing and Lewis Gun instruction.	
Do	14		Battn. training - Coys. allotted ranges and bombing ground, remainder of May. General training. Rolls allotted to	

Army Form C. 2118.

WAR DIARY 12th Bn. Gloucestershire Regt.
or
INTELLIGENCE SUMMARY.

(Erase heading not required.)

SEPTEMBER 1917

Place	Date	Hour	Summary of Events and Information	Remarks and references to Appendices
MAIZIERES	14		Battalion Bn. parade at 4.30 p.m. for right wearers in box helmets.	
Do.	15		Platoon competition. Platoon representing Coy. paraded at 10.15 a.m. and returned to billets at 1.30 p.m. Competition won by No.6 Platoon of "B" Coy. Remainder of Coy. practicing bays in attack.	
Do.	16		Battalion Church parade in the morning. Afternoon sports and shooting competition under Battalion arrangements.	
Do.	17		General training on the Brigade training ground.	
Do.	18		Battalion drill and tactics in their morning. Lecture by Major E.J. ANDERSON (Army School) on Bayonet fighting. Bn. Sports and competition in afternoon.	

Army Form C. 2118.

WAR DIARY 12th Bn. Gloucestershire Regt.
or
INTELLIGENCE SUMMARY.

SEPTEMBER 1917

(Erase heading not required.)

Place	Date	Hour	Summary of Events and Information	Remarks and references to Appendices
MAIZIERES	19		Battalion bands for ninth march. Afternoon-Buzzers Musketry Meeting - Rifle and Lewis gun competitions.	
Do	20		Two boys on Range, remainder of Bn. at the disposal of Coy Commanders for general training.	
Do	21		Lecture by Captain W.G. CHAPMAN M.C. at 9.30 A.M. was given by the WHIZZ BANGS (Divisional Concert Party) in MAIZIERES at 10.30 a.m. Bn. paraded at 3.30 p.m. for night operations. marched to GRAND RULLECOURT. Ref Sheet 51.C. 1/40,000. Bn. in support on LEFT to 1/D.C.L.I. with "DEVON'S" on RIGHT and 1/E. SURREYS in support on RIGHT. for an attack on German trenches from GRAND RULLECOURT RD in I.33.d inclusive to the Western boundary of Square I.33.C. (For fuller details of attack see O.O. attached)	

Army Form C. 2118.

WAR DIARY 12th Bn. R. Worcestershire Regt.
INTELLIGENCE SUMMARY.
(Erase heading not required.)

SEPTEMBER 1917

Place	Date	Hour	Summary of Events and Information	Remarks and references to Appendices
MAIZIÈRES	22		Bn. arrived in billets from night operations at 11 a.m. Afternoon and evening football match and boxing competition.	
Do	23		Bn. paraded at 11.30 am for Church Parade. Lecture by Divisional R.C. Officer to Bn. after Parade.	
Do	24		Bn. having under Company arrangements, bayonet fighting, bombing, musketry arrangements, bayonet allotted ranges Lewis Company	
Do	25		Bn. paraded at 6.30 am. for march to LIGNY ST FLOCHEL Stn. where it entrained for 5th Army Area. One Coy followed Bn. and entrained at 11.40 am. Bn. arrived at AUDRUICQ Stn. at 3.30 p.m. where it detrained and marched to billets at BAYENGHEM arriving in billets about 6.15 p.m.	

Army Form C. 2118.

WAR DIARY
or
INTELLIGENCE SUMMARY.
(Erase heading not required.)

Place	Date	Hour	Summary of Events and Information	Remarks and references to Appendices
BAYENGHEM	26		Bays. at disposal of Bgy. Commanders for instruction in gas masks, etc.	
Do.	27		Morning, Bgy. parade in marching order for drill. Afternoon firing on range. Bn. paraded at 5.45 p.m. and marched from BAYENGHEM to MOULLE, arrived and billeted at 8 p.m.	
MOULLE	28		Battn. paraded at 6.35 a.m. for march to LE NIEPPE where baths arrived at 12 noon. Dinners 12.30 p.m. and Battn. marched to billets at 2 p.m.	
LE NIEPPE	29		Bn. paraded at 8.30 A.M. and marched to METEREN. Halt was made on road for dinners, and Bn. arrived at METEREN at 4.15 p.m.	

Army Form C. 2118.

WAR DIARY 12th Bn. Gloucestershire Regt.
INTELLIGENCE SUMMARY.
(Erase heading not required.)

Instructions regarding War Diaries and Intelligence Summaries are contained in F. S. Regs., Part II. and the Staff Manual respectively. Title pages will be prepared in manuscript.

F. 8

SEPTEMBER 1917

Place	Date	Hour	Summary of Events and Information	Remarks and references to Appendices
METEREN	30		Church parade in the morning. Inspection of equipment etc. and cleaning up generally.	

W. J. Cow
Major
for Lt. Col.
Cmdg. 12th Bn. Gloucestershire Regt.

S.E.C.R.E.T.

OPERATION ORDERS No. 11 & 13
by
Lt-Col. R.I. RAWSON,
Commanding 12th Bn. GLOUCESTERSHIRE REGIMENT.

Ref. Map. 1/10,000 SUGAR FACTORY.
1/10,000 THE QUARRY.

2/9/17
7/9/17

1. **Relief.**
   The Battalion will relieve the 1st CHESHIRES in the front line trenches on the afternoon of the 4th instant, in the same Sector as when last in the front line.

2. **Dinners.** ~~11.30 a.m.~~ 12 noon Teas on arrival in trenches.

3. **Parade.**
   Coys will parade in time to move off at –
   1.10
   1.30 "C" Coy ~~12.40~~ p.m. to relieve left front.
   1.20 "D" Coy ~~12.50~~ p.m. to relieve left support.
   "A" Coy 1 p.m.   to relieve right front.
   1.40 "B" Coy 1.10 p.m. to relieve right support.
   Headquarters will parade under ~~Lieut A.K. Hicks~~ and move off at ~~1.30 p.m.~~ 2/Lt Wills
   All Companies
   ~~"A" and "B" Coy~~ will move via TOMMY TRENCH and will be at junction of ~~OLD KENT ROAD and~~ TOMMY at ~~3.45 p.m.~~ ~~where~~ guides will meet them. Red line at jn of ARLEUX LOOP & W trench.
   all movement re para 3. O.O.
   ~~"C" and "D" Coys will move via TIRED ALLEY and ARLEUX LOOP and will be at junction of SEVERN ALLEY and ARLEUX LOOP at 3.30 p.m. where guides will meet them.~~

4. **Attached.**
   ~~"D" Coy will detail two Lewis Gun teams to be attached to "C" Coy.~~

5. **Advance Party.**
   O.C. Coys and one N.C.O. per platoon, Signallers and Observers, ~~Regimental Sergeant Major~~, one runner, Bombing Officer and Bombing Sergeant will parade at 12 noon to go forward to take over Stores, etc.

6. **Taking Over.**
   O.C. Coys will pay particular attention to taking over Defence Schemes, Aeroplane Photographs and Log Books, etc. Special care must be taken as regards work in hand.

7. **Officers Trench Kits, Mess Stores, etc.**
   To be dumped outside Guard Room at 12 noon. Officers Valises to be dumped in a separate pile near Orderly Room by 12 noon.

8. **Transport – Lewis Guns.**
   One Limber will march with each Company to entrances of TOMMY ~~and TIRED ALLEY~~. Lewis Guns with Buckets must be carried forward from these points.
   Lewis Gun Officer will arrange with Coys for the dumping of Battalion Reserve Buckets.

9. **Rations & Water.**
   Rations and water will be drawn from the same place as when last in the front line. Quartermaster will arrange to bring rations to this Dump on night of ~~8th.~~

10. **Officers Rations.**

   The Transport Officer will detail one half limber for H.Q. Rations. Coy Officers Rations will be taken up by Lewis Gun Limbers. These rations will have to be carried forward by Servants from TOMMY or ~~THIRD~~ Trenches.

11. **Reports.** Completion of relief will be reported to B.H.Q. by Runner.

12. **Note.** Attention of Company Commanders is drawn to the correct way in which to send S.O.S.

   Troops coming out of the trenches will give way to troops coming in.

(Sd' J.H. Maywood. Lieut.
Adjt., 12th Bn. Gloucester Regiment.

(6)

Operation Order No. 14.
by
Lt. Col. R. S. Rawson
cg. 12th Bn. Gloucester Regt.
Ref. Map. ROCLINCOURT 1/10,000
Sheet 51 C 1/40,000

1. **Relief.** The Battn. will be relieved tomorrow 7th inst., by 10th Battn. E. YORKS Regt., which will arrive in following order.

   H.Qrs.
   D Coy. to relieve D Coy.
   A   "   "   B "
   C   "   "   C "
   B   "   "   A "

2. **Guides.** Two guides from Bn. H.Qrs. and 2 guides per Company (1 per Platoon) will be at junction of TOMMY ALLEY and KENT Road at 3.15 p.m. to guide respective relieving Platoons.

3. **Stores.** Lists of trench stores to be made out in duplicate with great care. One copy to be given to relieving companies and duplicate to be receipted and handed to the Adjutant by 9 a.m. on 8th inst. Instructions as to various articles have been issued to O.C. Companies and must be strictly complied with.
   Gas shell alarm rattles will be handed over. All periscopes taken over in the trenches will be handed over, but not those on Regimental charge. All petrol tins in trenches will be handed over, including those brought up by Battalion.

4. **Cleanliness.** Care must be taken to hand over trenches and shelters clean.

5. **Handing Over.** All defence & advance schemes, maps and photographs, log books etc., will be handed over & receipts obtained.
   All work including wiring, will be carefully explained to incoming Unit.

6. **Report.** Completion of relief to be reported by runner.

7. **March.** On relief, Companies will march to WELLINGTON CAMP, ROCLINCOURT.

8. Trench Kits etc. All trench kits etc., which cannot be carried with Companies must be sent to WEST entrance of TOMMY ALLEY during the morning, where a Regimental Policeman will take charge of it.
Lewis Guns & all Magazines will be carried out with Companies.
The Bombing Officer will arrange for all Bomb buckets on Regimental charge to be carried out.

9. Transport. The Transport Officer will arrange for Lewis Gun Limbers to be at WEST end of TOMMY ALLEY at 7 p.m., and also transport for Officers' trench & mess kits, also Officers' chargers.

10. Quartermaster. The Q.M. will arrange the following:-
Officers' Valises to be at WELLINGTON CAMP on arrival.
Haversacks of other ranks ditto.
He will take over WELLINGTON CAMP before the arrival of the Battalion.
A hot meal to be ready at 8 P.M.
Q.M. Sergeants to be at WELLINGTON CAMP to meet their Companies.

11. Move. The Battalion will be marching at 9 a.m. on the 8th. Reveille that day will be at 6 a.m., and the C.O. is sure that all ranks will endeavour to turn out as neatly as possible under the circumstances. Strict march discipline must be kept when leaving the trenches.

6/9/17.

J.W. Maywood, Captain,
Adjt., 12/Gloucester Regt.

12th Bn. GLOUCESTERSHIRE REGIMENT
OPERATION ORDER No. 15.
(For practice purposes).

Sept 20th 1917.

Ref. 51.c. 1/40000 and Sketch Map issued.

1. During the early morning of 22nd September, the 95th Infantry Brigade will attack and capture the German trench line system from the GRAND RULLECOURT Road in I.33.d. inclusive to the western boundary of Square I.33.c.

2. The Brigade will attack with two Battalions in front and two in Support as follows:-

   1st East Surrey Regiment on the RIGHT.
   1st D.C.L.I. on LEFT.
   1st DEVONS in SUPPORT on RIGHT.
   12th Gloucester Regiment in SUPPORT on LEFT.

3. The two front line Battalions will attack and capture the first objective (Blue Line)
   The two Support Battalions will pass through and capture and consolidate the final objective (Green Line).

4. After capturing the Green Line, "A", "B" and "C" Coys will push forward one post of at least 1 N.C.O. and 9 men with one Lewis Gun to the LIENCOURT-AVESNES Road with the object of obtaining observation towards the North but will not go beyond the Road.

5. Boundaries between Battalions will be a line drawn due South from Road junction at I.33 Central (as shown on map).

6. The Battalion will be formed for attacked on the line at E.F.G.H. by 5.30 a.m. on 22nd as detailed to Coy Commanders ready to move forward in three waves on a one platoon front. Move forward Zero plus 5.

   "A" Coy. G - H.   "B" Coy F - G.   "C" Coy E - F.

   "D" Coy one section bombers to follow first wave of each front line Coy and remain in first Battalion objective.
   One section of Rifle Grenadiers to follow second wave of each front line Coy and remain in second Battalion objective.
   Remainder of "D" Coy two platoon in one wave   ) in rear of
                 one platoon in second wave) "B" Coy.
   All moppers up will wear white armlets on left forearm.

7. At 4 a.m. the Battalion will form up as follows:-

   "A" Coy on Track D-B in order of battle.
   "B" Coy   do   B-C   do   do
   "C" Coy on Road E.C.   do   do
   "D" Coy (less moppers up) in rear of "C" Coy.
   Battalion H.Q. at Point D.

8. Objectives.   Leave Line E.H. Zero plus 5.

   1st Wave.   Pass Blue Line N-O Zero plus 19 capture 1st object P.Q. zero plus 22 and remain there.
   2nd Wave.   Pass first objective zero plus 24 capture 2nd objective S-T zero plus 26 and remain there.
   3rd Wave.   Pass second objective S-T. Zero plus 28 capture Green Line U-V zero plus 30 and consolidate.
   1st Wave will reinforce as necessary leaving moppers up behind.
   3rd wave will send forward posts to LIENCOURT-AVESNES Road.
   Distances between lines 25 yards.
   Distances between waves 75 yards.
   "D" Coy will occupy line P-Q and be in reserve ready to repulse counter-attacks.

(2)

Boundaries between Coys as detailed to Coy Commanders.

9. The Artillery barrage (represented by signal flags) will move at the rate of 50 yards a minute and the line will represent the inner line of the barrage which the attacking Infantry must keep within 50 yards of.

10. Battalion H.Q. will move forward with "D" Coy to the line P-Q

11. S.O.S. Three white Very Lights in rapid succession followed by two Golden rain.

12. Regimental Aid Post at point C.

13. All prisoners will be sent under escort to Battalion H.Q. and thence to Brigade H.Q. under escort.

14. A Contact plane will be in the air from 6 a.m. to 6.30 a.m. Flares will be lighted at 6.5 a.m. and 6.30 a.m. or when called for by the aeroplane.
White Very Lights will be fired when the Green Line has been captured.

15. Watches will be synchronized at 12.30 a.m. and 4.30 a.m.

16. Zero hour at 5.45 a.m.

ACKNOWLEDGE'

(Sd) R.I. Rawson, Lt-Col.
Cg. 12th Bn. Gloucestershire Regiment.

INSTRUCTIONS FOR ATTACK ON 22.9.17.

1. "A", "B" and "C" Coys will each carry 8 ground flares in their third wave.   12 White Very Lights.
   "A" and "C" two Signal Rockets.
   "B" Coy one Signal Rocket.
   8 Ground flares in third wave.

2. Certificates will be rendered on parade that all S.A.A. is left in billets.
   No grenades or "P" Bombs etc will be carried.
   No Grenade Buckets will be carried

3. Battalion will bivouac at O.2.d.5.2.
   Teas will be at 6 p.m. on 21st.
   Q.M. will arrange for tea at 3 a.m. on 22nd
   Breakfast at same place about 7.30 a.m.

4. Transport Officer will arrange for ~~two~~ wagons Cookers, water carts, two Lewis Gun Limbers, with Lewis Guns only, Mess Cart Medical Cart and one limber for Officers trench kits, to accompany the Battalion on 21st.

5. Greatcoats will be carried in packs on the march and will be dumped at W and recovered on return to bivouacs after the attack.

6. Tools will be issued after arrival in bivouac as far as possible every man to have a tool.

7. Moppers up to wear white armlets.
   Places for flares to be carefully selected.
   Trench dumps to be formed or marked.
   Consolidation to be kept up and proper digging to be carried out until ordered to stop.
   Great care must be taken to preserve touch and direction and not to bunch.

8. The 1/6 A. & S.Hrs will be Germans and represent two Battalions.
   They will probably not retire and will fight.
   They must be taken prisoner properly.
   Certain strong points are not to be considered taken until they hoist the white flag and even then action will be continued against them until the garrison is captured.
   There will be consolidated shell holes in front of and between all lines   Four Sandbags per man will be carried.
   There will probably be a vigorous counter-attack. We may be pushed out of the Green Line and if so all local Commanders will counter-attack with all forces at their disposal except the reserve Company which will wait for C.O's orders.
   3 Very Pistols per Company will be carried.

9. The Q.M. will arrange for dinners for 22nd to be prepared in billets and to be ready at 1 p.m.

20.9.17.

(Sd) R.I. Rawson. Lt-Col.
Cg. 12th Bn. Gloucester Regiment.

SECRET.

OPERATIONS ORDERS No. 15
BY
Lt-Col. R.I. RAWSON.
Commanding 12th Bn. GLOUCESTERSHIRE REGIMENT.

Copy No. 1

Ref Maps. Sheet 51c. N.E. 1/20,000.
Sheet 51b. N.W. 1/20,000.

1. **Parade.** The Battalion will parade at WELLINGTON CAMP at 8.50 a.m. on the 8th instant and will march to billets at ACQ. Dress – Marching Order. Steel helmets will be carried on packs. No parcels or sandbags etc to be carried. The Band will play. Regimental Transport, both A and B Echelons, will march in rear of the Battalion and will be drawn up on the ARRAS-LENS Road with its head 100 yards from ECURIE Cross-roads at 8.50 a.m. ready to follow on.

2. **Reveille, etc.**

    Reveille 6 a.m. Breakfasts 7 a.m. All Valises etc to be stacked ready for loading at 7.30 a.m. Mess Cart to proceed independantly to ACQ and report there to Major H.A. Colt. M.C. Not more than one brakesman or two Cooks to march in rear of each wagon. Remainder of Administrative H.Q. will march in rear of Battalion. Attention is drawn to the turnout of Cooks and employed men.

3. **Advance Party.**

    The Advanced Party consisting of 4 C.Q.M.S's., Sgt. E.W. Toogood and one N.C.O. from H.Q. to billet the Transport, will report to Major H.A. Colt. M.C. at 8 a.m. and proceed under his direction on Bicycles.

    Orders regarding the Advanced Party for new Area, the loading of Transport, refilling points, baggage, etc, have already been issued to those concerned.

4. **Synchronising of Watches.**

    2nd Lieut. E.M.T. Burges will report at Brigade H.Q. at ARGYLL CAMP at 7 a.m. on 8th instant and check watches.

5. **Cash.** O.C. Companies will render indents for cash required for pay before parade.

6. **March Discipline.**

    Strict march discipline must be observed.

7. **Draft.** The new Draft allotted to Companies will parade as a separate platoon in each Company for march purposes.
Companies will be organised in three platoons even when brought to full strength, with one complete Lewis Gun Section attached to Company H.Q. O.C. Coys will take steps to equalise their present strength in 3 platoons, so as to obtain a fair proportion of new drafts in each Platoon.

8. **Lewis Guns.**

    The Battalion Lewis Gun Officer is responsible for seeing all Lewis Gun Limbers properly packed and will arrange the earliest possible opportunity for cleaning guns.

10. **Cleaning Up, etc.**

    The afternoon of the 8th instant must be devoted to cleaning up and getting ready for the march on the 9th.

(2)

Men must be clean and tidy at all times and are not to be permitted to walk about streets or billets with their coats open or improperly dressed.   smartness
Strict attention is to be paid to ~~marching~~ and correctness in saluting.
When guards are found, the men must know their duties, and guards must turn out quickly and smartly at the double.

(Sd) J.H. Maywood, Captain.
Adjt., 12th Bn. Gloucester Regiment.

12th Bn. GLOUCESTERSHIRE REGIMENT OPERATION ORDER No. 16.

Reference Sheets HAZEBROUCK 5.A. 1/100000.
LENS 1/100000.

1. The Battalion, less "B" Company and "B" Coys Cooker with team complete will parade in marching order at 7 a.m. on Tuesday 25th instant and march to LIGNY ST. FLOCHEL for entraining at 8.40 a.m. Breakfasts under Coy arrangements.

   Order of March.   "D" Coy - "A" Coy - "C" Coy - H.Q.

   All Administrative details not required with Transport will parade with Battalion H.Q.

   Head of the Battalion at the North end of "B" Coys billets.

2. The Transport less "B" Coys Cooker and team will parade at 6.30 a.m. on 25th and will arraive at the Station Yard at LIGNY at 7.10 a.m.

   The train for paras 1 and 2 is timed to depart at 10.10 a.m.

3. "B" Coys Cooker and team will parade at 1.30 p.m. on 25th and will arrange at the Station Yard at LIGNY ready to entrain at 3.10 p.m. and will report to a Captain of 1st EAST SURREY Regiment in charge of the entrainment.

   "B" Coy will parade in marching order at 3 p.m. and will arrive at LIGNY Station at 4.40 p.m. and report to the same Officer. This train will depart at 6.10 p.m.

Train No.	March No.	Serial No of Unit.
19	T. 58	532

   1 Coy and Cooker 1st DEVONS, No. 3 Coy Divisional Train and 491st Field Coy R.E will also be on this train.

4. Baggage and Supply Wagons will march with the Battalion Transport and entrain loaded. Arrangements for supplies have been detailed to the Q.M. All Transport will entrain fully loaded and Water carts full.
   Watering facilities are detailed to the Transport Officer.
   Breast ropes will be provided by the Battalion, one breast rope and two head ropes per four horses.

5. The unexpended portion of the days ration and the iron ration will be carried on the man. Water bottles must be full before entraining.

6. The Brigade loading parties of two Officers, ten N.C.Os. and ninety men will be found by 1st EAST SURREY Regiment at entraining Station and 1st D.C.L.I. at detraining Station.
   These Battalions will provide a Major or Captain in addition to be in charge of entraining and detraining at their respective Stations.

7. All Officers are responsible that billets are left clean, all damages paid for and receipts obtained, and that the station rendezvous is left in a clean and sanitary condition. Temporary latrines should be dug and filled in prior to departure.
   Water in LIGNY Station Yard from a well.

8. The Battalion Billeting party consisting of 2nd Lt. E.G. Wills. four C.Q.M.S's and one N.C.O. from H.Q. with six bicycles will parade at 3.30 p.m. on 24th instant and report to the entraining Officer at LIGNY at 4.40 p.m. for entrainment on No. 1 train with 95th Infantry Brigade Headquarters.
   2nd Lt. E.G. WILLS must be in possession of Map 1/100000 HAZEBROUCK 5.A.
   Separate instructions re billeting are issued to him.

9. The Mess President will arrange for food for Officers for 25th instant.

10. All Officers Valises and Mess Kit must be loaded by 5.15 a.m. under arrangements made by the Transport Officer.

   The Q.M. will arrange to weigh Valises as they are loaded in accordance with Battalion Orders, Part 1, para 9 of 14th instant.

   Lewis Gun Limbers and all other Transport will be loaded by 9 p.m. on 24th instant.

23.9.17.

(Sd) J.R. Maywood, Captain.
Adjt., 12th Bn. Gloucestershire Regiment.

WAR DIARY 1/2th Bn. W. Lancashire Regt.

INTELLIGENCE SUMMARY.
(Erase heading not required.)

OCTOBER 1917   Vol 24

K.23

Place	Date	Hour	Summary of Events and Information	Remarks and references to Appendices
METEREN	1		The Battalion less transport & administrative section paraded at 6.30 a.m. and proceeded to support line to relieve 11th Bn. W. YORKS REGT. (68th Inf. Bde.) ROUTE - By bus to N.5.C.9.3 (Wet 28.40.800). where Busses were met, situation of Battalion arrived & explained to C.Os. Relief completed by 9 a.m. — positions of companies etc. as follows:	
			"B" Company on Left. FITZ + MACHINE GUN JUNCTION	
			"C" do do Centre. ROBERT JUNCTION L.I.C.	
			"A" do in Left Support.	
			"D" do in Right Support. WEST MINNEARSS COPSE	
			B.2H.Q. CLAPHAM JUNCTION. J.13.d.9.7.	
			Bn. war. in supports to 1/5 SURREY REGT.	
			N.O.C. 300. very heavy shelling by enemy during the night, and S.O.S. Rockets were seen on several occasions during the night in Dn.Counter.	

WAR DIARY

1/2nd Bn. Auckland Regt Army Form C. 2118.

INTELLIGENCE SUMMARY

OCTOBER 1917

Place	Date	Hour	Summary of Events and Information	Remarks and references to Appendices
MEREREN	1		Tonight an unsuccessful Labour party of 7.30 p.m. and marched to N.M.L. where a draw was noted for the time the batches were in the lines.	
IN RESERVE	2		Battalion in Reserve continued went inspecting and improving the trenches for a considerable day. The temporary unit was badly from the trenches trouble. 7K. L.H. BARDNER 27/H. WOOD died 22.8.H.M. was found and that altogether about 100 OR's casualty was until were buried.	
Do	3		Battalion in Reserve experienced of Listening Patrols. A heavy artillery was still very active throughout.	

WAR DIARY
or
INTELLIGENCE SUMMARY.

Army Form C. 2118.

12th Bn. Gloucestershire Regt.

OCTOBER 1917

Reference Map:- GHELUVELT 1/10,000

Place	Date	Hour	Summary of Events and Information	Remarks and references to Appendices
	3		For advance were being carried out, nothing of importance took place. Casualties were 2/Lt N.R.E. BLOODWORTH wounded and 20 OR.	
IN RESERVE	4		Battalion was in reserve to 1/5 SURREYS REGT during an attack on the second line formed by 95th Infy Bde. on a line in line of the Overworsh trench with 1/Devons on the Right and 1/5 SURR EYs on the Left with the 1/5 WORCESTERSHIRE Regt in support to the Right and 12th Bn. 1 LOO. GLO. ? Regt in support to the SURREYS. The 7 K.O.S.B's attacked on the night of 1/Devons with 64th Infy Brigade on the Left. Brigade Operations Order 16. A.S.G. - I.17. A. 2.2. - I.17. A.S.G. - I.H.G. 55/05.	

WAR DIARY 12th Bn. E. Lancashire Regt.

INTELLIGENCE SUMMARY

OCTOBER 1917

Army Form C. 2118.

Place	Date	Hour	Summary of Events and Information	Remarks and references to Appendices
	4 (continued)		The attack commenced at 6 a.m. and B.Coy on the battalion less "A" Company (which had been detailed for carrying) moved forward to occupy the line held by 1/E Surrey Regt. from I.15.b.5.6. through 1st PARM to I.16.a.55.72. as follows. B Coy Companies both N. of REUTEL BEEK (I.15.c. I.16.). Casualties had been heavy. Our remnants of the companies had deep shelly reversed in one going into our British own lines. No artillery was ready to give covering fire. At 10.10 the Bosch reported a counter attack on our right and "D" Coy (which was on the right) found to reinforce 4 DEVON REGT. At daybreak an enemy aeroplane came very low over our trenches. 2/Lt J.F. HAIRSTONE and 2/Lt D.W. BAILEY were KILLED. Captain C.S. PETHERAM, 2/Lt B.H. WHITE and 2/Lt F.H. MADDRENS wounded. Total Casualties O.R. 156.	

Army Form C. 2118.

WAR DIARY
INTELLIGENCE SUMMARY.

12th Bn. Gloucestershire Regt.

OCTOBER 1917

(Erase heading not required.)

Place	Date	Hour	Summary of Events and Information	Remarks and references to Appendices
IN RESERVE	5		The Battalion was very heavily shelled during the morning, the enemy's artillery became very active during the afternoon. Companies re-organized their men and formed new positions during the day. The battalion withdrew to SANCTUARY WOOD during the evening, owing to the darkness, and very bad state of the ground relief was not completed until 5 a.m. 6th inst. 2nd Lt R.A. BEER & 2nd Lt W.H. MILLS were killed. 2nd Lt J. SANDBACH WOUNDED and about 20 O.R. casualties during the day.	
SANCTUARY WOOD	6		Still later. The battalion was in dug-outs and shelters in SANCTUARY WOOD. movement by day was very limited, as fritz could easily be observed by the enemy, duck-boards and tracks in the vicinity of SANCTUARY WOOD.	

Army Form C. 2118.

WAR DIARY 12th Bn. Gloucestershire Regt.
INTELLIGENCE SUMMARY.
(Erase heading not required.)

OCTOBER 1917.

Place	Date	Hour	Summary of Events and Information	Remarks and references to Appendices
SANCTUARY WOOD	6		were constantly shelled during the day. A carrying party of 1 Officer and 50 O.R. were detailed for carrying rations to 1/CHESHIRES who were holding the front line. Casualties during the day were very light.	
SANCTUARY WOOD	7		The battalion furnished the following working parties during the day:- 1 Officer and 50 O.R. carrying rations to 1/CHESHIRE REGT. in the front line. 1 Officer and 40 O.R. employed on cable burying in vicinity of FITZCLARENCE FARM. 1 Officer and 30 O.R. carrying S.A.A. from CLAPHAM JUNCTION to CAMERON HOUSE. Enemy artillery was very quiet during	

Army Form C. 2118.

WAR DIARY 12th Bn. Gloucestershire Regt.

or

INTELLIGENCE SUMMARY.

(Erase heading not required.)

OCTOBER 1917

Place	Date	Hour	Summary of Events and Information	Remarks and references to Appendices
SANCTUARY WOOD	7		The morning but the duck-boards and trenches were shelled by the enemy during the evening and approach was hindered in bringing up the rations. 2/Lt. B.H. WEIR was wounded and several of his party were lost owing to the darkness and bad state of the ground, while taking rations to YORKSHIRES.	
Do.	8		Bn. found carrying parties as on 7th inst. Two Companies returned to SANCTUARY WOOD and found carrying parties up the line, holding the front line. Remainder of Bn. moved forward to relieve the 1/E. SURREY REGT. who were in supports to "CHESHIRES". "A" Company being on the left and "B" Company on the Right. Battn. H.Qrs. Mr. FITZCLARENCE FM. Rain fell very heavily during the night and	

WAR DIARY 12 Div. Gloucestershire Regt

INTELLIGENCE SUMMARY

(Erase heading not required.)

Army Form C. 2118.

Reference Map:- GHELUVELT
1/10,000

Place	Date	Hour	Summary of Events and Information	Remarks and references to Appendices
	8		...made the ground very muddy & was also very dark and the Companies found great difficulty in getting into position, consequently the relief was not completed until early morning.	
SUPPORT	9		The battalion was very tired & feeling much in need when an attack was being carried out against the enemys Pill boxes, which commenced at 5.30 a.m. Objective lay N. of 3 & CHATEAU in I.15.a. N. through I.16.b.& 3. through I.22.a. situation became quiet until about 5.30 p.m. when a very heavy barrage was put up our supports shelling and at south slope of SHREWSBURY WOOD situation again became normal. Sent two companies to SHREWSBURY WOOD	

WAR DIARY / 2nd Bn. Wiltshire Regt.
INTELLIGENCE SUMMARY.
(Erase heading not required.)

OCTOBER 1917

Army Form C. 2118.

Place	Date	Hour	Summary of Events and Information	Remarks and references to Appendices
SUPPORT	9		Until the usual amount of shelling and during which were put up by the enemy to keep up any attempt to... MAJOR H.A. COLT M.C. took over command of the Bn. in the line and Lieut. R.I. RAWSON proceeded to the transport lines.	
Do	10		The enemy heavily shelled the howitzer manning the morning, but there was nothing of importance to note. The Battalion again withdrew to SOMERGHY WOOD in the evening, movement was very difficult owing to the state of the ground. The enemy put over a barrage during relief and the companies were consequently held up...	

Army Form C. 2118.

WAR DIARY 12th Bn. Gloucestershire Regt.
or
INTELLIGENCE SUMMARY.

(Erase heading not required.)

OCTOBER 1917

Place	Date	Hour	Summary of Events and Information	Remarks and references to Appendices
SANCTUARY WOOD	10		Position unchanged. Lt. Col. R.I. RAWSON proceeded to England for long service leave off 6 months.	Reference Shell No. 28. 1/40,000
	11		The Bn. was relieved about 10 P.M. by 12th Bn. DURHAM L.I. and withdrew to RIDGEWOOD. Shooting bickering which was not good. On arrival at RIDGEWOOD the Batalion had dinner, and after a rest marched by bus to CURRAGH CAMP WESTOUTRE, where the bn. was billeted in huts, billeting completed about 7.30 A.M.	

Army Form C. 2118.

WAR DIARY 12th Bn. Gloucestershire Regt.
or
INTELLIGENCE SUMMARY.
(Erase heading not required.)

OCTOBER 1917

Place	Date	Hour	Summary of Events and Information	Remarks and references to Appendices
			Summary of Casualties for period 1st to 11th October 1917	
			KILLED 2nd Lt. P.W. BAILEY " J.F. HAINSTONE } 4.10.17 " R.A. BEER " W.H. MILLS } 5.10.17 59 Other Ranks Killed	
			WOUNDED Capt. L.S. PETHERAM 2Lt. H.B. McSHANE " A.W. SMITH } 4.10.17 " F.H. ANDREWS " L.D. SANDBACH } 5.10.17 " G.M. WEIR } 7.10.17 177 Other Ranks Wounded	
			GASSED 2Lt. J.A. BARDRICK " H. WOOD " L.C. MAY } 2.10.17 " N.C.E. BLOODWORTH } 3.10.17 91 Other Ranks Gassed 1 O.R. Wounded & Missing 9 O.R. Missing 8 O.R. Died of Wounds	
			TOTAL 14 OFFICERS 345 O.R.	

Army Form C. 2118.

WAR DIARY 12th Bn. Gloucestershire Regt.

INTELLIGENCE SUMMARY.

(Erase heading not required.)

OCTOBER 1917

Place	Date	Hour	Summary of Events and Information	Remarks and references to Appendices
CURRAGH CAMP. WESTOUTRE	12		Battalion cleaning up and reorganising stocking of Reg.tl equipments etc.	
Do	13		Companies at the disposal of Coy. Commanders to reorganising & hygiene. Anyone highly sent signal course and seeing the fun. Draft of 10 OR. joined the Bn.	
Do	14		Battalion paraded outside at 11 a.m. B. othes is to be added to [illegible] A.O.R [illegible] station.	
Do	15		Physical training and bayonet fighting during the morning. Weapon training afternoon.	

2353 Wt. W2344/1454 700,000 5/15 D. D. & L. A.D.S.S./Forms/C. 2118.

WAR DIARY 12th Wiltshire Regt.
INTELLIGENCE SUMMARY
(Erase heading not required.)

Army Form C. 2118.

OCTOBER 1917

Place	Date	Hour	Summary of Events and Information	Remarks and references to Appendices
CURRAGH CAMP WESTDOWNE	16		Shipped morning Bayonet fighting and Musketry, evening Platoon in attack, afternoon Road making etc. Musketry Road making etc. Seven other ranks the Lewis gun Officer sent down to Liverpool and rectied cleaves	
Do	17		Physical training Bayonet fighting and Musketry. Morning Platoon in attack, Musketry, evening Platoon and Sentry Drill. Received orders to have Junior Officers in the Cluster Reserve Btn to come Malta to be kept during the day. 6 OR joined the draft to leave	

WAR DIARY
or
INTELLIGENCE SUMMARY.

Army Form C. 2118.

12th Div. Gloucestershire Regt

Place	Date	Hour	Summary of Events and Information	Remarks and references to Appendices
CURRAGH CAMP, WESTOUTRE	15		Received orders to leave Nieuwer Stadtser theatre and signallers. The 5th Siege Howitzer Coy Received Oxygen cylinders for refilling & requisite to the battery at dan. Lindsay's cohorts waiting with O.C. 2nd Division at Wernen Received Howitzers 1 & 2	
O.O.	19		Special inspection by Col Smith the R.E.E disregard the day. History of our respirators given Battery drill and manual exercise during the day Instruction of transport by Lt S.S. Turner in afternoon	

Army Form C. 2118.

WAR DIARY 12th Bn Gloucestershire Regt.
or
INTELLIGENCE SUMMARY.

(Erase heading not required.)

Dato 3£ R 1917

Instructions regarding War Diaries and Intelligence Summaries are contained in F. S. Regs., Part II. and the Staff Manual respectively. Title pages will be prepared in manuscript.

Place	Date	Hour	Summary of Events and Information	Remarks and references to Appendices
CURRAGH CAMP WESTOURNE	19 (cont)		Lieut L.M. L. E Reading joined Bn as reinforcements. 58 O.R. joined. Lt. Col. Hudson Esq. had Reverence tanks and taken over strength of Bn.	
L.O.	20		B Station parade all recruits marched off 3 Bhr return to camp about 11.30 A.M. A Rugby Football match was played on the afternoon against Devon Regt. RESULT DEVON REGT. 17 pts GLOUCESTERS 3 pts 101 O.R. joined Battalion as reinforcements	

WAR DIARY 12th Bn. Gloucestershire Reg.

INTELLIGENCE SUMMARY

OCTOBER 1917

Place	Date	Hour	Summary of Events and Information	Remarks and references to Appendices
CURRAGH CAMP NEWBRIDGE	21		Church parade during the morning. Afternoon spent in reading. 7 O.R. joined battalion for reinforcements.	
DO	22		Inspection and Battalion training. One of the Lt. Col. paraded at 11 a.m. for an hour for Battalion parade at 11 a.m. to G.O.C. Lt. Col. then paraded to his members on the and told them his members for during the morning. Afternoon Regimental matches were held.	

Army Form C. 2118.

WAR DIARY 12th Bn 1 Leinster Rik Reg.
INTELLIGENCE SUMMARY.
(Erase heading not required.)

Place	Date	Hour	Summary of Events and Information	Remarks and references to Appendices
CURRAGH CAMP. WESTOUTRE	23		Westoutre. Bayonet fighting. Physical training and Musketry. Organised sports in the afternoon.	Reference Sheet No 28. 1/40.000
Do.	24		Physical training, Musketry, Bayonet fighting, and by Drill during the morning. Classes for Lewis Gunners, Signallers & Stretcher Bearers as usual.	
Do.	25		Boys at chapel at Company parades during the morning. Battalion paraded at 2 p.m. and moved forward to RIDGEWOOD. Transport and Administrative Branch proceeded to same area as when battalion was last in new line (N.W. sector). Opposite M.56. O.R. joined Bn. on reinforcement from the following Officers: 2nd Lts A.H. MAY, F. H. HARRIS, IN. DANN, G. H. ROGERS and T.R. BRIDGFORD). M. CALVERT,	

WAR DIARY 12th Bn. Worcestershire Regt.
or
INTELLIGENCE SUMMARY.

Army Form C. 2118.

OCTOBER 1917

Place	Date	Hour	Summary of Events and Information	Remarks and references to Appendices
RIDGEWOOD	26		Battalion in Divisional Reserve at RIDGEWOOD	Reference Map - GHELUVELT 1/10.000
Do	27 28		Bn paraded at 11 am and moved forward to relieve the 16th Bn R WARWICKSHIRE REGT in the front line. Battalion proceeded with BEDFORD HOUSE & SANCTUARY WOOD heavily bombarding road at J.30. One Company was in the front line, two supports in close support, one in reserve at "DEVON" J.19.d.2 B.H.R. SERR HOUSE J.15.b.4.6. 2 Lt E.G. FOWLER was killed J.7.B.9.6. Casualties were nearly light.	

Army Form C. 2118.

WAR DIARY 12th Bn. Gloucestershire Regiment

INTELLIGENCE SUMMARY.

(Erase heading not required.)

OCTOBER 1917

Place	Date	Hour	Summary of Events and Information	Remarks and references to Appendices
FRONT LINE	29		Battalion holding front line. Casualties nil. Coy's nothing of importance to report.	
Do	30		Battalion holding front line. Enemy's artillery very active during the morning and later party had great difficulty in getting proved out owing T.M. to enemy's war hits at B.4.P.H.A-I.Z.C.I.O.I.T. otherwise situation normal. Casualties high.	
Do	31		Battalion in front line. Situation normal, weather fine.	

J.A. Maynard Major
Cmdg. 12 Bn Gloucestershire Regt

Army Form C. 2118.

WAR DIARY 12th Bn Gloucestershire Regiment
INTELLIGENCE SUMMARY.

(Erase heading not required.)

NOVEMBER 1917

Place	Date	Hour	Summary of Events and Information	Remarks and references to Appendices
Front Line	1		Bn holding front line trenches. Casualties were very light. There was nothing of importance to report. Bn was relieved on night of 1/2 by Worcester Regt and withdrew to RIDGEWOOD	
RIDGEWOOD	2		Battalion in huts and shelters in RIDGE WOOD. Bn resting during the morning. Afternoon general clean up etc.	
Do	3		Companies at disposal of Coy Commanders for cleaning up. Remainder of equipment etc. Bath at Ridgewood were allotted to the Bn during the afternoon.	

K.24

Army Form C. 2118.

WAR DIARY 12th Bn. Gloucestershire Regiment

INTELLIGENCE SUMMARY

NOVEMBER 1917

(Erase heading not required.)

Place	Date	Hour	Summary of Events and Information	Remarks and references to Appendices
RIDGEWOOD	4		Remainder of Battalion were allotted the Baths during the day. Our Church parade at 9.30 A.M. The camp was inspected by the D.A. & Q.M.G. Second Army during the morning.	
Do	5		Battalion relieved 2 Companies of 1st Wiltshire & 1st Bedfords. One Company proceeded to CAMERON COVERT and two Companies to Spt Bn and Stirling Castle. Situation was very quiet during the relief which was completed with only 4 casualties. Captain C. S. PETHERAM & 2nd V.R. joined Bn. in Rear.	

Army Form C. 2118.

WAR DIARY /2nd Bn. Worcestershire Regiment.

INTELLIGENCE SUMMARY.

(Erase heading not required.)

Instructions regarding War Diaries and Intelligence Summaries are contained in F. S. Regs., Part II. and the Staff Manual respectively. Title pages will be prepared in manuscript.

Place	Date	Hour	Summary of Events and Information	Remarks and references to Appendices
OR IORT STIRLING TUNNEL	6		Bn. in tunnels. 1/c in 1st Jut. Making mutual reliefs one Company who had gone forward to EMERON COVERT. Bn. reinforced support blocks with 2 sections 'E' section Regt. to Coy. near VELDHOEK & TOWER near Bn. H. Qrs. on JERK HOUSE. Enemy artillery was very active during morning and unusual executive reconnoitering relief.	
FRONT LINE	7		Bn. in front line & usual artillery activity every 20. Any attempts of enemy to get at any O.P. by our bombers during the day	

Army Form C. 2118.

WAR DIARY 12th Bn. Gloucestershire Reg

or

INTELLIGENCE SUMMARY.

(Erase heading not required.)

NOV. 1917

Place	Date	Hour	Summary of Events and Information	Remarks and references to Appendices
Front Line	7		The Battalion was relieved on night of 7th & 8th Nov. by the Royal Warwickshire Regt. 13th Bn. Regt. and withdrew to huts & shelters in BEDFORD HOUSE	
Bedford House	8		Men in huts & shelters at BEDFORD HOUSE. Men cleaning up and inspection of arms etc	
Do	9		Bn paraded at 10.45 A.M. and marched to RIDGEWOOD and took over camp from 16th Bn. Royal Warwickshire Regt	

WAR DIARY 12th Bn. Gloucestershire Regt

Army Form C. 2118.

INTELLIGENCE SUMMARY.

Place	Date	Hour	Summary of Events and Information	Remarks and references to Appendices
RIDGEWOOD	10		Company tactics ended. Company arrangements to check Regimental equipment etc.	
DO.	11		Bn paraded at 9.30 am and proceeded to HARGON CAMP (M.7.d.8.4) sheet 28. Route- Cere Road- N.10.b. 9.5. - Scrupuea boues- Hollebeieke- Kn.b.lytte- Woitouke- Bn arrived in tent at HARGON Camp at 12 noon	
HARGON CAMP	12		Coys at disposal of Coy Cmdrs for checking Regtl equipment - organising etc. - Physical training morning. Platoon Commanders. Organised Games from 3pm to 4 pm	

Army Form C. 2118.

WAR DIARY 12 Bn. Norfolk Regiment

or

INTELLIGENCE SUMMARY.

NOVEMBER 1917

Place	Date	Hour	Summary of Events and Information	Remarks and references to Appendices
ARAGON CAMP	13		Battalion Units to the Bn during the day-being not occupy the Baths at disposal of by Commanders for Sections, bucking Drill & raising etc. Organised games from troops to attend	
do	14		Battalion paraded at 1 a.m. and marched to OUDERDUM Station where it entrained for NIELLES-BREQUIN en detraining the battalion marched to QUESQUES where they were billetted for the night. On arrival went on billets at 7 p.m. 5 p.m.	
QUESQUES	15		The Battalion paraded at 9 a.m. and marched to training ground at HENNEVEUX. On arrival at Henneveux at 12 noon	

WAR DIARY 12th Bn. Gloucestershire Regiment

Army Form C. 2118.

INTELLIGENCE SUMMARY.

NOVEMBER 1917

Place	Date	Hour	Summary of Events and Information	Remarks and references to Appendices
HENNEVEUX	16		Companies at disposal of Company Commanders during the morning for general clean up of billets, clothing, equipment etc. Inspection of arms and equipment by O.C. Coys. and B.M. will until 3pm – from 3-4 pm organised games.	
Do	17		Companies at disposal of Company Commanders to general training during the morning – Classes to Signallers, Observers & Stretcher bearers – Machine gun & equipment for work on transport lines, Rifle range and Bayonet fighting course. Afternoon – Half holiday.	

WAR DIARY

of

INTELLIGENCE SUMMARY

12th Bn. Gloucestershire Reg't. Army Form C. 2118.

NOVEMBER 1917

Place	Date	Hour	Summary of Events and Information	Remarks and references to Appendices
HENNEVEUX	18		Church parade at 11.30 a.m. voluntary service at 6 p.m. and	
	19		Coy Commanders at 6.45 a.m.	
	20		Battalion training included & Platoon training in open	
	21		Musketry and Bayonet Fighting, arm drill etc	
	22		Company firing on range & also Lewis Guns on	
	23		range for quarter proved.	
	24		Specialists training for Bombers, Rifle grenadiers,	
			Signallers and Stretcher bearers	
Do	25		On parade at 9.45 a.m. Inspected by him to station Area.	
			Buses meant turned up on to road BOULOGNE-LUMBRE	
			Rd, after embussing bn proceeded to LE PARCQ where bn	
			arrived & were billetted at 6 P.M.	

WAR DIARY 1/2 Mn. Monmouthshire Regiment

INTELLIGENCE SUMMARY

Army Form C. 2118.

NOVEMBER 1917

Place	Date	Hour	Summary of Events and Information	Remarks and references to Appendices
Le Parc	26		Inspection of billets & Brigadier Officer, remainder of morning trps at disposal of Coy Commanders for training. Lecture by Col. Bayly during the afternoon on discipline & esprit de corps.	
			Div. football match with R.E.'s during the afternoon. 1/2 Bn. gained two points from C.H & R.T. Coys.	
Do.	27		Companies at disposal of Coy Commanders for Reorganising of platoons, Musketry, exercise rapid firing, Kit inspections dry drill etc.	
			Final match for platoon competition played bet. Nos 16 Platoon, C Coy. & 15 Platoon D Coy. Result 4-0 to 15 Platoon 1.	

WAR DIARY or INTELLIGENCE SUMMARY

1/2 Bn. Lincolnshire Regiment

NOVEMBER 1917

Place	Date	Hour	Summary of Events and Information	Remarks and references to Appendices
LE PARC	28		Bn. paraded at 9.30 A.M. for route march & returned to billets about 12.15 p.m. Afternoon Sports.	
Do	29		6 companies at disposal of Company Commander for Physical training, Rapid loading, Bayonet fighting, Musketry etc. Afternoon - Lecture by Coy. Commander - Sports	
Do	30		Companies at disposal of Coy. Commander preparing for move etc. Lecture at 2.30 p.m. by Lt. R.J. FITZGERALD on "His recent experiences in Germany".	

Ha[?]
E.C.
Lieut 1/2 Bn. Lincs Regt

WO 95/1580/2

5th Division

12th Gloucesters – Disbanded

~~19th East 1918~~

1918 APR – 1918 OCT

(DISBANDED)

95th Brigade.

5th Division.

1/12th BATTALION

GLOUCESTERSHIRE REHIMENT

APRIL 1918.

Army Form C. 2118.

WAR DIARY
or
INTELLIGENCE SUMMARY.
(Erase heading not required.)

12th Battalion Gloucestershire Regiment
APRIL 1918

Place	Date	Hour	Summary of Events and Information	Remarks and references to Appendices
ITALY LONGARE	1	-	In billets at LONGARE and SEGULO. S. of VICENZA, under orders to entrain for FRANCE.	
	2		Battalion entrained at VICENZA station for FRANCE — Battalion - consisting of "A" + "C" Coys and Battn Headquarters under command of Lt Col Hajor m.c. at 1.30 p.m. Other ½ Battalion - "B" + "D" Coys and remainder of HQrs - under command of Capt J.H.Maywood - at 7.30 P.m.	
	3		In train en route from Italy to FRANCE	
	4			
	5			
	6		Battalion detrained at PETIT HOUVAIN Pas de Calais. First half Battalion about 4 p.m and second half about 9 pm. Marched to Ivergny and billeted About 15 Kilos	
IVERGNY Pas de Calais	7		In billets at IVERGNY. Weather dull + wet. No casualties	
	8			
	9	10 a.m	Battalion marched to POMMERA (via LE SOUICH LUCHEUX-(ESPERANCE) on DOULLENS- ARRAS Road About 15 Kilos. Weather fine. No casualties	
	10		Battalion left billets at POMMERA at 2 a.m. to march to BEAUVAL-sur-BOIS. When within 1 kilometre of destination orders were received cancelling move and Battalion returned to POMMERA and billeted	Appendix 1
	11		P.T.O	

Army Form C. 2118.

WAR DIARY 12th Battalion Gloucestershire Regiment
INTELLIGENCE SUMMARY.
April 1918

(Erase heading not required.)

Place	Date	Hour	Summary of Events and Information	Remarks and references to Appendices
POMMERA	11	noon	Battalion with A Echelon Transport entrained at MONDICOURT Station about 1 P.M. from POMMERA and proceeded via ST. POL & CHOCQUES to THIENNES, where they detrained and marched to billets at LES OGEAUX about 5 kilos weather fine. No casualties. Strength 3 officers	
	12		Battalion left billets and proceeded to take up position in support to 95th Bde. about K8 near LA MOTTE - MERVILLE Road. 2 O.R. Wounded	
	13		About dawn enemy attacked front line and B. Coy 12 Glosters were ordered up to reinforce. 1/Lt J. HULL S.O. Wounded, 2 Lt Avery 2/Lt G. J. RUTLAND and 2/Lt G.N. HARRIS wounded. Towards evening D. Coy went forward & took up position in close support to front line	
	14		Heavy enemy shelling but no infantry action. Casualties 3 O.R. Wounded.	
	15		Enemy attacked in morning & was repulsed. 2/Lt Leveaux 2/Lt Simmons wounded. 7 O.R. Wounded. Remainder of day was rather was fairly quiet and there was nothing of importance to report	

Army Form C. 2118.

WAR DIARY
INTELLIGENCE SUMMARY.
(Erase heading not required.)

1st/8th Worcester Regt
April 1917

Place	Date	Hour	Summary of Events and Information	Remarks and references to Appendices
	16		Situation fairly quiet during the day & no casualties occurred. Starting at 6 p.m. Battalion was relieved by 1/Bedfords (15th Bde) and went into reserve at LE TOUQUET (J 5 x 3 central). Capt. A.S. TAYLOR wounded during relief but remained at duty.	
LE TOUQUET	17		In reserve to 13th Bde. Battalion cleaning up, checking over. No casualties. Weather fine.	
			About 8 p.m. enemy commenced to shell village and continued at intervals throughout the night.	
LE TOUQUET	18		During to shelling it was found necessary to leave billets and occupy trenches near village. About 5 p.m. Battalion moved into FOREST and took up position in J 6 c. Two casualties. Weather fine.	
	19		In reserve to forces. No casualties. Nothing of importance to report.	
	20			
	21	9.20	Battalion relieved 14th R. Warwicks in the Lt front of the Right Divisional Sector. 1/5 Surreys on Right. 10th R Innis. & 1/Devons in support to left front sector. No casualties during relief and nothing to report. After completion of relief enemy commenced Trench Mortar and 3 or 4 gas shells	

C.H.P. ANDERSON
Capt.

WAR DIARY
INTELLIGENCE SUMMARY.

12th Battalion Gloucester Regt.
April 1917

Place	Date	Hour	Summary of Events and Information	Remarks and references to Appendices
K.20.c.96 to K.19.d.9.0	22		In front line. Heavy enemy shelling. 2 O.R. killed 7 wounded. Otherwise nothing of importance to report.	
	23		In front line. Usual enemy shelling. 3 O.R. killed 6 O.R. wounded	
	24		In front line. Enemy shelled front line and BOIS MOYEN heavily. Went gas shells. 2 O.R. wounded 8 O.R. gassed. Lt. Col. H.A. COLT. M.C. Gassed.	
	25		Usual enemy shelling. 12th Gloucesters were detailed to capture under cover of a creeping barrage:- Le Pelit Bois K.26.c.65.75 Houses + Bldgs K.20.d.C.9.1 Orchards K.26.d.3.0.5	
			Tank was allotted to 'A' Coy under Capt C.B.P.7.TH.59 Am.m with 'D' Coy in support, 'C' Coy with 'D' Coy in support were to keep in close touch with Bn on our left (Y Berylds St Bldg) and when Peter had captured their objective (Bldgs K.31.a.3.7) and report had been received that our 'A' Coy had taken	Le Petit Bois K.26.c.65.75 Houses + Bldgs K.20.d.C.9.1 to K.26.t.5a.5 Mon-Brown of Chinese Farm

WAR DIARY

12th Gloucester Regt Army Form C. 2118.

INTELLIGENCE SUMMARY

April 1918

(Erase heading not required.)

Summary of Events and Information

their objective at K 26 & 30.25. C Coy went to manoeuvre
forward and occupy line from left of own A Coy and
join up with 1/R.W.Fus on own left flank. Not
line to be about K 31 a.0.1 on railway line

All men were ready by nightfall and at 9 p.m.
supporting Coys B + D moved up into position immediately
behind attacking Coys A + C
Our Zero hour 9.30 p.m. barrage opened
At 9.33 left attacking party of A Coy (No 1 Platoon
under Sgt. Lewis) went her 1 Platoon of B Coy under 2/Lt
G.M. ROGERS in close support advancing under barrage
took all their objectives (group of bldgs Goureth Farm.
from K 20 c 9.1 to K 26 & 30.25) without further opposition
and by 10 p.m. were consolidating on that position.
line through K 30 + 30 e.s.

The right attacking party of A Coy - No 5 Platoon
of A Coy under 2/Lt G. Mills and No 3 Platoon
under Lt N. ARMITAGE in support, were to attack

(A7092) Wt. W12839/M1293. 750,000. 1/17. D. D. & L., Ltd. Forms/C2118'14.

WAR DIARY or INTELLIGENCE SUMMARY

Army Form C. 2118.

1st Gloucester Regt. April 1918

Place	Date	Hour	Summary of Events and Information	Remarks and references to Appendices
LE VERTBOIS			from north over a bridge at K 26 a 65.85 and from west over a temporary bridge which was to have been placed at K 26 a 3.5 but as this bridge did not arrive in time to be of use another route up road K 26 a 2.5 to K 26 a 5.6 had to be used. Our 9.33 p.m. party moved forward but met with considerable resistance while working up front. 2/Lt MILLS was wounded. Lt ARMITAGE was killed and numerous casualties were caused by M.G. fire at short range before M gun was disposed of by party which had entered LE VERTBOIS from the North (One bridge at K 26 a 65.85) having met with no resistance. Both parties then joined up and reinforced by a platoon of B Coy under 2/Lt GOSNEY which had been ordered up, advanced to final objective where they formed up and left attacking party of A Coy at K 26 b 30 at about 10.20 p.m.	

WAR DIARY
or
INTELLIGENCE SUMMARY.

Army Form C. 2118.

10th Bn Gloucester Regt

April 1918

Place	Date	Hour	Summary of Events and Information	Remarks and references to Appendices
	25		Remainder of B Coy under Lt A LAIRD were then sent up to reinforce front line which was still being held and to assist in consolidation. One platoon of 1/5 OCLI was sent forward in support along Road — Gloucester farm — le VERTBOIS. Party which had advanced through le VERTBOIS mopped up as every man had been needed to overcome enemy resistance and during consolidation of new line Lt A LAIRD obtained information from a wounded prisoner that a number of the enemy still remained in the cellars at le VERTBOIS. He proceeded with Corp. SMITH and 1 O.R. to le VERTBOIS and found about 30 Germans in a cellar. These surrendered without resistance. By daylight on 26th position was well consolidated. 1/5 Surreys on our right gave up about R.26.a.1 8.0 about 12 midnight.	

WAR DIARY
of
1st Bn. Gloucester Reg¹
INTELLIGENCE SUMMARY.
April 1918

Army Form C. 2118.

(Erase heading not required)

Place	Date	Hour	Summary of Events and Information	Remarks and references to Appendices
			"C" Coy on our left advancing as enemy was not only slight resistance and captured only 3 prisoners. Objective were reached except on left flank where line is 20 to 30 yards where objective laid down owing to failure 1 Bn. on our left to reach their final line. One platoon of "D" Coy moved H. behind Coy and dug in about 100 yards behind them when they consolidated. Remainder of "D" Coy was used for carrying Ammunition etc to front line. 1/O.C.L moved up into our 2d front line in support. Captured 3 M Guns. 35 unwounded prisoners 4 wounded prisoners. Heavy casualties are known to have been inflicted on the enemy.	

Appendix 4

Army Form C. 2118.

WAR DIARY
or
INTELLIGENCE SUMMARY.
(Erase heading not required.)

Instructions regarding War Diaries and Intelligence Summaries are contained in F. S. Regs., Part II. and the Staff Manual respectively. Title pages will be prepared in manuscript.

Place	Date	Hour	Summary of Events and Information	Remarks and references to Appendices
			Copy of Wire received from Genl Haking, Commanding XI Corps.	26.4.18
			"Please convey to Br-Genls Oldman and Aston Lt. Col Stafford and Major Chapman, and all ranks of Bedfordshire and 12th Gloucestershire Regts my congratulations for gaining their objectives last night and It was a most creditable performance and will greatly improve our situation."	
			Copy of Wire received from G.O.C. Commanding 5th Division.	26.4.18
			"The Divisional Commanders congratulates PRAY, PILLOW, and the Divisional and Heavy Artillery on the exceedingly neat and well-arranged operation that was carried out last night and PUTS and PEACOCK made a most gallant and successful attack and the determination with which PEACOCK fought their way into VERT BOIS farm is to be specially commended."	
			PEACOCK = 12th Gloucesters	

Army Form C. 2118.

WAR DIARY
of
12th Bn. Gloucester Regt
INTELLIGENCE SUMMARY.
April 1918

(Erase heading not required.)

Instructions regarding War Diaries and Intelligence Summaries are contained in F. S. Regs., Part II. and the Staff Manual respectively. Title pages will be prepared in manuscript.

Place	Date	Hour	Summary of Events and Information	Remarks and references to Appendices
	2/4		Casualties Lt N ARMITAGE Killed 2/Lt E.G WILLS " G.M ROGERS (since died) Wounded (of wounds) Lt Col H.A COLT Gassed 2/Lt T.J BENTAMIN Wounded or duty	21 OR Killed 30 OR Wounded
	26		Enemy shelled new front line and BOIS MOYEN heavily during day. Several casualties. On night 26/27 new front line was re-organised and 1/5 C.L.I. were withdrawn from immediate support.	
	27		About 1 am patrol from C Coy under 2/Lt T.J BENTAMIN went out but found all enemy posts unoccupied. A patrol encountered about K 26 b 9 4 was fired upon & 3 casualties caused. Patrol dispersed hurriedly. About 4.30 am on 27 under cover of a heavy barrage a hostile patrol of about 20 approached our line but were driven off with heavy losses by M.G. fire. During remainder of day enemy shelled our position doing a good deal of injury. 1 OR Killed 6 OR wded 2/Lt R.G. ROBERTS Gassed	

WAR DIARY
INTELLIGENCE SUMMARY.

Army Form C. 2118.

13th Gloucester Regt
April 1918

Place	Date	Hour	Summary of Events and Information	Remarks and references to Appendices
Front line	28	—	On night of 27/28 Batt. was relieved by 1/D.C.L.I / 61st Div /2nd Bde and went into support in BOIS MOYEN about K.13.D - K.19.b. Lt. W.H. COOMBS joined.	
BOIS MOYEN (FORET DE NIEPPE)	29		In support in BOIS MOYEN. Capt G.E. RATCLIFFE, Lt. W.T. HAGGART 2/Lt. F.J. CLIFTON, 2/Lt. D.J. ROBERTS + 2/Lt. E.E. SHEPHARD joined. An reinforcement. Lt-Col H.A. COLT rejoined from hospital	
-"-	30		In support. No casualties. Nothing of importance to report.	

K. Colt
D. Colt
Lt. Col.
Comdg 13th Bn Glouc Regt

SECRET.

OPERATION ORDER No. 55.
by
Lieut-Colonel H. A. COLT. M.C.
Commanding 12th Battalion THE GLOUCESTERSHIRE REGIMENT.

Reference Map:- LENS.

1. **Move.** The Battalion will move tomorrow to POMMERA.

2. **Route.** LE SOUICH - LUCHEUX - L'ESPERANCE.

3. **Starting Point.**

    Battalion:- "D" Coys Billets (No. 37 and 38).
    Brigade:- Forked Roads EAST of S in BREVILLERS.

4. **Order of March.**

    "D" - Band and "A" - "B" - "C" - H.Q.
    100 yards distance will be maintained between Coys on marching off.

5. **Parade.** The Battalion will parade in above order, head of column at Battalion Starting Point, ready to move off at 10.5 a.m.

6. **Halts.** Usual halts ten minutes to the hour.

7. **Watches.** Coys will send representatives to B.H.Q. at 8.30 a.m. to synchronise watches.

8. **Transport.**

    Will form up ready to move off in rear of the Battalion. Distance of 25 yards will be maintained between each group of six vehicles.

9. **Dinners.** Will be cooked on the march and eaten on arrival in billets about 1.30 p.m.

10. **Blankets.**

    Will be rolled in bundles of ten, distinctly marked and dumped at Q.M. Stores by 8 a.m.

11. **Officers' Valises.**

    To be dumped at Q.M. Stores by 9 a.m.

12. **Sick Parade.**

    At 8 a.m. The M.O. will render to Orderly Room immediately after sick parade a nominal roll of men unfit to march. These men will parade ready to proceed at 10.5 a.m.

13. **Officers' Mess Stores.**

    Mess Cart must be loaded by 9 a.m. and proceed independently and follow DEVONS Transport to POMMERA.

14. **Billets.**

    Must be left scrupulously clean. O.C. Coys will render a certificate to the Adjutant to this effect before passing Battalion Starting Point.

15. **Guard.** Regimental Quarter Guard will march with their Coy. Police will take over Prisoners.

16. **Billeting Party.**

   2nd Lt. S.H. Gillard and C.Q.M.S. Waldron will proceed by Lorry at 7.30 a.m. from Brigade H.Q.
   One N.C.O. from each Coy and one man each from B.H.Q. and Transport on bicycles will parade at H.Q. at 9 a.m. and proceed to POMMERA.   They will report to the Adjutant before proceeding and to 2nd Lt. Gillard on arrival at POMMERA.

17. **Unfit Men.**

   All unfit men who are likely to fall out will fall out at Battalion Starting Point and will parade under 2nd Lt. C.J. Rutland who will march them behind the Battalion to Brigade Starting Point.   He will then march them independently.

8.4.18.
(Sd) J.H. Maywood. Captain.
Adjt., 12th Bn. Gloucester Regiment.

Appendix

SECRET.

OPERATION ORDER No. 56
by
Lieut-Colonel. H. A. COLT. M.C.
Commanding 12th Battalion THE GLOUCESTERSHIRE REGIMENT.

Reference Map:— LENS.

1. <u>Move.</u> The Battalion will move tomorrow to BERLES-AU-BOIS (17 kilos).

2. <u>Route.</u> Main Road – LA CAUCHIE – POMMIER. 150 yards between Coys.

3. <u>Starting Point.</u> Battalion:– "A" Coys Mess.
Brigade:– On Main DOULLENS-ARRAS Road where 3rd class road crosses main road by the H in SOLERNEAU.

4. <u>Parade.</u> Ready to march off at 8 a.m. (eight a.m.).

5. <u>Halts.</u> Usual halts ten minutes to the hour.

6. <u>Order of March.</u> "A" – "B" and Band – "C" – H.Q. – "D".

7. <u>Watches.</u> Coys will send representatives to B.H.Q. at 7.30 a.m. to synchronise watches.

8. <u>Transport.</u> Will form up ready to move off in rear of the Battalion. Distance of 25 yards will be maintained between each group of six vehicles.

9. <u>Dinners.</u> Will be cooked on the march and eaten on arrival in billets about 1 p.m.

10. <u>Blankets.</u> Will be rolled in bundles of ten, distinctly marked and dumped at Q.M. Stores by 7 a.m.

11. <u>Officers' Valises.</u> To be dumped at Q.M. Stores by 7.15 a.m.

12. <u>Sick Parade.</u> At 6.45 a.m.

13. <u>Officers' Mess Stores.</u> Mess Cart must be loaded by 7.45 a.m. and proceed independently.

14. <u>Billets.</u> Must be left scrupulously clean. O.C. Coys will render a certificate to the Adjutant to this effect before passing Battalion Starting Point.

15. <u>Guard.</u> Coys will take charge of their own prisoners.

16. <u>Billeting Party.</u> 2nd Lt. S.H. Gillard, one N.C.O. from each Coy and one each from B.H.Q. and Transport on bicycles will parade at H.Q. at 8 a.m. and proceed to BERLES-AU-BOIS. They will report to the Adjutant before proceeding.

17. <u>Unfit Men.</u> All unfit men who are likely to fall out will fall out at Battalion Starting Point and will parade under 2nd Lt. C.J. Rutland who will march them behind the Battalion to Brigade Starting Point. He will then march them independently.

(Sd) J.H. Maywood. Captain.
Adjt., 12th Bn. Gloucestershire Regiment.

9.4.18.

SECRET.

OPERATION ORDER No. 57
by
Lieut-Colonel. H.A. COLT. M.C.
Commanding 12th Battalion THE GLOUCESTERSHIRE REGIMENT.

1. **Move.** The Battalion will entrain at MONDICOURT this morning. Journey will take about 6/8 hours.

2. **Starting Point.** "A" Coys Billet.

3. **Order of March.**

    H.Q. and Band — "A" — "B" — "C" — "D".

    (Dumped Personnel WILL march with the Battalion).

    The following vehicles will also march with the Battalion.

        2 L.G. Limbers.
        1 S.A.A. Limber.
        "D" Coys Cooker.
        6 pack Mules.

4. **Parade.** Coys will parade ready to move off at 10 a.m. (ten A.M.).

5. **Accommodation.** 20 Officers or 40 Other Ranks will be put in each covered van on the train.

6. **Blankets.** Will be taken in the train. They will be rolled in bundles of ten, marked clearly with names of Coys and dumped at Q.M. Stores for conveyance by lorry by 7.30 a.m. (seven-thirty a.m.).

7. **Officers' Trench Kits.** Will be dumped at Q.M. Stores by 8 a.m. These are only to be the equivalent of two blankets.

8. **Officers' Mess Kits.** Are to be made as small as possible and will be carried on Coy Lewis Gun Limber.

9. **Ammunition.** One Bandolier per man will be served out at the Station.

10. **Lewis Guns.** One extra Lewis Gun will be issued at MONDICOURT when entraining to "A" Coy and one to "C" Coy. There will be 16 (sixteen) magazines per gun.

11. **Rations.** Each man will entrain with rations for consumption today on them and Coy Commanders will issue a certificate to this effect to the Adjutant before marching off.

12. **Train Guards.** Coys will detail Guards for the train in accordance with the orders given for the recent train journey and the Orderly Officer will follow the same instructions as before issued.

13. **Train Orders.** The same orders issued form the train journey from ITALY will be adhered to.

14. **Billets.** Billets will be left scrupulously clean. O.C. Coys will render a certificate to the Adjutant to this effect before marching off.

            (Sd) J.H. Maywood. Captain.
            Adjt., 12th Bn. Gloucestershire Regt.

11.x.18.

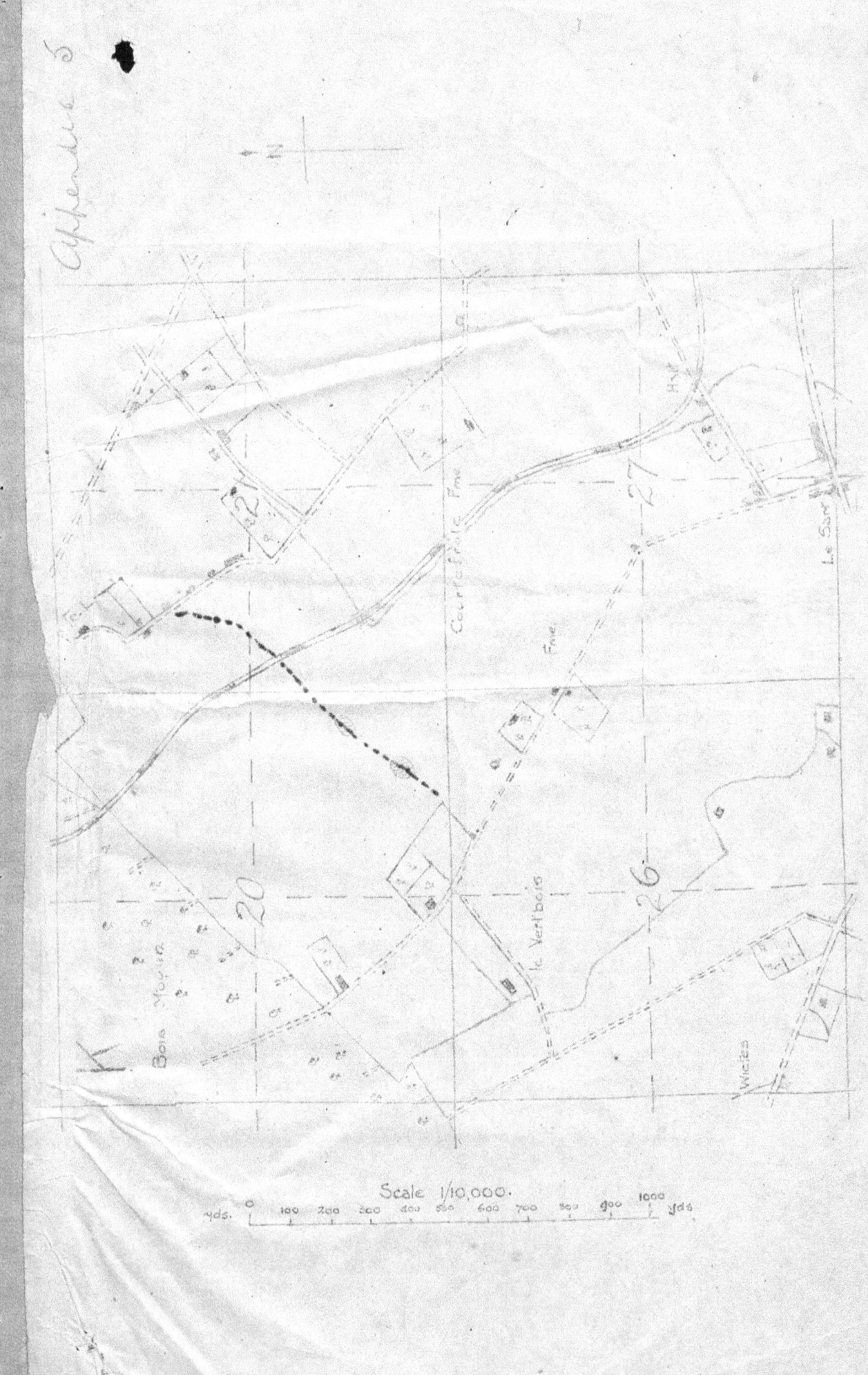

Confidential

War Diary
of
12th Battalion Gloucestershire Regiment
for the month of
May - 1918

W. G. Chapman Major
og 12th Battn. Gloucestershire Regt.

May 31/18

Vol 31

K.30

Army Form C. 2118.

WAR DIARY
INTELLIGENCE SUMMARY

12th Battalion GLOUCESTERSHIRE REGT.

MAY 1918

(Erase heading not required.)

Instructions regarding War Diaries and Intelligence Summaries are contained in F.S. Regs., Part II. and the Staff Manual respectively. Title pages will be prepared in manuscript.

Place	Date	Hour	Summary of Events and Information	Remarks and references to Appendices
In Support RE Sub Sector	1st		In support - no casualties - nothing of importance to report	See Appendix 1
	2nd		In support - nothing to report	
	3rd		In support during morning. About 4 pm Battalion moved to Camp at J.15.a, 95th Bde being Brigade in reserve. No casualties. Nothing to report.	
In Reserve J.15.a	4		In Divisional reserve - no casualties. Weather wet. Working parties found for work on Roads and tracks in Divisional Area	
"	5		One company working daily on new camp on W. Side of MORBECQUE. MERVILLE Road. about J.14 & J.23	
"	6		Capt N. HATHAWAY (RAMC), Lt TORGENHALGH, Lt F.H. LARRUBE MC, Lt A.K. HICKS, 2/Lt E.J. WILLIAMS, 2/Lt C.W. WEIR, 2/Lt C.O. MAY, 2/Lt A. BRACHER & 2/Lt C.J. BRUGG joined Battn	
"	7			
"	8			
	9		At dusk on 9th Battalion left Camp at J.15.a and marched via la Rue des MORTS to relieve 15th R. WARWICK REGT in left Subsector of left Bde front. Headquarters at K.26.8.9. No casualties nothing of importance to report	Appendix 2
In front line left Sub	10.		In front line. Weather fine. Casualties 1 O.R. Wounded.	

Army Form C. 2118.

WAR DIARY 12th Bn. Gloucestershire Regt.

INTELLIGENCE SUMMARY. May 1918.

(Erase heading not required.)

Place	Date	Hour	Summary of Events and Information	Remarks and references to Appendices
Left S Sector	11		In front line. Situation quiet and nothing of importance to report. Casualties 1 OR wounded 1 OR Gassed (slt.k)	
	12		In front line. Situation normal. Enemy snipers and M.G. active. Casualties 1 OR killed 2 OR wounded 2 OR wounded Gas (slt.k).	
	13		In front line. Situation quiet nothing of importance to report. Casualties 1 OR wounded	
	14		In front line. Situation quiet 1 OR Gassed. After dark Battn was relieved in front line by 1/D.C.L.I and moved back into support near ROUSSEL FARM with Headquarters in wood about K.8.a.2.5. Area shelled with gas shells which caused 4 casualties. Otherwise	Appendix 3
	15		In Support. Situation quiet. Usual working and carrying parties found for front line. 3 OR wounded.	

Army Form C. 2118.

WAR DIARY
or
INTELLIGENCE SUMMARY.

(Erase heading not required.)

12th Battn Gloucestershire Regt

May 1918

Place	Date	Hour	Summary of Events and Information	Remarks and references to Appendices
K 80~75	16		In support. Situation normal. Weather fine. Some shelling of our support line with H.E. and gas shells. Casualties 2 O.R. wounded 3 Wounded (shell gas) Capt J P Newman	
	17		In support. Usual enemy shelling but nothing of importance to report. 2 O.R. wounded 1 O.R. wounded (Gas)	
	18		In support. Situation quiet. No casualties. Weather continues fine	
	19		Situation quiet. Nothing to report. 1 O.R. wounded Lt R.S. SANDBACH + 4/Lt G N PARKINSON joined Battn	
	20		Quiet during morning. At 4.30 p.m. in afternoon 1E/SURREYS attacked and captured enemy post line opposite Right Brigade Right Subsector thus straightening our line. No immediate retaliation but about 11.30 pm enemy shelled roads + tracks to front line with all calibres. Our casualties - 3 O.R. wounded 2/Lt S R PHILLIPS 2/Lt C H Box joined Battn	
	21		In support. About 3 am enemy put down a heavy	

WAR DIARY 1/4th Bn. Gloucester. Regt 4
or
INTELLIGENCE SUMMARY. May 1918

Place	Date	Hour	Summary of Events and Information	Remarks and references to Appendices
In Support	21		Barrage on our own support line preparatory to counter attacking position gained by us yesterday. Shelling heaviest near B Coys HQ near ROUSSEL FARM. B Coy Headquarters were put on fire and our casualties were 3 OR killed Lt W J HAGGART and 14 OR wounded. 1 OR Gassed. Remainder of day enemy was exceptionally quiet	
	22		Commencing about 3 am enemy shelled our line heavily for about an hour. Casualties 1 OR killed 9/Appendix 4 3 OR wounded and 16 OR Gassed. After dark Battalion was relieved by 6th R. Warwickshire Regt and moved back to billets in STEENBECQUE, 9th Bde being Brigade in reserve to 5th Division. 2/Lt J H H WHITE rejoined	
STEENBECQUE	23		In reserve. Battalion bathing, cleaning up, refitting and checking deficiencies.	

Army Form C. 2118.

WAR DIARY
INTELLIGENCE SUMMARY.
(Erase heading not required.)

12th Gloucester Regt.
May 1918

Place	Date	Hour	Summary of Events and Information	Remarks and references to Appendices
STEENBECQUE	24		In Divisional Reserve. Training continued as usual	
	25		Classes formed under Specialist Officers.	
	26		Nothing of importance to report	
	27		Batt B.H.Q Route D50 June 27/48	
	28			
	29		At 1.40 pm Battalion moved off and proceeded via Pontoon Bridge at J.70.44 to VILLORBA CAMP J.K.e 02 and relieved 3/K.O.S.B in Brigade Reserve. No casualties.	Appendix 5
VILLORBA CAMP	30		In Brigade reserve. Weather fine. Usual working parties found. No casualties and nothing of importance to report.	
	31			

W. G. Chapman
Major
Commanding 12th Gloucester Regt.

Copy No.

Appendix 1

OPERATION ORDER No.
Lt-Col H.A.Colt. M.C. Cmdg.

1. **Move.** The battalion will move off to-morrow the 3rd inst. to camp atn J.15.a.
2. **Starting Point.** Red House at K.13.a. RSQ. 4/1
3. **Order of March.** B.H.Q. (as one platoon) A B C D Coys
4. **Time.** First party to pass starting point at 2 pm. remainder by platoons at 200 yards distance.
5. **Lewis Guns.** Coys will arrange to send their Lewis Guns down one at a time to the starting point, and will load up lewis guns and magazines in limbers. One man will accompany each limber, and the remainder will return to their Coys. Loading to be complete by 1.50 pm. sharp.
6. **Officers Kits.** Officers Mess and trench kits will be loaded in limbers at starting point by 2 pm. sharp.
7. **Camp Kettles.** Camp kettles will travel in Coy L.G.Limbers.
8. **Meals.** Dinners at 12 noon. Teas, as soon as possible after arrival in new area Quartermaster will arrange that they are ready on arrival.
9. **Advance Party.** Lt W.H.Coombs and 1 N.C.O. per Coy and 1 from B.H.Q. will proceed on foot to new area party will report at B.H.Q. at 10 am.
10. **Stores and S.S.A.** Will be dumped by Coys during the morning at present dressing station, care being taken that too much movement is not visible.
11. **Petrol Tins.** Coys will take steps to see that all petrol tins are carried to starting point, where they will be put into a limber detailed for the purpose.
12. **March Discipline.** Particular attention will be paid to march discipline. Care will be taken that men march about in formed bodies and that there are no stragglers. Any men unable to keep up must combine with other men similarly afflicted and form a slow party.
13. **Transport.** The following will be at starting point at 1.45 pm. ,-
    Lewis Gun Limbers.
    Limber for Officers T.&M.Kits.
    Limber for empty petrol tins.
    All chargers
14. **Reports.** On moving off Coys will send a report to B.H.Q. On arrival at new area Coys will report their arrival at new B.H.Q.

<u>Acknowledge</u>

2/5/18.

Lt. A/Adj.
PEACOCK.

SECRET! *file* OPERATION ORDER No 40.
By
Lieut-Colonel H.A.Colt M.C.
Commanding 12th Battalion THE GLOUCESTERSHIRE REGT

Ref Map- 36A NE 1/20000

1 Relief Battalion will relieve 15th R. WARWICKS tomorrow 9.5.18 as follows
"D" Coy relieves "D" Coy LEFT FRONT
"B" Coy ... "B" Coy CENTRE
"A" Coy ... "A" Coy RIGHT
"C" Coy ... "C" Coy SUPPORT

2 Starting Point Will be detailed as soon as known

3 Route do do do

4 Order of March "D" Coy "B" Coy "A" Coy "C" Coy BHQ

5 Distance 100 yards between platoons, Company HQ will march with one of the platoons.

6 Parade Will be detailed when known

7 Guides 3 Guides per Company and one for BHQ will be at K7 b 4/4 (near our original Camp on LA MOTTE ! MERVILLE Road) at 8 p.m.

8 Lewis Gun Limbers Will be detailed when route is known

9 Cooking There is a battalion cookhouse about K9 a 9/3 QM to arrange for cooking pots etc to be sent there

10 Water Will be sent up in petrol tins 10 to each Company

11 Stores Receipts for stores taken over to be at BHQ by 9 a.m. 10th inst

12 Officers Mess and Trench Kit will be detailed later

13 Completion of relief will be reported by code words as follows
HERRING ...... "A" Coy
BERRY ...... "B" Coy
BRAY ...... "C" Coy
COD ...... "D" Coy

14 Advance Party Officers Commanding companies with one runner and CSM will push on ahead of their companies as soon as it is dark enough, in order to take over stores etc.

(Sd) A Laird Lieut
A/Adj 12th Bn Gloucestershire Regt

SECRET.
URGENT.   Appendix to
                  OPERATION ORDER No. 40. dated 5/5/18

Appendix 2a

1. RATIONS : will be distributed as follows:-
        Our RATIONS for tomorrow 10th will be carried on the
                men up to the trenches.
        Quartermaster to arrange that all meat &c. for
        cooking is sent up, with sufficient cooking pots, to
        BATTN. COOK-HOUSE at R.O's H.Q..

2. WATER. Full petrol Tins will be sent up by Limbers to-night &
        dumped at B.H.Q. These will be refilled by Coys.
        on succeeding nights from water tanks at HALT X R.d.

3. TRANSPORT for LINE.
        *LEWIS GUN LIMBERS
        1 LIMBER for Petrol Tins
        1 do. for Officers Mess & Trench Kits.
        1 do. (or more if necessary) for Cooking Pots &
                Rations to be cooked by Cooks at Bn.Cook-Hse.
        The above will be at present Camp at 7 p.m. to-night

4. OTHER TRANSPORT. Transport Officer to arrange for vehicles to
        remove Officers Valises, Mens' Blankets,Shoemakers
        & Tailors, Canteen Stores &c.
             All the above must be ready to move at 5 p.m.

5. DUMPED PERSONNEL. will leave present Camp at 5 p.m and return to
        Transport Lines.

                ....
        * NOTE. As the road is very bad,LEWIS GUN LIMBERS will
                proceed independently after being loaded up,
                and will meet the Battn. at FORESTER'S HOUSE
                at J.10.d.6.7. First Limber to be there at
                6.30 p.m. (Order of March "D", "B", "A", "C".)
                ....

                                (Sd)   A. LAIRD, Lieut.
5/5/18   A/Adjt.13th Bn.Gloucester Regt.

Copies to:- Transport Officer
            Quartermaster
            War Diary.

Appx 3 / Bn Trench 56 A NE
Operation Order No. 4   1/20,000
By Lieut Col H.A. Colt M.C.

1. Battalion will be relieved on night 4/5 May by 1/O.C.L.I. On relief Battn will withdraw as follows:-
A Coy will take over trenches vacated by No 1 Coy /Devons. Position in trenches between river K15a 3.5 and forest at K 14 d 5.5
B Coy will take over trenches vacated by No 3 Coy /Devons ~~near A Coy Glouc~~ at about ROUSSEL FARM
C Coy will take over trenches vacated by No 2 Coy Devons near A Coy Gloucesters present position
D Coy will take over trenches vacated by No 4 Coy /Devons round orchard near K 9 Central

2. All stores, S.A.A. &c will be handed over and receipts obtained

3. Officers Mess & Trench Kits to be carried to new position under Coy arrangements

4. Dispositions
   C Coy in support b/p C.s for
                              counter attacking
   D Coy in support of Devons - - -
   1 platoon 'A' Coy under orders
      of Devons for counter attacking
   Officers of these Coys and platoon
   Commander of A Coy will report
   to the Officer commanding Unit to
   which they are attached

5. Cooking can be done by night at all
   Coy HQrs
6. Water will be brought up by Mules
   to Companies
7. Rations will be dumped:-
   A Coy at K 14 b 4 4
   B Coy   K 8 d 3 3
   C Coy   K 3 d 8 2
   D Coy   K 9 d 8 2
   HQrs   at BHQ
8. Reports On being relief - Coys to
   report by code word Henry
   and when in new positions
   by code word Archer
9. As soon as possible after relief
   Coys will send to BHQ rough
   sketch showing dispositions
   lists of stores taken over

10/ <u>Lewis Guns</u> to be carried
by teams; care being
taken that no magazines
are left in trenches

11 <u>Guides</u> Adjutant to detail
3 Runners or observers to
reconnoitre each Coy
trenches.
A Coy to send an Officer to
BHQ at 4 pm to take over
trenches
B. C. & D. will send Officers as
soon as light permits
to reconnoitre new trenches

A. Laird
Lt 6/A&S
PEACOCK

OPERATION ORDER No. 42

Ref. map. 36 a 1/40,000

Appendix 4

1. **Relief.** This Battalion will be relieved to-night 22/23 May by 16th. R.W. Regrt. After relief Battn. will withdraw to STEENBECQUE.

2. **Advance Party.** Capt. C.S.Petheram, N.C. and C.Q.M.S's. will proceed to STEENBECQUE as soon as possible after receipt of these orders to take over billets from 16th. R.War.Regt. Coys. will take over from their opposite number. C.Q.M.S's to meet their Coys at X Rds. I 5 d 5.9. and guide to billets.

3. **Trench Stores.** will be handed over to incoming Unit and receipts sent to B.H.Q. by 12 noon 23/5/18.

4. **Route.** After relief Coys. will move off by Platoons at 222 Yds. interval via La rue des Morts-Rd.Junc. J 11 b 85.70 - Rd.Junc. J 4.a.95.95 and then along Canal to PONTOON BRIDGE at J.7. 45/40 thence to X Rds. I 5. a 5-9- where C.Q.M.S'S will be waiting.

5. **Lewis Guns.** Lewis Gun Limbers will be sent up to meet Coys at 11.15 p-m-

6. **Cooks Utensils.** to be dumped at Rd. Junc. K.8 a 35/10 before 10.45 p-m- but not until after dusk. O.C.Hqrs. to arrange to place guard of 2 men over dump and load. TRANSPORT OFFICER to arrange transport

7. **Petrol Tins.** to be sent down with Cooks utensils.

8. **Teas** Cooks will be sent down as soon as possible after dark and will report to QMr. at Transport lines. to prepare tea for Battn on arrival in Billets.

9. **Trench Kits and Mess Stores.** to be taken on L.Gun Limbers. Transport Officer will detail 2 Limbers for BHQ. to be at Rd.Junc. K.8 a 35/10 at 11.15 p-m.

10. **Officers Valises & Blankets.** to be taken to new Billets.

11. **Officers Chargers.** To come up with Lewis Gun Limbers. BHQ. Officers chargers to be at old dressing station K. 13 b.5.5 by 12.30 a.m.

12. **Guides** Each Coy will find 1 Guide per platoon and 1 for Coy-HQ- BHQ. to find 2 guides. All guides to be at HALTE where Railway crosses Via Roma by 10.45 p-m-
    Relieveing Coys arrive in order.
    1. "B" Coy. 16.R.W.R. relieve "C" Coy-12/Glosters
    2. D   "   "   "   D   "
    3. C   "   "   "   A   "
    4. A   "   "   "   B   "

13. Completion of Relief to be reported as follows.
    "A" Coy- Want Message Pad
    "B" Coy Burnt Out
    "C" Coy Want Revolver Amm.
    "D" Coy Information Weird.
    O.C. Coys on reaching billets will send an Orderly to HQ. to report arrival of Coy and to wait for orders

22/5/18

Sd. J.P.Webb, Capt.
A/Adjt. 12th.Bn.Glouc.Regt

OPERATION ORDER No. 43   Copy no.

1. Relief.   The Battalion will relieve 2nd K.O.S.B. in Brigade Reserve
                  in VILLORBA CAMP to-day.

2. Starting Point.   Where Road crosses Railway in I.12.a.7/6.

3. Route.   Rd. Junc. L.12.b.5/9 – Pontoon Bridge J.7.c.45/45 – Cross roads
                  J.8.a.9/6 to VILLORBA CAMP J.15.c.0/2.

4. Time of Starting.
                  First Company to pass Starting Point 1.40 p.m., remainder at
                  five minute intervals in the following order,– B.H.Q. A.
                  B. C. D.

5. Advance Party.   As detailed.

6. Officers Trench Kits.
                  To be dumped outside Bn Orderly Room by 12.30 p.m.

7. Officers Valises.
                  To be dumped outside Bn Orderly Room by 12 noon. T.O. will
                  have them taken back to Transport Lines.

8. Blankets.   To be rolled in bundles of ten, distinctly marked and dumped
                  as under, by 12 noon.
                     B.H.Q.)
                     A   )   At Bn Orderly Room.
                     B   )
                     C   )   On edge of road about I.5.d.8/3.
                     D   )
                  These blankets will be taken to VILLORBA CAMP.

9. Officers Mess Kit.
                  To be carried on Lewis Gun limbers, Transport Officer will detail
                  2 limbers to carry extra stores and B.H.Q. Mess Kit. To be at
                  B.H.Q. Mess at 1.30 p.m.
                  Messing will be by Coys.

10. Lewis Gun Limbers.   Will march with their Companies.

11. Cookers.   Will be in position in VILLORBA CAMP in time to make teas by
                  4.30 p.m.

12. Band.   Will play Battalion out and will then come up, independently
                  parading at 3 p.m. T.O. will provide 1 limber to carry band stores
                  to be at Bn Orderly Room at 3 p.m.

13. Orderly Room.
                  Surplus orderly room stores will be dumped with Officers valises
                  by 12 noon, to be taken to Transport Lines.

14. Stores.   Lists of stores taken over will be handed in to B.H.Q. by 6 p.m.
                  to-day.   Receipts will be obtained for all tents, shelters and
                  stores handed over in this area to 14th R.War Reg. These will
                  be handed to B.H.Q. by 6 p.m. to-day.

15. Water.   Water carts and petrol tins will be brought up to new area.

16. Cleanliness of Billets.
                  Billets must be handed over scrupulously clean.

17. Completion of Relief.
                  Will be reported personally by Coy. Comdrs. to C.O.

                                              (Sd) J.P. Webb. Capt. A/Adjt.
                                              12th Bn Gloucestershire Regiment.

Confidential

War Diary

of

12th Gloucestershire Regt

for the month of

JUNE 1918

Army Form C. 2118.

WAR DIARY
or
INTELLIGENCE SUMMARY.

(Erase heading not required.)

Instructions regarding War Diaries and Intelligence Summaries are contained in F. S. Regs., Part II. and the Staff Manual respectively. Title pages will be prepared in manuscript.

Place	Date	Hour	Summary of Events and Information	Remarks and references to Appendices

Army Form C. 2118.

WAR DIARY 12th Battalion Gloucestershire Regt
of
INTELLIGENCE SUMMARY. June 1918.

(Erase heading not required.)

Instructions regarding War Diaries and Intelligence Summaries are contained in F. S. Regs., Part II. and the Staff Manual respectively. Title pages will be prepared in manuscript.

Place	Date	Hour	Summary of Events and Information	Remarks and references to Appendices
VILORBA CAMP T.15.c.o.v Sheet 36a	1 2 3		In Brigade reserve. Right Sub-Sector. No casualties. Weather fine. Large working parties found daily for work on Divisional Reserve lines. Little training carried out.	
	4		Battalion left Vilorba Camp & moved via Va Roma to 4.2 Subsector and relieved 1/D.C.L.I. in front line No casualties. Nothing of importance to report. (see Appendices 1)	
L2 S. Sector	5		In front line. Enemy artillery and T.M's active. Night of 5/6 June 9/47. E.E. SHEPHERD, A/C.S.M. J. LEWIS & Sgt F.C. SMITH & 1 O.R. were killed by H.T.M. & O.R. killed by M.G. Fire 1 O.R. Wounded.	
	6		In front line. Situation normal. 1 O.R. wounded. Enemy artillery activity nothing of importance to report.	
	7		Situation quiet. 1 O.R. Wounded. Weather dull nothing to report.	

Army Form C. 2118.

WAR DIARY

12th Bn. Gloucestershire Regt

June 1918

INTELLIGENCE SUMMARY.

(Erase heading not required.)

Instructions regarding War Diaries and Intelligence Summaries are contained in F. S. Regs., Part II. and the Staff Manual respectively. Title pages will be prepared in manuscript.

Place	Date	Hour	Summary of Events and Information	Remarks and references to Appendices
L3 Sector	8		In front line. Situation quiet. Nothing to report. 2/Lt W.B. COGNOCK joined	
	9		-Do- Some enemy artillery activity. No casualties. Nothing to report. Capt J.H. MAYNOOD rejoined	
	10		-Do- Situation normal. Nothing of importance to report. 2/Lt ROWE & PAWSON joined	
	11		In front line. Enemy shelled front and support lines with HE and Gas. 4 OR wounded - Gas. Otherwise situation normal.	
	12		Battalion was relieved night 12/13 by 1/4 Oxfords (1st Bde) and marched to ARCADE CAMP J.28.a. 3 casualties during relief. 95th Bde in Div Reserve (Appendix 2)	2/Lt W.G. SHEPHERD
"ARCADE" CAMP J.28.A.	13		Training commenced. Hours cleaning up and specialists. Bathing, cleaning & checking deficiencies	

WAR DIARY 12 Bn. Gloucestershire Regt
INTELLIGENCE SUMMARY
June 1918

Place	Date	Hour	Summary of Events and Information	Remarks and references to Appendices
ARCADE CAMP	15		In Bde Reserve in ARCADE Camp. Usual training carried out. At 1 am on morning of 18th enemy shelled camp with 4.2" HE. dropped 1 O.R. killed 5 O.R. wounded. camp again shelled about 9 pm 18/6/18 but no casualties	7/K.O.S.B. joined 14/6/18 Appdx 3
	16			
	17			
	18			
	19		On night 19/20 Battalion moved forward and relieved 7/KOSB 131 Bde and 4/Bord in Support in M S. Sector. no casualties. Nothing to report	
	20		In support line situation quiet. 2 O.R. wounded some shelling of our back areas in early morning. 1 O.R. killed returning to Transport lines.	
tenth to Support				

WAR DIARY

13th Br. Cheshire Regt   June 1918

Army Form C. 2118.

INTELLIGENCE SUMMARY.

Place	Date	Hour	Summary of Events and Information	Remarks and references to Appendices
Support Line	21/22		In support line. No casualties. Situation quiet. Nothing of importance to report. 1/5 R.W. Devons in front	
	23		On night of 23rd Bn relieved /Devons in front line - Left front enemy shelled tracks and trenches heavily with HE and Gas during relief. 3 OR wounded. 23 OR Gassed.	
Front Line	24		In front line. Some enemy artillery activity. 2 OR Wounded Otherwise nothing of importance to report.	
	25		In front line. 2 OR Wounded. Lt R.N.DREW & Lt J.G.ABBOTT and 1 OR killed while on patrol about 9 P.M. On night of 25/26 Battn was relieved by 1/5 Surreys and went into Bde Reserve at SPRESIANO CAMP 3.50	Appendix

Army Form C. 2118.

WAR DIARY
INTELLIGENCE SUMMARY.
(Erase heading not required.)

June 1918

Place	Date	Hour	Summary of Events and Information	Remarks and references to Appendices
SPRESIANO CAMP J. 14 B (Sheet 36a)	26/6/18		In reserve. Battalion resting and cleaning up. Weather fine. Nothing of importance to report.	
-"-	27		In reserve. During the morning Battalion carried out a Practice Scheme.	Officers
		7pm	At 7pm Battalion moved off from Camp to march to trenches. While crossing road about K.7 & 8.1, Battalion was caught by enemy shell fire (HE + gas) - and 47 casualties were sustained. Most of these were caused by gas and these cases returned to duty next day. Battalion lay down at edge of wood to wait for nightfall when they moved up to "Assembly" positions - i.e. front line trenches then held by Devons.	

WAR DIARY
or
INTELLIGENCE SUMMARY.
(Erase heading not required.)

Army Form C. 2118.

12th Bn Gloucester Regt
June 1918

Instructions regarding War Diaries and Intelligence Summaries are contained in F. S. Regs, Part II. and the Staff Manual respectively. Title pages will be prepared in manuscript.

Place	Date	Hour	Summary of Events and Information	Remarks and references to Appendices
GRUDESCOURT	28		12th Gloucester attacked and captured enemys positions as shewn on attached Meange hypo Dispositions for attack B Coy on right A " " left C " in support A " Reserve The 10th E Yorks (92nd Bde) attacked on our left and 1 DCLI on our right. During night 27/28 Battn moved up and took up position in Assembly trenches. B.D Coy in our front line. C Coy in the hedge behind B. D Coys and A Coy in trenches in orchard around B.H.Q. (K+a2b) One Coy of 4th Surreys were also disposed around Bristol Park K.3d & 2. Before daybreak B Coy moved out and lay down in open about 100yds in front of our line. C Coy moving into the trenches thus vacated.	See Appendices 6 through indi...

WAR DIARY
or
INTELLIGENCE SUMMARY.

Army Form C. 2118.

B. Lincolns Regt June 1918

Place	Date	Hour	Summary of Events and Information	Remarks and references to Appendices
CRU DEGURE	21		The Attack

At Zero hour - 6 a.m - Barrage opened and continued as shown on attached Barrage table. There was no preliminary bombardment.
Troops moved forward under barrage to its attack and at first met with little opposition although some casualties were caused by our men pushing forward too close under the barrage.

Method of Attack

B. & D. Coys were to capture all objectives up to Le CORNET PERDU which they were to contain and push on to final objective Road N side at O.5.
C. Coy to be responsible for taking Le CORNET PERDU and for filling gap in attacking line | An Appendix 6
An Appendix 9 |

WAR DIARY
of 1st Battalion Glasgow Regt
INTELLIGENCE SUMMARY.
(Erase heading not required.)

Army Form C. 2118.

June 1918

Place	Date	Hour	Summary of Events and Information	Remarks and references to Appendices
CRUPEILLE XX			Having completed their duty 'C' Coy to dig in on line K 5d 10.30 to K 5 b 40.30. As soon as protective barrage ceased front line Coys to send out patrols to Run-PLATE BECQUE to destroy bridge and to watch enemy movements. Air Intentional patrol consisting of 1 Officer and 2 sections 12/Glors and a similar party of 10. E/YORKS on our left is move well in rear of attacking force to K 6a 36 to keep touch with Bn on our left.	
			General. All objectives were taken with little opposition according to schedule. When nearing final objective enemy machine guns became [active]	

WAR DIARY
or
INTELLIGENCE SUMMARY

Army Form C. 2118.

12th Bn Gloucesters Regt June 1918

Place	Date	Hour	Summary of Events and Information	Remarks and references to Appendices
	27		Bombardment and severe arm craters enemy artillery opened with shrapnel on our front line at 2am & 2 and at 2am & 12 with HE (4, 5, 6, 9) on front line and area around SAUDESCURE CHURCH. At 7.10am heavy m.g. fire was opened our front objective to be taken also being engineered by mortar at 7.30am. Gr Jt. Offen J. International patrol reported himself to be in touch with 10th Notts on left and our left Coy. Enemy artillery active and S.9 on area around "CAUDESCURE R" from 8.30am until 9.30 a.m. From 9.30 a.m. until midday situation fairly quiet	

WAR DIARY or INTELLIGENCE SUMMARY

Army Form C. 2118.

12th Bn Gloucester Regt
June 1916

Place	Date	Hour	Summary of Events and Information	Remarks and references to Appendices
CANDESCENT	3½		except for machine gun fire which was continuous. About 12.15 pm enemy artillery opened on our new forward positions and on our artillery retaliating. A general shelling duel ensued until 5 pm. During the afternoon a few parties were rounded up from amongst the corn in rear of, but just in our front line. About 3 pm patrols were sent out under cover of a barrage but could find no trace of enemy on our side of PAUL FRANC BEROUF. During the afternoon "C" Coy were up and reinforced B + D Coys in the Line. "A" 1E SURREYS taking up A Coys position in moving up into support coming Company in Reserve	

WAR DIARY
INTELLIGENCE SUMMARY.

(Erase heading not required.)

Army Form C. 2118.

1 Bn Gloucester Regt
June 1918

Place	Date	Hour	Summary of Events and Information	Remarks and references to Appendices
ONUBESCURE	29		Casualties. 2/Lt L.C. MAY, 2/Lt E.W. FARRINGTON Killed, Capt WIBRAY 2/Lt GUNYEIR wounded. In front line. Companies improving positions to. Enemy shelled our positions heavily throughout the day. W.R.E. GUISE killed. 2/Lt T.F. BENJAMIN Wounded (Gas) and 2/Lt F.H. LATROBE me wounded (this officer returned to duty same day) About 100 OR Casualties	2 Officers killed 2 wounded 4 O.R's Total Gasses Gassed 2 man Wounded about 100
"	30		In front line. Situation fairly quiet and nothing of importance to report. After dark. Battalion was relieved by 12th Royal Scots Fusiliers (9th Bn) and marched to reserve Billets at STEENBECQUE, which were reached about 4 am. 1/7/18. To commanding	

W.A.C. Lt Col.
Cdg 1/1 Bn Gloucester Regt

OPERATION ORDER No. 44.   Appendix   Copy No. 9
by
Major W.G. Chapman. M.C.
Cmdg. 12th Battalion the Gloucestershire Regt.

Ref. Map. Sheet 36A N.E. Edition 7. 1/20,000.

1. **Relief.** 12th Glosters will relieve 1st D.C.L.I. in L2 Sub-sector to-night.

2. **Starting Point.** Exit to Camp.

3. **Time of Starting.** First Company will pass starting point at 8.30 pm. 200 yards distance between Coys, and 100 yards between platoons.

4. **Order of March.** B.H.Q. - A. - D. - C. - B.

5. **Route.** Round outside of wood and up VIA ROMA.

6. **Guides.** 4 guides per Coy, and 2 for B.H.Q. will be at K.13.b.25/70 at 9.45 pm.

7. **Taking Over.**
   "A" Coy will take over from "D" Coy D.C.L.I.
   "B" Coy   "   "   "   "B" Coy   "
   "C" Coy   "   "   "   "A" Coy   "
   "D" Coy   "   "   "   "C" Coy   "

8. **Advance Party.** O.C. B.H.Q. will send an advanced party to take over stores, telephones etc.
   O.C. "B" Coy will send an advanced party to take over stores.

9. **Lewis Guns.** Lewis Gun limbers will march with their Coys, under orders of O.C. Coy.
   28 Magazines per gun will be taken up, remainder will be dumped by Coys on track by Cookhouse by 5.30 pm.
   They will be taken to Transport.

10. **Officers Trench Kits.** To be carried on Lewis Gun limbers. Any surplus Kits Officers wish to return to Transport will be stacked on track by Cookhouse by 5.30 pm.

11. **Officers Mess Kit.** To be carried on Lewis Gun Limbers. Transport Officer will detail two limbers to carry extra stores and B.H.Q. Mess Kit to be on track behind B.H.Q. Mess at 7.45 pm. Surplus mess kit for return to Transport should be dumped with Officers surplus kit.

12. **Cooks.** Will return with Cookers to Transport Lines when the Battn. moves off.

13. **Band.** Will return to Transport when Battn. moves off. Band Sergt. will detail 6 men to stay behind to guard Dump at Cookhouse until it has all been cleared. Band stores will be dumped by Cookhouse before 8 pm.

14. **Orderly Room.** Surplus orderly room stores will be dumped near Cookhouse by 5.30 pm. for return to Transport.

15. **Packs.** All packs must be distinctly marked on side nearest back with Regt. No. Name and Coy.
   They will be dumped by Coys on track near Cookhouse by 5.30 pm. Transport Officer will arrange to take them to Transport Lines and to keep them by Coys.

16. Canteen.   Canteen will close at 7.30 pm., and stores will be packed and d
                dumped with band instruments before 8 pm.

17. Trench Stores.   Signed lists of Trench Stores taken over, including
                maps, orders, etc., to reach B.H.Q. before dawn 5/6/18.

18. Work.   Work in hand to be carefully taken over and carried on with.

19. Dispositions.   Sketch of dispositions to be sent to B.H.Q. as soon as po
                possible after relief.

20. Completion of Relief.   To be reported to B.H.Q. by following Code.-
                "A" Coy   Want another D.C.M.
                "B" Coy   Lost short MAC.
                "C" Coy   C of CENTRE.
                "D" Coy   BLACKMAY.

21. Cleanliness of Camp.   The Camp must be left scrupulously clean.

22. Water.   Will come up in petrol tins with rations.

23. Cooking.   Meat will be cooked at Transport.   Tea will be made in the
                line under Coy arrangements.   Soup will be sent up in
                containers as often as possible.

Copies to:-
    O.C. B.H.Q. 1
          A Coy   2
          B Coy   3
          C Coy   4
          D Coy   5
    C.O.   6
    2nd in Command. 7
    Adjutant.   8
    File   9
    T.O.   10

                                        (Sd) J.P. Webb, Capt. A/Adj.
                                        12th Bn Gloucestershire Regiment.

Appendix 2

OPERATION ORDER No. 48.
by
Major W. G. Chapman, M.C.
Cmdg. 12th Battalion Gloucestershire Regiment.

Ref. Map - Sheet 36 A N.E. Edition 7. 1/20,000.

1. RELIEF. The Battalion will be relieved on the night 12/13th by 1/Ches Regt. After relief Coys will withdraw to Divl. Reserve in ARCADE CAMP about J.7.d. 100 yards distance to be maintain between platoons.

2. GUIDES. Each Coy will send 5 guides to B.H.Q. by 9 pm. (The 1/Cheshires are organised in 4 platoons & Coy H.Q.) 2/Lt Davidson will collect these guides and will take them to Rendez-vous K.13.a 7/4 he will remain there until all reliefs have moved up.

3. COMPLETION OF RELIEF. To be reported to B.H.Q. by code words as under:-
"A"   Peter wants leave.
"B"   Military Cross.
"C"   Gollywog.
"D"   Redney.

4. ARRIVAL IN CAMP. O.C. Coys will report personally to C.O. as soon as their Coys are all in.

(Sd) J.H. Maywood. Capt.
Adj. 12th Bn Gloucestershire Regiment.

Appendix 3

OPERATION ORDER No 50.   Copy No...3...
                    by
        Major W.G. Chapman, M.C. Commanding
        12th. Bn. Gloucestershire Regiment.

Reference Map FRANCE 36 A N.E. Edit.7 1/20,000

1. **Relief.** 12th. Gloucesters will relieve 2nd. K.O.S.Bs. and 1st DEVONS in Support in Left Brigade Sector to-night.

2. **Dispositions.**
    Coys will be disposed as under-
    "A" Coy K 14 d 50.60 – K 14 d 80.75
             K 14 b 60.20 – K 15 a 05.45
             K 15 a 10.50 – K 9 c 55.30

    "B" Coy. About FARM K. 14 b 65.95

    "C" Coy K. 9 b 35.85 – K 3 d 40.10
             K 3 d 35.45 – K 3d 15.50
    "D" Coy K. 9 c 55.30 – About CHINESE CAMP. K 9 b 20.25

    BHQ.   K 7 d 95.95

    As soon as Company Commanders are satisfied that their men are in position they will inform Officers Commanding any men of 2/K.O.S.B. or 1/Devons in their vicinity that they can go, and will report relief complete.

3. **Starting Point.** – OFFICERS MESS.

4. **Time of Starting.** First Company will pass Starting Point at 6.30 p-m.

5. **Order of March.** "C" – "A" – "D" – "B" – BHQ. will proceed independently under Orders of O.C.

6. **Route.** TRack 7 – which leaves MORBECQUE – HAVERSKERQUE Rd about 400 yards S.E. of CROWE Station and passes through OLD SPRESIANO CAMP.

7. **Advance Party.** O.C. Coys will send forward advance party to take over Stores &c.

8. **DRESS** Fighting Order.

9. **Lewis Guns.** Lewis Gun Limbers will march under orders of O.C. Coy via VIA ROMA. A Party will be detailed to proceed with limbers to unload them and dump under Coy arrangements so that limbers are not kept waiting for Coys. 28 Magazines per Gun will be taken up ; remainder will be dumped outside Orderly Room by 5.30 pm. They will be taken to Transport.

10 **Officers Trench Kits.** To be carried on Lewis Gun Limbers.

11. **Officers Valises.** To be stacked outside Orderly Room by 8 p;m.

12. **Officers Mess Kit.** To be carried on Lewis Gun Limbers. Transport Officer will detail 2 Limbers to carry extra stores & BHQ. Mess Kit, to be outside Orderly Room at 7.45 p.m. They will proceed via VIA ROMA to K 7 d 85.90 where they will be unloaded under orders of O.C. BHQ.

13 **Cooks.** Will return with Cookers to Transport Lines after Battn moves off.

14 **Band.** Band will return to Transport when Battn. moves off. Band Sgt. will detail 6 men to stay behind to Guard dump at Orderly Room until it has been cleared. Band stores will be dumped there after Bn. moves off.
    Band will play Battn out.

2.

15. Orderly Room.	Surplus Orderly Room stores to be dumped outside Orderly Room by 5.30 p-m for return to Transport.
16 Packs.	To be dumped BY COMPANIES outside Bn. Orderly Room by 5.30pm. Transport Officer will arrange to take them to Transport Lines and to keep them by Companies.
17. Canteen.	Will close at 8 p.m. and stores will be packed and dumped with Band instruments.
18 Trench Stores.	Signed Lists of Trench Stores, Maps &c. to reach BHQ by 9 a.m. 20/6/18
19. Dispositions	Sketch of Dispositions to be sent to BHQ. as soon as possible after relief.
20 Cleanliness of Camp.	Camp must be handed over scrupulously clean.
21 Water -	To come up in Petrol Tins with Rations. To-night - water will be taken to BHQ. O.C.Toys. will make arrangements to fetch same. T.O. Will detail one extra Limber for water
22. Cooking	Meat will be cooked at the Transport. Tea will be made in Line under Company arrangements. SOUP will be sent up in containers as often as possible.
23. Completion of relief.	To be reported to BHQ by following code words.

      "A" Coy - ACKNOWLEDGE
      "B" Coy. - Frankly Commanded.
      "C" Coy - Salvage to be sent home.
      "D" Coy - DON Done.

24. Officers Chargers.   To be at Camp by 8.25 8.15 p-m-

Copies to-

    1 C.O.
    2. 2nd in Command
    3 Adjutant
    4. T.O.& Q.Mr.
    5; O.C. BHQ.
    6. "A" Coy
    7. "B" Coy
    8 "C" Coy
    9 "D" Coy
   10 File.

                                         Sd J.H.Maywood. Capt.
                                 Adjt. 12th. Bn. Gloucester Regt.

SECRET.

To – All recipients of O.O.No. 50.

AMENDMENTS.

1. DISPOSITIONS. Dispositions stated in above order are cancelled, and the following substituted :-
There are two lines of trenches W. of R. BOURRE astride CHAPELLE BOOM – CAUDESCURE Road,
these will be occupied as under.

  Right of Road. "A" Coy in front.
         "B" Coy in support.
  Left of Road.   "C" Coy in Front.
         "D" Coy in support.

Trenches will probably want considerable improvement, which must be taken in hand, if any Coy is too crowded O.C. Coy must try and arrange with neighboring Coys for accomodation Sketch of dispositions and report on accomodation must be submitted according to O.O. No. 5p

2. There must be no unavoidable movement by day as enemy shell these trenches if any movement is seen.

            (Sd) J.H. Maywood, Capt.
         Adj. 12th Bn Gloucestershir regiment

OPERATION ORDER No. 50.
by
Lieut-Col H.A.Colt. M.C.
Cmdg. 12th Battalion Gloucestershire Regiment.

Ref. Map - FRANCE 36 A N.E. 1/20,000 Ed.7.

Appendix 4

1. RELIEF. The Battalion will be relieved to-night 25/26th as follows:-
"C" Coy by 1 Coy 1/E Surreys.
Remainder of battalion by 1/Devons as follows:-
"D" Coy by No.3.
"B" Coy by No.1.
"A" Coy by No.4.

On completion of relief, Coys will withdraw to SPRESIANO CAMP
(J.14.b.6/6.)

2. GUIDES. "C" Coy will detail 1 guide per platoon, and 1 from Coy H.Q. Guides to report to B.H.Q. at 10.15 pm.

3. ROUTE. After relief Coys will move indepedently by platoons at 100 yards interval to SPRESIANO CAMP via VIA ROMA, and track along southern edge of wood to MORBECQUE - HAVERSKERQUE main road.

4. TAKING OVER. Major W.G.Chapman M.C. will arrange to take over SPRESIANO CAMP from 1/E.Surreys and arrange for billeting.

5. COMPLETION OF RELIEF. Will be reported to B.H.Q. by code words as follows:
"A" Coy   R.E.Material.
"B" Coy   Elephant Dugout.
"C" Coy   Latrine Seats.
"D" Coy   No Maps.

(Sd) J.H.Maywood. Capt.
Adj. 12th Battalion Gloucestershire Reg

SECRET.   OPERATION ORDER No.51. Appendix 5   Copy No. 10
                                    by
                          Lt-Col H.A.Colt. M.C.
                       Cmdg. 12th Bn The Gloucestershire Regiment.

1. RELIEF.   12th Glosters will relieve the Coys of the 1/Devons who are at
                  present occupying our assembly position in the front line.
                  "B" & "D" Coys relieve these Coys
                  Remainder take up positions as already detailed.

2. STARTING POINT.   Exit to camp.

3. TIME.   First Coy will pass starting point at 7 pm. 100 yards interval
                  to be kept between platoons.

4. ORDER OF MARCH.   B.H.Q. - "D" - "B" - "C" - "A".

5. ROUTE.   No. 7 Track.

6. HALTS.   There will be frequent halts on the journey. On arriving at the
                  edge of the wood in the WARWICK CASTLE area, battalion will halt
                  until dark. No one will move outside the wood until 10.30 pm.

7. ADVANCE PARTY.   2/Lt G.M.Weir will move at 2 pm. accompanied by RSM
                  Crossman. They will report at Devon Headquarters WARWICK CASTLE
                  and from there go forward to take over the stores at the advance
                  dump.

8. DRESS.   FIGHTING ORDER. All Mills bombs, extra S.A.A. smoke bombs etc.
                  will be served out to the men after tea. Lewis guns and 28
                  magazines per gun will be carried up by gun teams(Coy Cmdrs to
                  detail extra men to assist them).

9. PACKS ETC.   Packs and Officers kits will be dumped at officers mess and
                  collected subsequently by Transport. Officers trench kits (if any)
                  and mess kits to be dumped at B.H.Q. by 6 pm.   TAKEN TO TRANSPORT LINES
                                                                  LATTER

10. TRANSPORT.   T.officer will arrange that these kits are taken up to BRISTOL
                  PARK. Extra lewis gun magazines will be dumped at B.H.Q. by 6 pm.
                  and will be taken up to BRISTOL PARK by transport.

11. DUMPED PERSONNEL.   Dumped personnel, Cooks, and band etc. will return to
                  Transport Lines after tea.

12. TRENCH STORES.   Lists of trench stores taken over to be sent to B.H.Q. as
                  soon as possible after relief.

13. DISPOSITIONS.   A rough sketch of dispositions to be sent to B.H.Q. as
                  soon as possible after relief.

14. COMPLETION OF RELIEF.   To be reported to B.H.Q. by runner.

15. CLEANLINESS.   This camp must be left scrupulously clean.

16. WATER - RATIONS.   T.Officer will arrange to send up 50 tins of water to
                  BRISTOL PARK to-night.
                  Rations for to-morrow will be cooked this afternoon and issued
                  to the men after tea.

17. TOOLS. BRIDGES ETC.   Will be drawn from B.H.Q. by Coys as soon as possible
                  after relief. No more picks and shovels than are necessary are
                  to be drawn.

18. CHARGERS.   Officers chargers to be at Camp by 6.45 pm.

                                              (Sd) J.H.Haywood Capt. Adj.
                                              12th Bn Gloucestershire Regiment.

SECRET.

Appendix 6

Copy No.

OPERATION ORDER No. 49.
by
Lt-Col H. A. Colt. M.C.
Cmdg. 12th Bn The Gloucestershire Regiment.

Ref. Map - Message Map Issued.

1. **INTENTION.** On a date and at an hour to be notified later 12th Bn Gloucester Regt will attack and capture enemy's position as shown on Message Maps.

2. **FLANKS.** The 10th E.Yorks will attack on our left, and 1/D.C.L.I on our right.

3. **DISPOSITIONS FOR ATTACK.** Coys will attack as follows:-
   FRONT LINE. "B" Coy on right.
   "D" Coy on left.
   SUPPORT. "C" Coy
   RESERVE; "A" Coy
   One Coy 1/E.Surreys.

4. **ASSEMBLY.** "B" & "D" Coys will be in the front line trench during the night. "C" Coy in hedges behind "B" & "D" Coys, "A" Coy in trenches in orchard round B.H.Q. and Coy of 1/E.Surreys in BRISTOL PARK. Before daybreak "B" Coy will cross stream in front of their trenches and lie down in the grass about 100 yards in front of them. "C" Coy will then take up their position in the trench thus vacated.
   The greatest care must be taken that no movement is observed and that all troops are under cover both from ground and from the air.

5. **THE ADVANCE.** At ZERO "B" & "D" Coys will advance as close as possible to the barrage and go forward with it, "C" Coy will leave the front line trench and follow 75 yards in rear of "B" & "D" Coys. "A" Coy will move forward and consolidate in shell holes about 200 yards in front of the front line trench. Unless otherwise ordered "A" Coy will remain there. O.C. "A" Coy and 2 runners will remain at B.H.Q. awaiting orders.

6. **METHOD OF ATTACK.**
   Each Coy will attack on a Two Platoon Frontage. Each platoon in formation laid down in S.S. 143.
   "B" & "D" Coys will capture all objectives up to LE CORNET PERDU which they will contain and push on to Final objective. "C" Coy will be responsible for taking CORNET PERDU and also for filling any gap there may exist between "B" & "D" Coys on their taking final objective, having completed this duty they will withdraw and dig in on a line about K.5.d.10/30 to K.5.d.40/80. Care must be taken that this thinning out of the line is not construed into an order to withdraw.
   If it is necessary for "C" Coy to send forward men to fill any gap in the front line O.C. "B" & "D" Coy will arrange to relieve these men as soon as possible so that they may be sent back to rejoin their Coy, and the front line will be held by "B" & "D" Coy only, who will consolidate in depth as detailed, if they consider they require more men they will inform B.H.Q.
   On reaching final objective and as soon as Protective Barrage ceases at ZERO plus 90 attacking Coys will push forward patrols to R.PLATE BECQUE, these patrols will destroy any bridges and will then lie out and watch the crossing so as to give the alarm in case of counter attack. they will themselves deal with any hostile patrols who appear.

7. **BARRAGE.** Barrage will open at ZERO according to barrage table attached. Machine guns will barrage 300 yards in advance of artillery barrage.

8. INTERNATIONAL PATROL.
O.C. "A" Coy will detail 1 Officer and 2 sections to be in the front line trench, where we join the 10th E.Yorks, at daybreak. Here he joins a similar party of the 10th E.Yorks. The senior officer will take charge of the amalgamated force and will march them <u>well in rear of the attacking force</u>. When the final objective has been captured and NOT BEFORE, he will post his men at K.6.a.3/0 where our left joins 10th E.Yorks right.

9. WIRE.
It appears quite possible that uncut wire may be encountered. In this case wire must be cut by wire cutters and breakers while Lewis guns keep down any enemy fire.

10. LIGHT SIGNALS.
S.O.S. - Green over Red over Green fired by rifle grenade rocket. Brigade Sector for S.O.S. will be known as L4.
On reaching final objective Three White Very lights in rapid succession will be fired.
Flares will be lit by front line troops only when called for by Contact Aeroplane.

11. PRISONERS.
Prisoners will be sent down to B.H.Q. under 10% escort.

12. WATCHES.
An officer from each Coy will be sent to B.H.Q. at 3 am to synchronize watches.

13. DRESS. FIGHTING ORDER.
170 rounds S.A.A.
2 Mills Bombs (to be carried in bottom pockets of S.D. Jacket)
1 round V.P.A. 1 inch White.
2 Red flares per man of B. C. & D. Coys.
4 Sandbags per man
2 Rifle Grenades.
12 S.O.S. rifle grenades per Coy.
24 No. 27 rifle grenades per Coy. to B & C Coy.
6 Box No 27 Smoke Bombs per Coy.

14. TOOLS.
Men of third platoon of attacking Coys will carry a shovel per man. "B" & "C" Coys will carry picks and shovels in proportion of 4 shovels to 1 pick. The two leading platoons of "C" Coy will dump these in first objective and O.C. "A" Coy will be responsible for collecting them.
Tools will be drawn during the night from B.H.Q.

15. R.A.P.
Aid Post will be at X.3.d.5/5.

16. Further Administrative details will be issued as a seperate order.

Copies To. 1 95th Bde.
2 C.O.
3 2/in Command.
4 Adjt.
5 T.O. & QM.
6 O.C. BHQ.
7 " "A" Coy
8 " "B" Coy
9 " "C" Coy
10 " "D" Coy
11 " 10th E.Yorks.

(Sd) J.H.Heywood, Capt Adjt.
10th Bn Gloucestershire Regiment.

BARRAGE TABLE.

Zero to Zero plus 4 — Standing barrage on enemy's Front Line i. First Objective, and creeping barrage 200 yards East of our Front Line.

```
Zero plus  4 to Zero plus  8 )
  "    "   8   "    "   "  12 )
  "    "  12   "    "   "  16 )
  "    "  16   "    "   "  20 )
  "    "  20   "    "   "  24 )   Barrage lifting at rate of 100 yards in
  "    "  24   "    "   "  28 )   4 mins.
  "    "  28   "    "   "  32 )
  "    "  32   "    "   "  36 )
  "    "  36   "    "   "  40 )

  "    "  40   "    "   "  46      Barrage on CORNET PERDU for 6 mins.

  "    "  46   "    "   "  50 )
  "    "  50   "    "   "  54 )
  "    "  54   "    "   "  58 )
  "    "  58   "    "   "  62 )
  "    "  62   "    "   "  66 )   Barrage lifting at rate of 100 yards in
  "    "  66   "    "   "  70 )   4 mins.
  "    "  70   "    "   "  74 )
  "    "  74   "    "   "  78 )
  "    "  78   "    "   "  82 )
  "    "  82   "    "   "  86 )

  "    "  86   "    "   "  92      On PLATE BEC UE.

  "    "  92   "    "   " 111      Creeps S.E. at 100 yards every 2 minutes.

  "    " 111   ——————————————————— All Batteries CEASE FIRE.
```

ADMINISTRATIVE ORDERS
ISSUED WITH
OPERATION ORDER No. 49 d. 26/6/18.

1. **DRESS.** FIGHTING ORDER. Packs will be dumped on leaving this Camp. Care is to be taken that no articles such as Caps, etc. are taken into the line. The following will be carried on the man:-
   (a) Unexpired portion of days ration.
   (b) Iron Rations.

2. **DUMPED PERSONNEL.** Each Coy will detail as dumped personnel -
Sergeants.	1
Corporals.	1
L/Corpls.	1
Other Ranks.	8
Lewis Gunrs.	8
	19

   The following will also be DUMPED PERSONNEL :-
RSM Bailey.	A.
CSM Leahy.	W.
Sgt Elley.	R.
Signallers.	9 - to be detailed by Sig. Off.
Runners.	15 - 2/Lt N. Davidson to arrange.
L/C Weekes.	1
Cpl Lambert.	1
Cpl Goslett.	1
Sgt Boobyer.	1
Sgt Brine.	1
Observer Cpl.	1
Sgt Harris.	1

   In considering above Coy Cmdrs are reminded that men sick at Transport, men on courses or on leave are to be made "Dumped Personnel".
   NOMINAL ROLLS to be at Orderly Room by 4 pm. 27th.

3. **WATER.** A dump of 300 petrol tins filled with water will be made at TANKARD FARM. The greatest care must be taken to bring back empty petrol tins to this point. In this way a continual supply of petrol tins filled with water may be maintained.
   A water point is being made on the Railway near CHAPEL BOOM K.8.b.9/2. Units will be notified when this is functioning.

4. **WIRECUTTERS AND BREAKERS.** Coys will go into action with full establishment of wire breakers and cutters. In addition "B" & "D" Coys will be each issued with 10 long handled wire cutters and "C" Coy with

5. **DESTRUCTION OF BRIDGES.** "B" & "D" Coys will be issued with 3 petrol tins of petrol for this purpose.

6. **AMMUNITION SUPPLY.** Coys requiring ammunition to send party to B.H.Q.

7. **TRANSPORT.** T. Officer will arrange to bring up all stores, rations etc and water on the night following the assault by pack animals.

8. **EXTRA S.A.A. AND MILLS BOMBS.** Will be issued to each man before leaving this Camp.

9. **BRIDGES.** Arrangements have been made for each Coy to be supplied with 3 light portable bridges.

10. **SMOKE BOMBS.** Each Coy will detail 6 men from Coy Hqrs. Each man will carry 2 smoke bombs. In the event of a smoke barrage being found necessary to mask a M.G. &c. Coy Cmdrs will detail this party to make a smoke screen.

11. **YUKON PACKS.** 40 of these are available at TANKARD FARM.

12. **MESSAGE CARRYING ROCKETS.** 5 of these have been allotted to this Battalion Signalling Officer to deal with these

13. LEWIS GUN MAGAZINES. Coy Cmdrs will arrange to take forward with them
    to attack 28 magazines. Remainder will be loaded at this Ca
    into a seperate limber which will deliver them to B.H.Q.

Copies to,-   All Coys
              Sig. Officer.
              Int. Officer.
              C.O.
              2nd in Command.
              T.O.
              QM.
                                            (Sd)   J.H.Maywood.   Capt. Adjt.
                                      12th Bn Gloucestershire Regiment.

Copy to all Coys. Such copies to be read on Coy. Parade

XI Corps No. G.S. 68/11.
5th Divn. No. S.56/1/29.

Major-General R.B. STEPHENS, CB., CMG.,
Commanding 5th Division.

1. I wish to convey to you and your Staff and to all ranks of your Division my appreciation and thanks for the very successful operation carried out by them on the 28th June.
The skilful manner in which your plan was prepared and secrecy preserved were among the chief causes of success.

2. The 13th Infy. Bde. under Br.Gen.JONES, DSO., had to attack two lines of trench and the buildings and enclosures about BONAR and DITCHIN FARMS. Their attack was carried out with great energy and determination and a fine offensive spirit was displayed by the 15th Bn. R.Warwickshire Regiment under Lt.Col. MILLER, DSO., 1st Bn. Royal West Kents under Major KAY, and the 2nd King's Own Scottish Borderers under Lt.Col. FURBER, DSO. The fine way in which these battalions pushed beyond their objectives and drove the enemy across the PLATE BECQUE not only secured the objectives allotted to the Brigade but afforded great assistance by securing the flank of the whole operation.

3. The task of the 95th Bde. under Brig.-Gen. NORTON, DSO., involved an advance of nearly 2,000 yards, and the capture of the Farms of L'EPINETTE and LE CORNET PERDU. The energy, dash and determination with which the 1/D.C.L.I. under Lt.Col. KIRK, DSO., and the 12th Bn. Gloucestershire Regt. under Lt.Col. COLT, MC., fulfilled their tasks is deserving of the highest praise. The arrangements made to ensure touch with the Division on the left successfully safeguarded the left flank of your Division.

4. The 15th Bde. under Lt.Col. GORDON HALL, CMG., DSO., co-operated successfully with the main operation by a demonstration on their right front. The attack carried out by a party of the 1st Cheshire Regt., under Major ANGUS in order to secure the right flank of the main operation was boldly conceived and gallantly executed.

5. The action of the artillery throughout was most carefully planned by Br.Gen. HUSSEY, CB., CMG., and Br.Gen. WALTHALL, and all ranks of 5th and 34th Divisional Artilleries and of the 282nd Army Bde. R.F.A. and 9th Canadian F.A.Bde. deserve great credit for the manner in which they supported the attack.

6. I particularly wish to thank the troops in the front line who worked so hard during the night 28th/29th June to consolidate the position and establish an efficient wire obstacle in front of their line. The patrol work carried out by them both by day and night and the destruction of the bridges over the PLATE BECQUE were a further means of securing the permanent establishment of the position.

7. I wish the 5th Division every good fortune and a continuation of their victorious action in attack which they displayed during the battle of the 28th June.

XI CORPS,
1st July, 1918.

(Sd.) R. HAKING, Lieut.-General,
Commanding XI Corps.

-2-

Devons.
Surreys.
D.C.L.I.
Gloucesters.
M/T.M.Bty.
M.G.Coy.

For information.

2nd July, 1918.

Capt.,
Brigade Major,
95th Inf. Brigade.

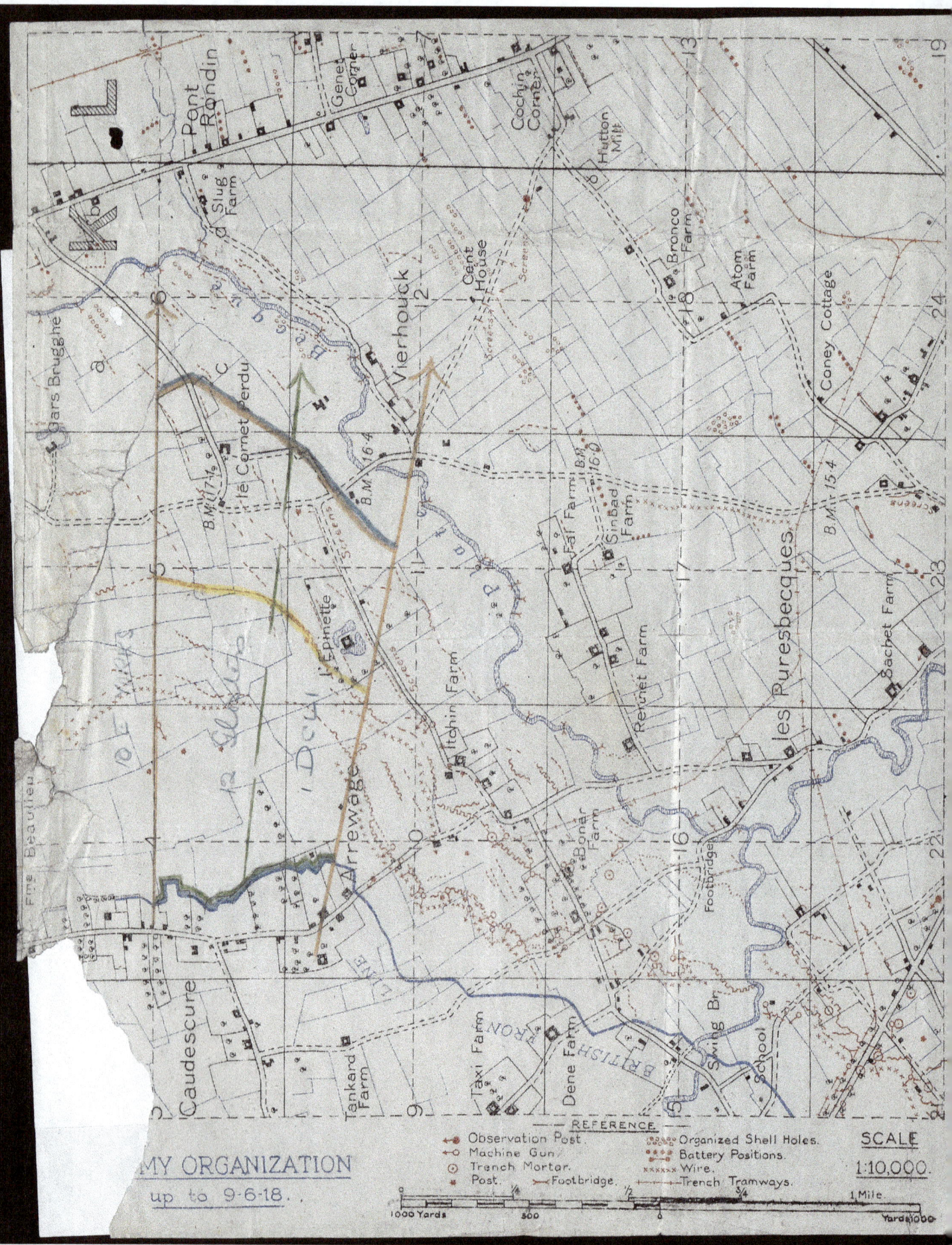

Confidential

War Diary
of the
13th Bn Gloucestershire Regiment
for the month of
July, 1918

July 31st 1918

WAR DIARY - 12th Bn GLOUCESTER REGIMENT

INTELLIGENCE SUMMARY. JULY 1918

Army Form C. 2118.

(Erase heading not required.)

Instructions regarding War Diaries and Intelligence Summaries are contained in F. S. Regs. Part II and the Staff Manual respectively. Title pages will be prepared in manuscript.

Place	Date	Hour	Summary of Events and Information	Remarks and references to Appendices
STEEN BECQUE	1		In Divisional Reserve. Battalion cleaning up & checking deficiencies, bathing &c.	
"	2		In Divisional Reserve. Battalion training cont. met. weather fine and nothing of importance to report.	
"	3		On 3rd 7/Lt S.J. BAYLIS 7/Lt L.D.SEARE 7/Lt L.W.HALSE and 7/Lt R.H. ANSTEY and 104 O.R. joined as reinforcements.	Officers
"	4			
"	5		On 4th 57 O.R. joined as reinforcements.	
			Afternoon of 5th 2.30 pm Battalion left Reserve in STEENBECQUE and relieved 1 NORFOLKS (5th Bde) in left sector of Regt. Brigade front (HQ at K.13.d.05.75) no casualties. Nothing to report. 7/Lt J.G. IBBOTSON and J.G. GARLAND and 16 O.R. joined.	
In Support	6		In support. One O.R. wounded. Nothing to report.	
"	7		In support. No casualties. Usual working and carrying parties found. Situation normal.	
"	8		In support. Situation quiet. Usual working parties found.	
	9		On morning of 9th when returning from working party 7/Lt J.G. GARLAND was killed. 7/Lt S.J. BAYLIS + 3 O.R. were	

WAR DIARY
of
INTELLIGENCE SUMMARY.

13th Bn Gloucestershire Reg

July 1917

Army Form C. 2118.

(Erase heading not required.)

Instructions regarding War Diaries and Intelligence Summaries are contained in F. S. Regs., Part II. and the Staff Manual respectively. Title pages will be prepared in manuscript.

Place	Date	Hour	Summary of Events and Information	Remarks and references to Appendices
Support Left G Sector A. Sector	10	-	In support. Situation quiet. No casualties and nothing to report.	
	11		In support. Situation normal. After dark Battn. relieved 1/0.C.L.I. in front line, same sub-sector. No casualties. Nothing to report.	Appendix 1
Front line	12		In front line. Usual trench warfare. Our patrols being active at night. No casualties and nothing of importance to report.	
Rgt G/Sector Right Sector	13		In front line. Situation normal. 2 O.R. wounded. Otherwise nothing to report. 15 O.R. joined as reinforcement.	
	14		Front line. No casualties. Nothing to report.	
	15		In front line. Situation normal. 3 O.R. wounded by shell fire. Otherwise nothing to report.	

WAR DIARY
INTELLIGENCE SUMMARY

Army Form C. 2118.

July 1918   12th Cheshire Regt

Place	Date	Hour	Summary of Events and Information	Remarks and references to Appendices
Front Line Left / Section Regnie Sain	16		In front line at 11.30 pm Patrol from each of C & D Coys. left our line with the object of capturing enemy posts at N.26.0.3/1.6 and N.31.9.3/6. Patrol attacking right post were seen by enemy who immediately commenced bombing, some bombs falling amongst patrol causing heavy casualties. Patrol then withdrew. Post to be attacked by left patrol were alarmed by the bombing of right post and immediately commenced bombing themselves, the alarm being taken up by whole enemy line. Left patrol therefore withdrew. Casualties. One man killed, 3 men missing, believed killed. 3 wounded.	
	17		In front line during the morning enemy shelled our front line with HE & shrapnel. Casualties 6 men killed. On night of 17/18th Battalion was relieved by 1st Royal Warwick Regt. and entrained for	Appendix 3

WAR DIARY

Gloucestershire Regt

INTELLIGENCE SUMMARY.

July 1918

Army Form C. 2118.

Place	Date	Hour	Summary of Events and Information	Remarks and references to Appendices
	17		Prevailed Station. Light Railway Running for La Jacques Camp, last company arrived camp about 3 am on 18th. Nothing to report	
La Jacques Camp	18		Battalion cleaning up taking on Weather fine hot casualties nothing to report	
La Jacque	19		In Divisional Reserve. Training continued. Weather changeable. Nothing of importance to report	
	20			
	21			
	22			
	23		Battalion left La Jacque camp by train and detrained at CROWE station, returning 1 Norfolk Regt (151st Bde) in Bde Reserve in SPRESIANO Camp (54 3) No casualties.	Appendix II
SPRESIANO Camp 3.14.6.	24		In Bde Reserve. 2 companies front for work in trenches line. Guards and fund do regimental training and work on camp entrance	
Do	25		About 1 am — enemy shelled camp with H.E and shrapnel 6 casualties. 6 O.R. Observer	

Army Form C. 2118.

WAR DIARY
or
INTELLIGENCE SUMMARY.
(Erase heading not required.)

July 1918 1/5th Gloucester Regt

Instructions regarding War Diaries and Intelligence Summaries are contained in F. S. Regs., Part II. and the Staff Manual respectively. Title pages will be prepared in manuscript.

Place	Date	Hour	Summary of Events and Information	Remarks and references to Appendices
SPRESSANO Camp f.10.b	26		In Reserve. Nothing to report on this day	
	27		Work continued on camp building up officers mess etc.	
	28		Front protection round hut making roads	
	29		Cleaning drains etc. On morning of 29th enemy high shells nearly of camp but no casualties.	
	30	About 6.30 pm	Battn. left SPRESSANO CAMP and marched via L'EPINETTE and VIA ROMA to relieve 1/DCLI in left subsector. No casualties. Nothing to report.	
Front Line Left S.Sub.	31		In front line. Weather fine. Patrols sent. Nothing to report	

W. B. Price
Lieut Col
C.O. 1/5 Bn Gloucester Regt

SECRET.   Appendix 1.

Copy No.

OPERATION ORDER NO. 52
by
Lt-Col H.A.Colt M.C.
Cmdg. 12th Bn The GLOUCESTERSHIRE REGIMENT.

Ref. Map - 36A 1/40,000.

1. **RELIEF.** Battalion will relieve 1/NORFOLKS in the SUPPORT LINE, RIGHT BRIGADE sector, to-morrow the 5th inst.
Each Coy will relieve the same lettered Coy of the 1/NORFOLKS.

2. **STARTING POINT.** Road Junction I.12.b.4/9.

3. **TIME.** Leading Platoon will pass starting point at 2.25 pm. Remainder at 100 yards interval.

4. **ORDER OF MARCH.** B.H.Q. - "C" - "B" - "D" - "A".
Lewis Gun limbers will move with their Coys.

5. **ROUTE.** PONTOON BRIDGE - straight through to VIA PADOVA - No.7 track - down road running through K.17 A. - VIA ROMA.

6. **GUIDES.** 4 guides per Coy will be in VIA ROMA at K.13.a.7/5.

7. **DRESS.** MARCHING ORDER - mess tins inside the pack.

8. **COOKING.** Will be done near B.H.Q.

9. **WATER-CART.** 1 Water cart will be at B.H.Q.

10. **ADVANCE PARTY.** 2/Lt A.Brucher, RSM and 4 CSMs will leave present billets at 10 am. and take over stores etc.

11. **RATIONS** Will come up by train as usual.

12. **OFFICERS' VALISES.** Will be stacked in the SQUARE by 1 pm.

13. **OFFICERS' TRENCH KITS & MESS KITS.** To be stacked in SQUARE by 1.30 pm.

14. **TRENCH STORES etc.** Care will be taken that all Stores, aeroplane photo, defence schemes and work in hand are taken over. Lists of stores taken over to be at B.H.Q. by 9 pm. the 5th inst.

15. **STAND TO.** Battalion will "Stand To" night and morning. Equipment will be worn excepting 8 am and 5 pm. when it may be removed.

16. **COMPLETION OF RELIEF.** Will be reported by Code word, "BISHOP".

(Sd) J.H.Maywood. Capt.
Adj. 12th Bn Gloucestershire Regt.

SECRET.

Copy No.

OPERATION ORDERS No. 53.
by
Lieut-Col H.A.Colt M.C.
Cmdg. 12th Bn GLOUCESTERSHIRE REGIMENT
Ref. Map - 36A. N.E. Edition 7. 1/20,000.

---

1. **RELIEF.** The Battalion will relieve 1/D.C.L.I. in LEFT SUB SECTOR tomorrow 11th. inst.

2. **DISPOSITIONS.**
   - B.H.Q   K.13.b.90/55.
   - A Coy.   RIGHT FRONT.
   - B Coy.   LEFT FRONT.
   - C Coy.   RIGHT SUPPORT.
   - D Coy.   LEFT SUPPORT.

3. **GUIDES.** If necessary will be arranged by Company Commanders with the O.Cs. Relieving Company.

4. **ADVANCE PARTY.** Company Commanders will send forward an ADVANCE PARTY to take over stores etc. before dark.
   Captain J.P.Webb and the R.S.M. will take over from B.H.Q.

5. **TRENCH STORES.** S.A.A., bombs, aero. photographs, and defence schemes will be taken over and receipts forwarded to B.H.Q. by 9 A.M. 12th inst.

6. **RATIONS.** Rations will come up by train as usual. A & D Coys. will be dumped at end of INFANTRY ROW., B.H.Q., B & C Coys. in VIA ROMA near B.H.Q.

7. **LEWIS GUNS, MESS KITS etc.** To be carried forward by Coys.

8. **COOKING.** Cooking will be done at the Transport Lines.

9. **WATER.** Water will be drawn from tanks in VIA ROMA. 12 tins now in possession of Coys. will be taken up full. 1 water-cart will be kept at B.H.Q. as a reserve supply.

10. **COMPLETION OF RELIEF.** This will be reported by the code word "WIDOW".

Date 10/7/18.

(Sd) J.H.Maywood. Capt.
Adjt. 12th Bn Gloucestershire Regiment.

Copies to
1 C.O.
2 Adjt.
3 Lt S.H.Gillard.
4 B.H.Q.
5 4 Companies.
9 T.O. and Qm.
10 File.

SECRET.   OPERATION ORDER N°55
          by Lt. Col. J. CHAPLIN. M.C.
          Comdg. R.E.H.I.   C.O.

Ref. Map 26ᴬ 1/40,000

1. **Relief.** The battalion will be relieved by 14th
   WARWICKS to-morrow night 17/3.
   On completion of relief Bn will with-
   draw by train from MEREDITH STN to
   LA LACQUE.

2. **Guides.** Each Co. will send 1 guide per
   platoon, and 1 for Coy. HQ to be at
   CASTADUS - VIA ROMA to meet incoming unit at 9 pm. Guides are
   to ask for incoming Coys' "nms",
   Right Front, Left Support etc. and not
   by letter.

3. **Trench Stores.** All trench stores, S.A.A,
   bombs etc to be handed over and
   receipts obtained. Receipts to be handed
   into Orderly Room by 12 noon 18/3.

4. **Lewis Guns, Mens kit etc.** To be brought
   out by Coys and taken back on the
   train. All water cans must be
   brought out and put in Salvage
   Limber. Coys will inform Orderly

Room by Room i.e., number of tins to light with. Two dust trucks will be at end of Claumin line, one for A & B and one for C & D, for the conveyance of 4.6 magazines, Salvage, and Surplus kits to VII ROMA.

6. Taking over of Billets. The Quartermaster will arrange for the taking over and allotting of billets. He will also arrange for a hot meal for the men on arrival in new billeting area.

7. Officers Valises etc. The Transport Officer will arrange for Officers' valises to be taken to LA JACOVE. And for the transport of Orderly Room, Workshops and Canteen.

8. Transport. 1 limber to be in VIA ROMA near BHQ to take back Salvage and water tins to Transport; also horses to bring back water cart.

9. Chargers will be sent to LA JACOVE and will be picketed at Camps.

10. Completion of Relief. Will be reported by Code to BHQ as under:—
    A   months home service
    B   M.C.

        C   Tony Cross
        D   STAFF

Coy Commanders will also call in at Bn Q earlier pass.

1. Train Arrangements. Lt. V.D. Davidson will arrange to allot trucks to Coys

Copies to
   All Coys
   C.O
   2 Command
   Adj.
   T.O Q.M
   8 etc

                              J H Maywood
                                    Capt
                            Adj. R.H.I.

SECRET.

OPERATION ORDER No. 56,
by
Lt-Col H.A.Colt M.C.
Cmdg. 12th Bn The GLOUCESTERSHIRE REGIMENT.

Ref. Map.- 36 A. 1/40,000.

1. RELIEF.   Battalion will relieve 1/Norfolks at SPRESIANO CAMP to-day. Relief to be completed by 6 pm.

2. STARTING POINT.   T roads by SCHOOL (K.20.c.1/1.)

3. ROUTE.   School (K.20.c.1/1.) - Fork Roads near T of THIENNES - Fork Ro about K.21.b.8/9. - Fork Roads about K.22.a.2/5. - Fork Roads about K.21.a.8/4. - Pontoon Bridge - along path by Canal - Down Road to SPRESIANO CAMP.

4. HALTS.   Usual halts from 10 minutes to the hour to the hour itself.

5. DRESS   Marching Order, mess tins inside packs.

6. ORDER OF MARCH.   H.Q. - Band - A. - B. - C. - D.   Movement will be by platoons at intervals of 100 yards.

7. TIME OF STARTING.   Leading platoon will pass starting point at 3 pm.

8. OFFICERS' VALISES, MESS KITS.   will be dumped in the CINEMA by 2 pm. Transport Officer to arrange to transport them to Camp.

9. ADVANCE PARTY.   Will move off at 1 pm., to take over Camp.

10. LEWIS GUN LIMBERS.   will be packed by 1.30 pm. and proceed with their Coys to the Camp.

1. COOKERS will march in rear, independently, to new Camp.
2. TEA will be served on arrival at Camp, Corporal Cook to arrange.
3. CLEANLINESS OF BILLETS. Billets must be handed over scrupulously clean and certificates to this effect will be rendered by Coy Commanders.
4. LISTS OF STORES TAKEN OVER, will be handed in to Orderly Room by 9 pm. to-day.

/7/18.

(Sd) J.H. Maywood. Capt.
Adj. 12th Bn Gloucestershire Regiment.

Addition to Para 12. Officers Mess Kit. Surplus Mess Kit to be returned to Transport to be dumped outside Orderly Room by 8 a.m with Officers valis

Confidential

Register No.
Serial No.
Vol. No. WR 34

F. 33

War Diary
of the
12th Bn. Gloucestershire Regiment
for the month of
August 1918

W. G. Chapman Major
O/C 12th Bn. Gloucestershire Regt

Sept. 5/18

Army Form C. 2118.

WAR DIARY
INTELLIGENCE SUMMARY.

(Erase heading not required.)

12th Bn Gloucestershire Regiment
August 1918

Instructions regarding War Diaries and Intelligence Summaries are contained in F.S. Regs., Part II. and the Staff Manual respectively. Title pages will be prepared in manuscript.

Place	Date	Hour	Summary of Events and Information	Remarks and references to Appendices
Front line Lys Sector	1, 2, 3, 4		In front line Nieuf Warjou. Enemy fairly quiet and nothing of importance to report. Usual shelling of our back areas every evening.	
	5		On night of 5/6 Battalion was relieved by 7th Gloucestershire Regiment (61st Division) and marched to SPRESIANO CAMP. No casualties although enemy shelled trenches and roads behind lines. Heavy wet and relief difficult.	
SPRESIANO CAMP	6	2 pm	Battalion left SPRESIANO Camp and marched via THIENNES - BOESEGHEM - WITTES to ORCHARD CAMP, RACQUINGHEM. About 14 kilos. March stormy. No casualties.	
ORCHARD CAMP	7, 8, 9, 10		In Orchard Camp 5/Division in GHQ Reserve. Cleaning up & bathing on 7th. Training continued on subsequent days.	

Army Form C. 2118.

WAR DIARY
or
INTELLIGENCE SUMMARY.
(Erase heading not required.)

12th Gloucestershire Regt
August 1916

Instructions regarding War Diaries and Intelligence Summaries are contained in F. S. Regs., Part II. and the Staff Manual respectively. Title pages will be prepared in manuscript.

Place	Date	Hour	Summary of Events and Information	Remarks and references to Appendices
ORCHARD CAMP	11		Battalion & Company training continued, special attention being given to "Open Warfare"	
	12		Weather fine and nothing unusual to report	
RACQUINGHEM	13			
	14	3.45 a.m.	Bn marched from RACQUINGHEM and proceeded via HEURINGHEM - BILQUES - HELFAUT-NOIR CORNET to WIZERNES STATION. Entrained at WIZERNES and detrained at DOULLENS about 2.30 pm same day. Marched via main DOULLENS AUXI LE CHATEAU Road to REMAISNIL (about 11 kilos) Weather very hot and march very trying.	
REMAISNIL	15		Battalion resting and preparing to continue training	
	16		Reorganization of Bn. Billeting area Battalion marched to BOFFLES and FORTEL. A, B & C Coys being billeted in BOFFLES and D Coy and HQrs in FORTEL.	

Army Form C. 2118.

12th Gloucestershire Regt.
August 1918

WAR DIARY
or
INTELLIGENCE SUMMARY.
(Erase heading not required.)

Place	Date	Hour	Summary of Events and Information	Remarks and references to Appendices
Field	17		In billets at BOFFLES and FORTEL. Nothing of importance to report.	
"	18		Battalion ordered to move at short notice to DOULLENS. Left Billets about 9.30 pm and reached DOULLENS about 2.30 am & billeted in CITADEL.	
"	19		About 9.30 pm Battalion left DOULLENS and marched via FRESCHEVILLERS - ORVILLE - AUTHIE - ST-LEGER COIGNEUX to ROSSIGNOL FARM (1 mile N. of COIGNEUX) Weather close and slight drizzle.	
ROSSIGNOL FARM	20		During the day Battalion was preparing to go into the line. Extra SAA, Bombs etc being distributed. About 10.30 pm Battalion moved off and marched via SAILLY au BOIS and HEBUTERNE to trenches around BOIS du BIEZ with HQrs in ROTTENOI FARM. Battalion being in reserve to 75th Inf Bde.	

Army Form C. 2118.

WAR DIARY
— or —
INTELLIGENCE SUMMARY.

(Erase heading not required.)

12th Gloucestershire Regiment
August 1918

Place	Date	Hour	Summary of Events and Information	Remarks and references to Appendices
	21.		Orders were received that 95th Bde would capture enemy's positions up to and including a line through G.31.d.7.5 to G.26.o.8.6 The 37th Division, starting from British front line N.d. BUCQUOY were to capture enemy positions through L.14.b. L.9.c. & L.10.a to L.4.c.D. The 5th Division then to pass through to the capture of their allotted objectives. There was no preliminary bombardment - Infantry advancing under a creeping barrage, supported by tanks. At 2.40 a.m. = 4.45 a.m. Barrage opened and 37th Division advanced and captured their objective without much trouble. 95th Brigade then passed through 37th Division	Ref 57D NE 5/c NW 1/c

WAR DIARY
1/2 Gloucester Regt
INTELLIGENCE SUMMARY. August 1918

Army Form C. 2118.

Place	Date	Hour	Summary of Events and Information	Remarks and references to Appendices

and advanced to the capture of their first
objective - BROWN LINE - running through L 16 D.
This was captured with little resistance, although
owing to a thick mist which rendered the
keeping of direction difficult, there was
some confusion and tanks were frequently
lost sight of. Battalion of Brigade -
1/Devons + 1/E/Surreys in front line - 1/D.C.L.I in
support with 12/Gloucesters in Reserve.
About 12.30 pm 12/Gloucesters moved forward
and advance was resumed - 1/E/Surreys
being on left front, 12 Gloucesters on Right
front and 1/DCLI in support with 1/Devons
in Reserve.
The next objective - Red Line - running

Ref O 1/E } 1/10,000
    O 2/NW

WAR DIARY

12th Gloucester Regt.
August 1918

INTELLIGENCE SUMMARY

Place	Date	Hour	Summary of Events and Information	Remarks and references to Appendices
	21		Through L.34c – G.30 a + b along ARRAS – ALBERT railway was reached and consolidated, although more resistance was met with. Owing to the mist, which considerably hampered Artillery and Tanks it was impossible to continue the advance to the final objective. Casualties in 1st day's fighting Capt. J.P. Webb, 2/Lt L.N. Maise, 2/Lt L.S. Holman, 2/Lt J.D Seake wded and about 100 O.R. casualties + 2/Lt Belmonk	Ref map 51cNW 1/20,000
	22		Battalion resting and reorganizing as far as possible. About 4.30 p.m. the was some shelling of our positions and about 5.30 p.m. S.O.S was sent up on our right and left. At 5.30 p.m. enemy was seen to be advancing	

12 Gloucestershire Regt August 1918

WAR DIARY
INTELLIGENCE SUMMARY

Army Form C. 2118.

Reference 57 C.N.W. 1/20,000

Place	Date	Hour	Summary of Events and Information	Remarks and references to Appendices
	22		for a counter-attack and 2/Lt. R H ANSTEY with 2 platoons of "A" Coy was sent out to enfilade the advancing enemy. This he succeeded in doing and captured about 180 prisoners and 5 machine guns. The 1/DEVONS also succeeded in rounding up some 300 prisoners and counter attack then broke down. Enemy was quiet afterwards except for some slight shelling of our line.	
	23		Orders were received for the capture of the Final Objective — viz — line through G.31.b. 7.5. & G.26.c.8.6. — At 11 a.m. attack commenced, troops moving forward under creeping barrage. Enemy had constructed machine gun nests along railway and these caused numerous casualties before they were finally overcome	

WAR DIARY
INTELLIGENCE SUMMARY

Gloucestershire Regt

August 1918

Army Form C. 2118.

There was also a considerable amount of M.G. fire from the direction of MIRAUMONT which had not yet been taken by N.Z. Division.

Owing to losses 12 Glosters (who had been reinforced by "B" & "D" Coys of 1/D.C.L.I.) were unable to advance beyond ridge before IRLES and reinforcements were asked for. Before these arrived however Lt. Col. H.A. COLT M.C. 1/4 Gloucestershire Regt. at the head of the remainder of the 1/Glosters & 2 Companies of Cornwalls had succeeded in reaching the Village and consolidated on the final objective i.e. at COLT being wounded however whilst superintending consolidation.

On 23rd Casualties were very heavy in addition to Lt. Col. H.A. COLT M.C. the following Officers were wounded:

Lt. A. LAIRD M.C, 2/Lt R.H. ANSTEY, 2/Lt G.G.L. NICKS, 2/Lt J.T.N. MILES, Lt. F.H. LATROBE M.C, Lt. T.C. GREENHALGH M.C, 2/Lt T.P. GUNNING, 2/Lt J. IBBOTSON and Capt. & Adjt. J.H. MAYWOOD was Killed. Losses in O.R. about 200 on this day.

WAR DIARY or INTELLIGENCE SUMMARY

Army Form C. 2118.

12th Bn Gloucestershire Regt

August 1917

Place	Date	Hour	Summary of Events and Information	Remarks and references to Appendices
	23		Officers remaining Capt. W.R. HATHAWAY, 2/Lt A BRACHER and 2/Lt T.T. BENJAMIN.	
	24		Orders were issued for 12/Gloucesters to withdraw to line N.q. IRLES which was dug at 3 a.m. on 24th. Major W.G. CHAPMAN M.C. assumed command of Battalion and 2/Lt A.BRACHER took over duties of Adjutant about 10.30 am. Battalion withdrew to Reserve about 4.17.	
	25		Battalion moved to G.23. 2nd Btn. being in Div Reserve. 2/Lt T.T. BENJAMIN + 2 O.R. were wounded during day. In reserve in same position	
	26			
	27		Weather dull + stormy. Situation quiet. No Casualties to report. Holding 1 importance is	
	28		Battalion resting and reorganising as much as possible. Salvaging and clearing of Battlefield commenced.	

WAR DIARY

12th Gloucestershire Regt

INTELLIGENCE SUMMARY.

August 1918

Army Form C. 2118.

Place	Date	Hour	Summary of Events and Information	Remarks and references to Appendices
	29		95th Bde relieved 13th Bde in assembly position for attack to take place later. Gloucesters believing 3/K.O.S.B. in Brigade Reserve. 1/Devons and 1/D.C.L.I. on front line and 1/E Surreys in support. 12/Gloucesters HQrs at H.7.c.0.0	
	30	5am	Orders were received for Battalion Brigade to attack and capture Beugny village and ground on each side. At zero hour 5am. Bn. moved forward to trenches vacated by 1/E Surreys who took up position in old front line on attacking Battalions moving forward. Attack was held up. 1/D.C.L.I. being unable to reach objective owing to wire and M.G. fire. Low flying Enemy Aircraft were very active all thro' day.	

WAR DIARY 12th Bn. Gloucestershire Regt. Army Form C. 2118.
or
INTELLIGENCE SUMMARY. August 1918
(Erase heading not required.)

Place	Date	Hour	Summary of Events and Information	Remarks and references to Appendices
	31		In same position. During night 31/1 Sept. 13th Gloucesters relieved 1/Devons in left sector of Brigade front from I.14.d.5.0 to Ervick junction I.14.6.33. 2/Lt W.J. HAGGART killed and 2 O.R. wounded. During the relieving 31st to 31st August 12/Gloucesters captured some 9 Officers and 300 Oranks prisoners, 1 Howitzer, 2 field Guns and some 40 machine Guns most of these could not be salved owing to lack of men. W. G. Chapman Major Commanding 12th Bn Gloucestershire Regt	

Confidential

Registers No
file no
Vol No 9 Vol 35

R.34

War Diary
of the
12th Bn Gloucestershire Regiment
for the month of
September 1918

G. Chapman
Lieut Col
C.O. 12th Bn the Gloucestershire Regt

Army Form C. 2118.

WAR DIARY / INTELLIGENCE SUMMARY.

(Erase heading not required.)

12th Battalion Gloucestershire Regt
September 1918

Place	Date	Hour	Summary of Events and Information	Remarks and references to Appendices
Reserve	4	10.45 am	57th Division relieved by 37th Division. Battalion moved back to hutted camp H.18.a. H.12.a arriving about 1.30 p.m. Remainder of day spent in cleaning up, repairs to huts &c. No casualties. Weather fine.	
	5		Battalion cleaning up, reorganizing &c. Bathing &c.	
	6		Battalion reorganizing Training &c. Specialist classes formed and specialist training continued	
	7			
	8		Weather changeable. No casualties.	
	9			
	10		Training orders received on 12th and 13th notifying move. Battalion sports on 11th	
	11			
	12			
	13			
"	14th		Battalion moved off at 8.40 am via H.19.a.4.1 P.8.a.7.0 to NEUVILLE - Route. BIEFVILLERS - BAPAUME - BANCOURT - HAPLINCOURT - BERTINCOURT - YTRES to NEUVILLE - and relieved N.Z. Division.	

WAR DIARY

Army Form C. 2118.

12th Bn. Gloucestershire Regt.

September 1918

INTELLIGENCE SUMMARY.
(Erase heading not required.)

Place	Date	Hour	Summary of Events and Information	Remarks and references to Appendices
NEVILLE	14		Battalion in position at P 24.a.c. & P 30.a with B.H.Q. at P.24.8.0. 12th Gloucesters being support battalion to 13th Bde and coming under orders of 13th Inf. Bde.	
	15		Enemy attack expected at dawn. 2 enemy divisions being known to be in Reserve. Owing to our heavy barrage the expected attack failed to materialise. About 8pm our positions were shelled with Blue cross gas shells. Enemy aircraft active. 4 of our balloons being destroyed. Working party of 350 O.R. found for work in forward area. Enemy aircraft active bombing back areas at night.	
	16		Battalion cleaning up and repairing trenches. Enemy aircraft active. Trenches bombed and machine gunned at night. Otherwise nothing to report.	
	17		Work during morning. Rest during afternoon.	

Army Form C. 2118.

WAR DIARY 12th Bn. Gloucestershire Regt.
INTELLIGENCE SUMMARY. September 1918

(Erase heading not required.)

Place	Date	Hour	Summary of Events and Information	Remarks and references to Appendices
	17		In the evening Battalion moved up to main line of Resistance. Intention - The Corps on our right to continue advance towards HINDENBURG LINE - the 5th Division to form a defensive flank hinging about Q.23.a.7.3. This operation to be performed by 13th Inf Bde and 12th Gloucesters. This Battn moved into position from Q.23.a.7.7. to Q.23.d.1.2. A.B.C. Coys in front with 2/K.O.S.B. D Coy in support. Enemy hostile planes active. Few casualties.	
	18	5.30am	Advance continued. Barrage opened and attack commenced. Our troops were slow. Heavy shelling of our trenches during the day with gas shells. This Battalion was not called upon to support advance. About 9 pm owing to operations of morning following relief took place. 13th Bde - 1RWKents relieved	

Army Form C. 2118.

WAR DIARY 12th Bn. Gloucestershire Regt
INTELLIGENCE SUMMARY. September 1918

(Erase heading not required.)

Instructions regarding War Diaries and Intelligence Summaries are contained in F. S. Regs., Part II. and the Staff Manual respectively. Title pages will be prepared in manuscript.

Place	Date	Hour	Summary of Events and Information	Remarks and references to Appendices
	18		7/KOSBs in right S. Sector. 12th Gloucesters being made responsible for main line of resistance. Move delayed owing to heavy enemy shelling with H.E. and gas shells.	
	19		Battalion withdrew to trenches around P 24 B H.Q being in NEUVILLE. Relief complete by 11.30 am nothing of importance to report.	
	20		95th Bde relieved 13th Bde in front line 7/Gloucesters being in reserve, relieving 7/KOSBs. Bn HQ in Quarry Q20c44. Some enemy shelling but Relief complete 6.3 pm. Nothing of importance to report.	
Ricamble Line	21		Improving trenches shelters &c. Nothing unusual to report. Raining	
	22		In front line. This Battalion found numerous carrying and working parties for the Brigade. No casualties.	

WAR DIARY
INTELLIGENCE SUMMARY.
(Erase heading not required.)

12th Bn. Gloucestershire Regt
September 1918

Army Form C. 2118.

Place	Date	Hour	Summary of Events and Information	Remarks and references to Appendices
In reserve	23		Usual working parties found. 6 Coy. trenches heavily shelled - 4 OR being wounded - and the Company then moved to -Q.21.c.8.6- Q.v.1.c.+3. Transport lines at YPRES shelled with H.V. during the morning 22 animals being killed. METZ and district bombed by enemy aircraft 10-11 p.m.	
In Reserve	24		Usual working parties and carrying parties found. No casualties. Capt. RATCLIFFE(mg) 2/Lt H LODGE 7/Lt FEARMAN and 2/Lt COX sent to Transport lines for transfer to 1/5 Gloucester Regt.	
	25		In reserve. At 1 dark Battalion was relieved by 4th K War Regt. and march back to trenches in O.12 Relief complete and Coy in new positions by 1.30 am 26th except "A" working parties which arrived about 3 a.m. "A" Coy heavily shelled - 3 OR wounded.	
In Reserve	26		Battalion cleaning up + reorganizing generally	

WAR DIARY
INTELLIGENCE SUMMARY

Army Form C. 2118.

12th Bn. Gloucestershire Regt.
September 1918

Place	Date	Hour	Summary of Events and Information	Remarks and references to Appendices
	27	11.30am	Battalion left position in O.13 and occupied trenches in P.17.C. - P.23.a.c - P.29.b + P.30.a with Bn HQrs in NEUVILLE. Operation Orders received as follows:- III Army to continue advance at a time + date to be notified later. 5th Divn to capture BEAUCAMP RIDGE - HIGHLAND RIDGE with a flank along AFRICAN TRENCH and - 4 advance of troops on N. of MARCOING to advance to WELSH RIDGE. Attack of 5th Divn to be carried out by 13th Bde on Rght 15th Bde on left with 95th Bde in Reserve. Zero hour + 152 minutes. RED OBJECTIVE - AFRICAN TRENCH - SIRELY along YORK AVENUE to be gained by zero. BROWN OBJECTIVE - QUEN IN along LINCOLN RD - TRENT ALLEY - R7.d.7/5 to be captured by zero plus 27½. Should attack to N be successful 13th Bde will continue to "GREEN DOTTED LINE". After capture of GREEN DOTTED LINE 95th Bde will attack S. from R.14 - NEWPORT TRENCH - R.26.d.06 and from R.15 - JAM TRENCH - FERN TRENCH to R.27.d.20 at which final track will be attained with Durroso to Right.	

WAR DIARY
or
INTELLIGENCE SUMMARY.
(Erase heading not required.)

12th Bn. Gloucesters Army Form C. 2118.
September 1918

Instructions regarding War Diaries and Intelligence Summaries are contained in F. S. Regs., Part II. and the Staff Manual respectively. Title pages will be prepared in manuscript.

Place	Date	Hour	Summary of Events and Information	Remarks and references to Appendices
	28		On night 27/28th 95th Bde. moved forward and relieved 1st Inf. Bde. At 11 pm Orders were received that 95th Bde. would capture objectives assigned to 1st Inf. Bde. Brigade attacked 2:40 am on 28th. 12th Gloucesters being in Reserve owing to late hour at which Orders were received, Battalion did not reach their position until after 2:40 am and although caught in enemy barrage there were no casualties. BHQ at Quarry Q.16.c.3.5. Coys in trenches QUOTIENT QUACK QUALITY and QUOTIENT AV... Battalion was not called upon during the day 1.28th. A warning order was received that attack would be resumed in morning of 29th and Ops were sent forward to reconnoitre Operation Orders were issued that 12 Gloucesters would capture line of Sunken Rd R.27.a.95/25 - R.21.b.7/4 and on the capture of this line 1st Bde. would continue the advance.	

WAR DIARY

INTELLIGENCE SUMMARY

Army Form C. 2118.

12th Bn Gloucestershire Regt

September 1918

Place	Date	Hour	Summary of Events and Information	Remarks and references to Appendices

Orders for attack were subsequently altered with great difficulty was experienced in finding Companies so as to their attack instructions companies being already on the move before amended orders were received.

Bns moved off commencing at 11 pm on 28th guides being found by Devons

March was without incident to assembly position R 20 a 7/6 along Sunken Road - Railway to junction of GREEN line + Railway at R 19 d 3/7

A B + D Coy attacking Coys with C Coy in Reserve

BHQ at Q 18 d 82

At Zero hour - 3.30 a.m. - Creeping barrage came down 200 yds in front of our line and remained there 3 minutes then moving on at rate of 100 yds per 3 minutes. Touch obtained with 1 DCLI on left but we could not get into touch with 21st Division on our right.

WAR DIARY
or
INTELLIGENCE SUMMARY.

Army Form C. 2118.

1st Bn. Gloucestershire Regt.

September 1918

Place	Date	Hour	Summary of Events and Information	Remarks and references to Appendices
			Owing to late hour at which orders were received and distance Battalion had to march, Coys only arrived in assembly position as barrage commenced and Action it could not be properly organised in its darkness. This and the fact that the men had no reliable information made it difficult to attain complete control. Attack commenced but owing to facts already stated and the darkness direction was extremely difficult to maintain. Progress was good and casualties small. At 4.30 am a report was received that objective had been gained and it was not for some hours that this information was found to be incorrect. Sunken Road R.20.b.& d. having apparently been taken for the real objective. The Battalion came under very intense M.G. fire frontally and from both flanks, especially from Gonnelieu on the right.	

WAR DIARY *September 1918*
INTELLIGENCE SUMMARY *12 Bn Gloucestershire Regt*

Army Form C. 2118.

At first this could not be obtained with units on flanks but eventually DCLI came up on our left but all reports agree that no one came up on our left right thus leaving this flank entirely exposed.

Casualties 2 Officers killed 12 OR killed 38 wounded — this number is considered very small. Enemy shelling very slight. In view of the heavy machine gun fire encountered must be considered very small.

About 120 prisoners captured.

Owing to incomplete mopping up by Division on our left isolated enemy machine gun posts existed which caused no considerable trouble. Men could be seen handling these guns although it was known that Division on left had gone forward. Thus posts had to be disposed of by means of Rifle Grenades Lewis Guns firing from top of Ridge in front & up were silenced by our counted batteries.

WAR DIARY 1=Bn Gloucestershire Regt   Army Form C. 2118.

INTELLIGENCE SUMMARY. September 1918

Place	Date	Hour	Summary of Events and Information	Remarks and references to Appendices
	29		Battalion consolidated in HOLLY SUPPORT LINE R 20c - SAME SUPPORT + FRIENDLY TRENCH. Patrols sent out during the day reported enemy to be holding HOLLY TRENCH & FERN TRENCH. New Zealanders were reported to be holding Northern part of our next objective. In the evening patrols 1/4 PCLI entered LA JACQUERIE and found enemy in S.E. corner only. During the night 29/30 the whole of our immediate front was evacuated by the enemy.	
	30		1st Sd Bde passed through 95th Bde & 12 Gloucesters withdrew to A Railway R 13 + R 19. Gloucesters afterwards withdrew to Q 7c.d + Q 8a where they were relieved by a unit of 112th Bde (37 Division) afterwards moving into old positions near METZ.	

W. G. Chapman
Lieut Col
C.y.12 15 Bn Gloucestershire Regt

War Diary
of the
13th Bn Gloucestershire Regt
for the month of
October 1918

B B Thur, Major
O/C 13th Bn Gloucester Regt

War Diary 12th Bn. Gloucestershire Regt
October 1918

Place	Date	Hour	Summary of Events and Information	Reference to Appendices
VELU WOOD	1		Battalion left positions near METZ and marched to hutments in VELU WOOD. Weather fine. Nothing to report.	
	2 3 4		In hutments in VELU WOOD. On 4th October G.O.C. 5th Division, Major Genl PONSONBY. C.B. CMG DSO reviewed 12th Gloucestershire Regt. 1st Royal Warwickshire Regt and 1/6th Bn. A. & S. Highlanders, the first two Battalions being about to be disbanded and the 1/6 A. & S. H. to be transferred to another Division	
	5th 6th	10am	Orders received for disbandment to commence on 6th inst. Farewell dinner given to G.O.C. & Brig. 15th Bde Staffs. Ceremonial Church Parade. Disbandment commenced. Other ranks transferred to other units of 5th Division as follows 246 Royal West Kents 334 1/ O.C.L.I 102 1/ Devon 88 1/ E. Surrey 7 Hants. Rgt 40 1st Cheshires 90 1 Bedfords	

Authority 5th Divn. C.C. 570/1/3 dated 5/10/18

War Diary 12 Bn Gloucester Regt
October 1918

Place	Date	Hour	Summary of Events and Information	
VELU WOOD	7		Details of Bn preparing for complete disbandment	
	8			
	9		Details moved to Bus	
	10			
	11		Details of Bn completing records &c. Disbandment finally completed on 19th.	
	12		Lt Col N S Chapman M.C. proceeded on leave 11/10/18 to arrange affairs of Bn at home. Major B B KIRBY M.C. assumed command of details until 19th on which date he ceased to command + details sent to Bn Reception Camp – following Officers up to this time remaining with details –	
	13			
	14			
	15			
	16			
	17			
	18			
	19		Bn finally respective units 20/10/18	

Capt & adjt A BRACHER 1/5 CLI
Lt S H GILLARD 1/Devons

O/c 12 Bn Gloucesters Regt
Major
12 Bn Gloucesters Regt

WO 95/1580/3

5th Division
95th Inf. Bde.

95th Mach. Gun Coy
Jan — Dec 1916

95th Brigade.
5th Division.

Company formed 26.12.15
as 14th M.G.C.: Designated
95th M.G.C. 12.1.16.

95th BRIGADE MACHINE GUN COMPANY

JANUARY 1 9 1 6

Army Form C. 2118.

WAR DIARY
or
INTELLIGENCE SUMMARY.
(Erase heading not required.)

Instructions regarding War Diaries and Intelligence Summaries are contained in F.S. Regs., Part II. and the Staff Manual respectively. Title pages will be prepared in manuscript.

Hour, Date, Place	Summary of Events and Information	Remarks and references to Appendices
11 A.m. Dec. 26. 1915. Suzanne	Transport assembled on ground vacated by 5th R. Fusiliers. Weather bad. Difficult to clean harness & facilities. Very poor lot of horses, many suffering from mud fever & / change shot.	JWKerr
Dec. 27. Suzanne	First half company formed from details from 1st Devons & 1st Dorsets. Drivers and East Surreys returned from trenches same night. Lieut F.A. Weekes & 2nd Lieut C.W. Snow & Hon. L.G.A. Bentinck joined up. Equipment & of these units taken over	JWKerr
Dec. 28. Suzanne	Day devoted to sorting cleaning and overhauling guns and equipment. ½ Company proceeded to trenches and relieved gun positions occupied by 1st D.C.L.I. and 2nd Manchesters. Relieds from there two units joining up same night. The following officers joined up 2nd Lieut C.A.E. Stein, G.R.H. Bailey, D.G. Kydd, and F.G. Scott. The Company billetted in Château grounds in Chatian grounds	JWKerr

Army Form C. 2118.

WAR DIARY
or
INTELLIGENCE SUMMARY.
(Erase heading not required.)

Hour, Date, Place	Summary of Events and Information	Remarks and references to Appendices
Dec 29 Suzanne	Guns required slips re taken over from various units. Checked and cleaned. Company personnel organized. Company divided into 8 sections of two gun teams each. Each section under an M.G. officer. 2/Lieut K.W. Burton joined up.	WMount
Dec 30 Suzanne	Sections E-H relieves Sections A-D in trenches.	WMount
Dec 31 Maricourt & Suzanne	Considerable amount of Enemy Shelling about Maricourt	WMount
1 January 1916 Maricourt & Suzanne	Relief of sections in trenches carried out. Sections C-E occupied defence positions around village of Maricourt	WMount
2 Jan. Maricourt & Suzanne	Six sections in trenches, 2 resting at Suzanne	WMount
3 Jan. Maricourt & Suzanne	Inter Company relief carried out.	WMount

Army Form C. 2118.

INTELLIGENCE SUMMARY
WAR DIARY
or
INTELLIGENCE SUMMARY.
(Erase heading not required.)

Instructions regarding War Diaries and Intelligence Summaries are contained in F. S. Regs., Part II. and the Staff Manual respectively. Title pages will be prepared in manuscript.

Hour, Date, Place	Summary of Events and Information	Remarks and references to Appendices
4 January Maricourt & Suzanne	Two Sections in trenches, 2 in rear billets Suzanne	
5 January Maricourt & Suzanne	do	
6 January Maricourt & Suzanne	do	
7 January Maricourt & Suzanne	(2) 4 sections relieved by 2 new Brigade and proceed to their Suzanne	
8 January Maricourt & Suzanne	Remains 2 sections of Company relieved by new Brigade. Company takes over billets in Suzanne	
9 January Suzanne	In billets	
10 January Suzanne	In billets	

Army Form C. 2118.

WAR DIARY
or
INTELLIGENCE SUMMARY.
(Erase heading not required.)

Instructions regarding War Diaries and Intelligence Summaries are contained in F. S. Regs., Part II. and the Staff Manual respectively. Title pages will be prepared in manuscript.

Hour, Date, Place	Summary of Events and Information	Remarks and references to Appendices
11 January, 1916 Suzanne	Company, with Bde. Hqs. Signaling section & other Bde. details march to Vaux-sur-Somme arriving 2.45 p.m. and go into billets	
12 January Vaux-sur-Somme	In billets	
13 January Vaux-sur-Somme / Beaucourt	Company & move off at 10 a.m. for Beaucourt, marching via Corbie. Arrived Beaucourt at 2 p.m. and went into billets. Billets scattered and poor.	
13 January Beaucourt	Name of Company changed as from 12 noon of this day from 14th Bde M.G. Coy. to 95th Bde M.G. Coy.	
13 January Beaucourt	In billets	
14 January Beaucourt	In billets, commenced training	
15 January Beaucourt	In billets, training	
16 January Beaucourt	do	
17 January Beaucourt	do	

Army Form C. 2118.

WAR DIARY
or
INTELLIGENCE SUMMARY.

(*Erase heading not required.*)

Instructions regarding War Diaries and Intelligence Summaries are contained in F. S. Regs., Part II. and the Staff Manual respectively. Title pages will be prepared in manuscript.

Hour, Date, Place	Summary of Events and Information	Remarks and references to Appendices
18 January Beaucourt	In billets, training	
19 January Beaucourt	In billets training	
20 January Beaucourt	In billets training	
21 January Beaucourt	do	
22 January Beaucourt	do	
23 January Beaucourt	do	
24 January Beaucourt	do	
25 January Beaucourt	do	
26 January Beaucourt	do	

INTELLIGENCE SUMMARY.

or

WAR DIARY

or

INTELLIGENCE SUMMARY.

(Erase heading not required.)

Instructions regarding War Diaries and Intelligence Summaries are contained in F.S. Regs., Part II. and the Staff Manual respectively. Title pages will be prepared in manuscript.

Army Form C. 2118.

Hour, Date, Place	Summary of Events and Information	Remarks and references to Appendices
27 January Beaucourt	In billets training	
28 January Beaucourt	In billets training	
29 January Beaucourt	do do	
30 January Beaucourt	do do	
31 January Beaucourt	do do	

95th Brigade.
5th Division

Arrived HAVRE from U.K. 11.3.16

95th BRIGADE MACHINE GUN COMPANY

20th FEBRUARY to 30th APRIL 1916

95-MG-Coy
Vol 4

War Diary V

of

95th Brigade Machine Gun Company

Period ending — — — . 30-4-16

War Diary

INTELLIGENCE SUMMARY.
(Erase heading not required.)

95th Brigade Machine Gun Company

Place	Date	Hour	Summary of Events and Information	Remarks and references to Appendices
Belton Park	20.2.16	9 AM	The Company received orders to mobilize (weather wet)	
Belton Park	10.3.16	2.45 AM	The Company left Belton Park to entrain at Grantham station	
Grantham	10.3.16	6.40 AM	Train left Grantham Station for Southampton, arriving there 3.15 pm	
Southampton	10.3.16	4 pm	Each Company split up into two parties one consisting of 6 officers and 3 N.C.Os and men. The other 3 officers all transport and the remainder of the officers and men. The two parties going on different boats (weather fine)	
Southampton	10.3.16	5 pm	Parties embarked. No 1 Party set sail at 7 pm. No 2 set off at 11.15 pm	
Le Havre	11.3.16	2 AM	No 1 Party arrived & all disembarked at 7 am. They marched up to rest camp above the town. No 2 Party arrived at Le Havre at 4 pm but did not disembark until 11 AM - 12 AM. After drawing extra differences from army ordnance at Havre they marched to the rest camp arriving there at 11 pm (weather fine)	
Le Havre	12.3.16	9.30 AM	Paraded for inspection by Camp Commandant & any deficiencies of clothing and kit made good. Night. (weather fine)	
Le Havre	13.3.16	9 AM	Parade and Kit inspection (weather fine)	
Le Havre	14.3.16	1 AM	Paraded and marched down to Le Havre station, entrained and left 6 AM with No 1 Coy	

T2134. Wt. W708—776. 500000. 4/15. Sir J. C. & S.

INTELLIGENCE SUMMARY.

(Erase heading not required.)

Place	Date	Hour	Summary of Events and Information	Remarks and references to Appendices
			95th Brigade Machine Gun Company.	
			Ports taken Rouen, Busby (halt for 2 hrs how) Doullens, Mondicourt 2°9¹.	
			Coy left us at Doullens Company arrived at Mondicourt at 6 pm and immediately detrained (weather fine)	
Mondicourt	14.3.16	9 pm	Set out from Mondicourt station and marched to Le Grand Rullecourt arriving there at 3 am 15.3.16 Company were put into billets	
Le Grand Rullecourt	15.3.16	6.30 pm	The Company left Le Grand Rullecourt and marched to Agney-les-Duisans arriving there at 12.30 am 16.3.16 Been put into billets (weather fine)	
Agney les Duisans	18.3.16	8.20 am	No.1 Section marched up to the trenches north of Arras for 24 hrs instruction (weather fine)	
Agney les Duisans	19.3.16	8.20 pm	No.2 Section marched up to the trenches for 24 hrs instruction (weather fine)	
Agney les Duisans	20.3.16	2.20 am	No.3 Section marched up to the trenches for 24 hrs instruction (weather fine)	
Agney les Duisans	21.3.16	8.20 am	No.4 Section marched up to the trenches for 24 hrs instruction (weather fine)	
Agney les Duisans	22.3.16	8.30 pm	The Company marched to the trenches to relieve No.13 Machine Gun Coy relief carried out successfully	
Arras	3.4.16	8.30 pm	Two men of No.4 Section hit by rifle grenade one killed and one wounded.	
Arras	5.4.16	7.30 pm	Company relieved by No.13 Machine Gun Coy and marched back to Agnez.	

Army Form C. 2118.

WAR DIARY
or
INTELLIGENCE SUMMARY.

(Erase heading not required.)

95th Bde Machine Gun Company

Period from 6/7/16 to 30/7/16

Place	Date	Hour	Summary of Events and Information	Remarks and references to Appendices
ARRAS	6/7/16	6.30pm	The Company was relieved in "J" SECTOR by the 13th Bde. Machine Gun Company. Relief was carried out and completed by 12.15 am 6/7/16.	
ARRAS-AGNEZ	6/7 to 7/7/16	12.30am	Left ARRAS for AGNEZ, sections marching independently, arriving at 4.45 am.	
AGNEZ	7/7 to 12/7/16	—	In rest billets from 7/7 to 13/7/16, the rest being spent in checking equipment, stores, and instructional practice, when the whole of the Gun & Transport Equipment were overhauled.	
AGNEZ-ARRAS	13/7/16	8.30pm	The Company paraded and marched to ARRAS, the 16th Bn. Gun company forming the Transport as they were afterwards relieving, taking over the rest billets vacated by this Company. Relief completed by 12.35 am 14/7/16 the whole of the Guns when relieving by which was some place.	
ARRAS	16/7/16	—		
ARRAS	17/7/16	—	Between the 14th and 19th the extreme hot weather was experienced.	
ARRAS	18/7/16 12AM-1AM		No. 7659 Pte Rogers was transferred to M.G.C. Depot. Grantly.	
ARRAS	19/7/16	—	From 14th to 19th April much time was spent in improving + strengthening emplacements and dug-outs.	
ARRAS	20/7/16	9.AM	No. 11284 Pte James H. rejoined from Hospital. 42nd C.C.Stn	
ARRAS	21/7/16	1.53am	No. 12484 Pte Hill was slightly wounded in foot, and transferred to O.C. Sector	

INTELLIGENCE SUMMARY

Army Form C. 2118.

Instructions regarding War Diaries and Intelligence Summaries are contained in F.S. Regs., Part II. and the Staff Manual respectively. Title pages will be prepared in manuscript.

(Erase heading not required.)

Place	Date	Hour	Summary of Events and Information	Remarks and references to Appendices
ARRAS	22/16	—	Nº 1 & 25 Bn. Evans was transferring to Cavalry Claim letter and notes of strength	
	24/16		160 "Stopping trumpets to Base in advance. He & Evans which were in with Distortion let mine now taken to support line making 16 guns in line. Pts Delahaye to casfation	
	28/16 to 29/30	8pm to 5:35pm	Reinforcements from H.A.C. Base Depot arrived (½ & ¾ mm.) Relief commenced - 13th Mm. of taking over, then was rather a long affair owing to all gun & ammunition being in the line and it thirty necessitated some of the teams making three and four journeys yet relief was completed by 1.35 am 90/16 when all sections marched to Headquarters where a hot supper awaited them. Living ~~fresh~~ fine weather it was visited to march to AGNEZ by detours, the rear section arriving in Rest Billets at 5.0am, after a very interesting march.	

5th May 1916

W. Atkinson Captain
Commdg 95th Bde Machine Gun Company

95th Brigade.
5th Division.

95th BRIGADE MACHINE GUN COMPANY

MAY 1916

95 MG Coy
Vol 5

Army Form C. 2118.

WAR DIARY
or
INTELLIGENCE SUMMARY.
(Erase heading not required.)

Vol. 3.

War Diary
of
95th Brigade — Machine Gun Company
From 1 – 31 May 1916

In the field
1st June 1916.

E. H. Horton Captain
Commanding 95th Bde. Machine Gun Company

WAR DIARY

INTELLIGENCE SUMMARY.
(Erase heading not required.)

Instructions regarding War Diaries and Intelligence Summaries are contained in F. S. Regs., Part II. and the Staff Manual respectively. Title pages will be prepared in manuscript.

Place	Date	Hour	Summary of Events and Information	Remarks and references to Appendices
HGNEZ	MAY/16 1st	10.0am	Received orders to take over line from 41st Bay M. Gun Coy.	
	2nd	—	Cleaning and overhauling Equipment and Guns, taking inventory of all gear preparatory to taking over trenches.	
AGNEZ-ARRAS	3rd	—	Paraded at 7P.M. and marched to ARRAS — arrived at Billets 10 P.M.	
ARRAS	4th	8.0am	Nos 1, 2 & 3 Sections paraded with 12 Guns, and moved off independently to take over positions and implements. Guides being furnished by 41st Bde M. Gun Coy. No 4 Section resting.	
			The present Billet is a very roomy & strong one, but shells continually burst near to and on the building, up to the present only one man being injured, i.e. No 7716 Pte Midderon J. who has since been struck off the strength.	
—	5th			
—	6-11th	—	On 9th, private orders to move to a fresh Billet & same have left the Billet, no shelling has taken place	
	12-20th	—	Very hot weather experienced	
	21-25		Lieut V.C. Wassom & 1 N.C.O. proceeded to M.G. Corps Base Depot on a Course	

T2134. Wt. W708—776. 500000. 4/15. Sir J. C. & S.

WAR DIARY
or
INTELLIGENCE SUMMARY.
(Erase heading not required.)

Place	Date	Hour	Summary of Events and Information	Remarks and references to Appendices
	MAY 1916			
ARRAS	25th		Sgt Barker & 2 NCOs proceeded on a M. Gun Course at Denh. School. The line held by No 3 Section was shelled during the night, none of the NCOs hurt. The Section were slightly affected by "tear" shells were being used.	
ARRAS	31st		Our Artillery carried out a bombardment of Enemy's line during the early hours – Remainder of the day – quiet.	

In the field
1st June 1916.

R.K. Hobson Captain
Comming 95th Bde M. Gun Coy

95th Brigade.
5th Division.

95th BRIGADE MACHINE GUN COMPANY

JUNE 1916

Army Form C. 2118.

95. M.G Coy
Vol 4

WAR DIARY
or
INTELLIGENCE SUMMARY.
(Erase heading not required.)

Vol. 4.

War Diary
of
95th Brigade - Machine Gun Company
Period 1 - 30 June 1916.

In the field
1st July 1916

WHobson Captain
Commdg 95th Bde M.Gun Coy.

Army Form C. 2118.

WAR DIARY
or
INTELLIGENCE SUMMARY.
(Erase heading not required.)

VOL 4

Place	Date	Hour	Summary of Events and Information	Remarks and references to Appendices
ARRAS	1-15th		Nothing unusual to report. Warm weather experienced during this period.	
ARRAS	16-20th		Shelling of Sector held by Company, also vicinity of billet.	
SIMONCOURT	21st		Moved from ARRAS to SIMONCOURT. No 1 & 2 Sections with 1 & 2 Guns — then on 21st No 3 & 4 Sections with No 3 & 4 Sections with 14.2 & remaining guns. All in Billets by 5 a.m.	
SIMONCOURT	22-26th		In reserve. — Working parties of 40 NCOs & men found daily — digging.	
SIMONCOURT	26th	6:30 pm	Moved to BERNEVILLE arrived in Billets 7:30 pm.	
BERNEVILLE	27th		Reserve 27th. Found working parties — digging fresh trenches.	
BERNEVILLE	28th		Digging parties as 27th.	
BERNEVILLE	29-30th		All C.O's Checking & cleaning guns, equipment & limbers, and inspecting water tests &c &c by Company.	
			Sicca.	
			1-7-16.	

R. Moss Captain
Comdg. 95th Bde M.G.M.Coy

95th Brigade.

5th Division.

95th BRIGADE

MACHINE GUN COMPANY

JULY 1 9 1 6

Army Form C. 2118.

WAR DIARY
or
INTELLIGENCE SUMMARY.
(Erase heading not required.)

95th M. G. Coy.

Instructions regarding War Diaries and Intelligence Summaries are contained in F.S. Regs., Part II. and the Staff Manual respectively. Title pages will be prepared in manuscript.

Place	Date	Hour	Summary of Events and Information	Remarks and references to Appendices
BEAUDRICOURT	1.7.16		In Billets. Nothing to report. Under orders to move.	
"	2.7.16		Left BEAUDRICOURT at 3.6 pm for BERNVILLE arriving there at 9 pm. Rained during march. Distance marched about 18 K.	
BERNVILLE	7.7.16 to 12.7.16		In Billets at BERNVILLE. Nothing to report.	
"	13.7.16		Left BERNVILLE at 9.30 pm for BEAUDRICOURT arriving there at 5 pm + billeted. Weather fine + cool.	
BEAUDRICOURT	14.7.16		Left BEAUDRICOURT at 12 PM for CANDAS arriving there at 7 PM at (billets) weather fine + cool.	
CANDAS	15.7.16		Left CANDAS 12 AM + marched to RU BEMPRE arriving at 5 PM (billets) fine weather.	
RUBEMPRE	16.7.16		Left RUBEMPRE at 7 AM for BRESSE arriving there at 12 noon. Bivouac stay. Weather showery.	
BRESSE	17.7.16		Left BRESSE at 1.30 AM for BECOURT BECORDEL arriving there at 12 noon. Bivouaced. Weather fine	
BECOURT BECORDEL	17.7.16 to 18.7.16		Nothing to report. Weather fine	

Army Form C. 2118.

WAR DIARY
or
INTELLIGENCE SUMMARY.
(Erase heading not required.)

Instructions regarding War Diaries and Intelligence Summaries are contained in F. S. Regs., Part II. and the Staff Manual respectively. Title pages will be prepared in manuscript.

Place	Date	Hour	Summary of Events and Information	Remarks and references to Appendices
MAMETZ	19.7.16		Left BECOURT (BECORDEL) for MAMETZ at 9 P.M. & Bivouaced in a field at 9 P.M. No 3 Section went into action in the line at LONGUEVAL. No 1 Section followed at 10.30 P.M., No 1 Section moving up in Support in the valley with No 2 Section in Reserve at MAMETZ.	
In the field	20.7.16 to 21.7.16		No 1, 3, & 4 Sections were all in the line + No 2 Section in Support in the valley. During the time there were a lot of attacks & counterattacking by the Germans. Guns M.G. did very good work in helping to smash a German counterattack & doing good plenty of audible targets on German flanking parties.	
In the field	22.7.16 to 23.7.16		No 2 Section moved up into line + #3 relieved guns of No 1, 3 & 4 Sections who had had a very thin time owing to heavy shelling. Heavy fighting & little activity.	
In the field	24.7.16		Composite Section relieved No 1 Section (6 guns) + No 1 Section (6 guns). These guns teams went out in Support. Heavy fighting & shelling still continues. Tonight getting difficult to find.	

T.2134. Wt. W708—776. 500000. 4/15. Sir J. C. & S.

WAR DIARY

or

INTELLIGENCE SUMMARY.

(Erase heading not required.)

Army Form C. 2118.

Place	Date	Hour	Summary of Events and Information	Remarks and references to Appendices
In the field	26-7-16 to 27-7-16		= 95th Machine Gun Company = The Company was relieved by 15th. G. Cy. & moved out into support to POMMIERS REDOUBT. Except 2 guns No 3 Section who returned 2 guns of 99th M.G.C. in LONGUEVAL VILLAGE + two guns of No 1 Section were left in position just outside LONGUEVAL VILLAGE. The two teams of No 3 Section were very heavily shelled & the two gun teams were all killed or wounded. Heavy shelling	
In the field	28-7-16 29-7-16		& fighting still continue. Kept strengthening the two guns of No 3 + two guns of No 1. Front line was started in German posts & trenches	
In the field	30-7-16		No 4 Section relieved by 13th M.G.C. & the section moved into POMMIERS REDOUBT.	
POMMIERS REDOUBT	31-7-16		Nothing to report. German shelled in vicinity of the REDOUBT.	
In the field	1-8-16			

S.H. Alison Captain
Commanding 95th M.G. Coy

95th Brigade.

5th Division.

95th BRIGADE MACHINE GUN COMPANY

AUGUST 1916

WAR DIARY
INTELLIGENCE SUMMARY. 95 M.G. Coy.

Army Form C. 2118.

Vol 8

Place	Date	Hour	Summary of Events and Information	Remarks and references to Appendices
POMMIERS REDOUBT	1/9/16		Relieved here by 51 M.G. Coy marched to D.18.d & bivouacked	REF MAP
D.18.d	2/9/16		Still here. Men bathed in ANCRE. Weather very hot.	
D.14.d	3/9/16		Bathing parade. Weather still very hot.	
D.18.d	4/9/16		Left Camp at 1.45 & marched to MERICOURT RIBEMONT Station & entrained at 11 PM. Weather fine.	
AIRINES	5/9/16		Arrived here at 3 AM. Weather fine & left at 11 AM & marched to VERGIES & billeted. Weather fine.	REF MAP 4 BAN) ADMIN MAP PART II
VERGIES	6/9/16 to 24/9/16		Here at Machine Gun Gunnery during this period. Weather very fine & hot. Nothing unusual to report.	
	24/9/16		Left VERGIES at 4 AM & marched to AIRINES & entrained weather wet. Detrained at EDGEHILL & marched to D.18.d & camped.	
D.18.d	24/9/16		Left D.18.d at 1 PM & marched to CITADEL men went into huts.	
CITADEL	25/9/16			
In the field	26/9/16 to 27/9/16		Left CITADEL at 2.15 PM and moved up into the Line relieving 106 M.G. Coy. No 2 Section went into the front line with the DEVON R No 3 Section the same and went Fire Positions (AGA No 1 & No Reserve)	REF MAP GUILLEMONT 1/20,000 No 3

95.11.6.H.C.

Army Form C. 2118.

WAR DIARY
INTELLIGENCE SUMMARY
(Erase heading not required.)

Place	Date	Hour	Summary of Events and Information	Remarks and references to Appendices
In the Field	28/8/16		No 4 Section relieved No 2 Section in FRONT LINE No 1 Section relieved No 3 Section in Support. Nos 2 & 3 being in Reserve	
In the Field	29/8/16		1/2 Section relieved 1/2 section of No 4 Section in FRONT LINE. No 3 Section went ½ Section of No 2 & No 4 moved up into Indirect Fire position	BERNARD
In the Field	30/8/16		No 3 Section relieved ½ Section of No 2 & Section in FRONT LINE No 1 Section relieved ½ Section of No 4 in Indirect Fire position. No 2 & No 4 Sections moved back into	GUILLEMONT 1500 ↔
In the Field	31/8/16			
TALUS BOISE	1/9/16	8 PM	received word that 15 M.G. Coy were going to relieve Sections of this company in the Line. Relief of Indirect Fire position took place at 2 A.M. 1/9/16 & FRONT LINE at 8.0 A.M. 1/9/16. No 1 & 3 Sections moved into camp at TALUS BOISE the whole company now being here.	

1-9-16

J.H. Adams. Captain.
Comdg. 95th M.G. Coy. M. Gun Corps

95th Brigade.
5th Division.

95th BRIGADE MACHINE GUN COMPANY

SEPTEMBER 1916

WAR DIARY
INTELLIGENCE SUMMARY.

95 M.G. Coy

Vol 9

Place	Date	Hour	Summary of Events and Information	Remarks and references to Appendices
TALUS BOIS	1/9/16		Company still resting	RE=MAP GUILLEMONT 1/20,000 T.M.
"	2/9/16		No 1 & 3 Section left at 3 PM & No 4 & 2 Section left at 4 PM arriving at SUNKEN ROAD (Coy H/Qrs) The Company took up the following position in the line in preparation for the attack on the German line.	
			No 1 Section (Indirect fire position) SUNKEN RD A6 a 6.6	
			No 3 " (Bill) ANGLE WOOD B1 c 6.5.	
			No 2 " attached to the DEVONS R	
			No 4 " " E SURREY R	
In the Field	3/9/16		95 INF BDE attacked. Section 1 & 3 duly carried out Indirect fire No 2 & 4 Section went over to 2nd Obj. & dug themselves in. No 2 section turned its covering fire. then firing in 15 Inf Bde.	
"	4/9/16		95 INF BDE still attacking. No 4 Section attached to E. SURREY. R in W.EDGE S WOOD	
"	5/9/16		No 1 Section relieved No 2 Section T 25 D No 3 Section N EDGE WOOD 2 guns of No 3 Section with D.C.L.I.	
	6/9/16		GERMANS attacked but were driven off Company were relieved by 168 M.G Coy	
HAPPY VALLEY	7/9/16		Company marched to HAPPY VALLEY & went into CAMP.	

Army Form C. 2118.

WAR DIARY
or
INTELLIGENCE SUMMARY.

No 2

(Erase heading not required.)

Instructions regarding War Diaries and Intelligence Summaries are contained in F. S. Regs., Part II. and the Staff Manual respectively. Title pages will be prepared in manuscript.

Place	Date	Hour	Summary of Events and Information	Remarks and references to Appendices
HAPPY VALLEY	8/9/16		Still resting at rest	
"	9/9/16		"	
VILLE SUR ANCRE	10/9/16		Company moved from HAPPY VALLEY to VILLE SUR ANCRE & went into Billets	
"	11/9/16			
VILLE SUR	12/9/16		Company Training	
ANCRE	13/9/16			
TREUX	14/9/16		Moved from VILLE SUR ANCRE to TREUX & went into Billets	
"	15/9/16		Company Training	
"	16/9/16			
SAND PITS	17/9/16		Moved into Camp at the SAND PITS.	
In the Field	18/9/16		Sections 2, 3 & 4 moved into the Line E. of GINCHY	
	19/9/16		6 guns with GLOUCESTER R	
	20/9/16		1 Section D.C.L.I	
	21/9/16		2 guns with E. SURREY	ALBERT (continued over)
			1 Section in Reserve at F 14 D	

INTELLIGENCE SUMMARY.

No 3

(Erase heading not required.)

Place	Date	Hour	Summary of Events and Information	Remarks and references to Appendices
In the field	22/9/16		Company Relieved by 13 M G Coy & moved in Camp at F14 D	ALBERT (Contoured Sheet)
"	23/9/16		Company resting F14 D	
"	24/9/16		Company moved into the line for the attack on MORVAL	
"	25/9/16		" in position for attack on MORVAL	GUILLEMONT 57d 1/20.000
			No 2 Section & 2 guns of No 1 Section in QUARRIES (Indirect fire position)	
			2 gun No 1 & 2 guns No 3 in QUADRILATERAL TRENCH (Indirect fire position)	
			2 gun No 3 Section in SUPPORT in QUADRILATERAL TRENCH	
			No 4 Section in Reserve in trench WEDGWOOD – CINCHY ROAD	
			6 PM 2 gun No 4 Section (Coupar) STRONG POINT near MORVAL CHURCH	
			" 2 " " " " " ORCHARD (Too)	
	26/9/16		German shelled MORVAL putting in 3oro shells of heavy calibre guns in STRONG POINT near MORVAL CHURCH moved into FRONT LINE clear of VILLAGE.	
			Company relieved at 11 PM by 60 & 61 M G Coys & moved into camp at F14 D	
CITADEL	27/9/16		Company moved into Camp at CITADEL	ALBERT (Contoured Sheet)

INTELLIGENCE SUMMARY. No 4

(Erase heading not required.)

Place	Date	Hour	Summary of Events and Information	Remarks and references to Appendices
CITADEL	28/9/16		Company resting	
FONTAINES	29/9/16		Company entrained at HAPPY VALLEY STATION at 5 PM arriving at LONGPRÉ at 2.30 AM & marching to huts at FONTAINES	
"	30/9/16		Company moved off from FONTAINES at 11.15 PM for entraining at 'PONT REMY'	
"	30/9/16		arriving at STATION 12 AM (midnight)	

E.H.Hobson Capt
o/c 95" M.G. Coy

95th Brigade.

5th Division.

95th BRIGADE MACHINE GUN COMPANY

OCTOBER 1916

Army Form C. 2118.

WAR DIARY
or
INTELLIGENCE SUMMARY
(Erase heading not required.)

95 M.G. Company

Vol 10

Place	Date	Hour	Summary of Events and Information	Remarks and references to Appendices
BETHUNE	1/10/16		Coy detrained at CHOQUES at midday & marched to billets in BETHUNE.	
"	2/10/16		2nd Lt. T.J. WILSON is awarded his Military Cross for his excellent work in the LEUZE WOOD operations. No 7737 Sgt H Travers to awarded the D.C.M for the same operations.	
GORRE	3/10/16		Coy marched to GORRE & took over the lines just North of the LA BASSEE Canal from 93rd M.G. Coy. 12 guns in the line.	
LE RREOL	10/10/16		13th M.G. Coy takes over positions held by 9 left guns of the Coy and the Coy took over the positions from 96 M.G. Coy just South of the LA BASSEE Canal.	
"			Coy H.Q. Moved to LE RREOL.	
"			Line North of canal very quiet but fires to considerable Trench Mortar Cohorts South of Canal round the BRICK STACKS	
"	28/6/16		No 12067 Pte HARNETT is awarded the Military Medal for his excellent work in the LEUZE WOOD operations.	
"			M.Gs of the Coy fire about 2000 rounds Indirect Fire nightly.	
"			33 Men are transferred from Battalions of the Brigades to the Company	

WAR DIARY
or
INTELLIGENCE SUMMARY.

Army Form C. 2118.

95 M.G. Company

In accordance with First Army letter O.B./181 to complete new establishment

J.H. Wilson Capt
Comdg 95 M.G. Coy
Nov 1st 1916.

95th Brigade.
5th Division

95th BRIGADE MACHINEGUN COMPANY

NOVEMBER 1916

INTELLIGENCE SUMMARY.

95 Machine Gun Company Vol XI

Place	Date	Hour	Summary of Events and Information	Remarks and references to Appendices
CUINCHY	1/11/16		13 Machine Guns in the line - Enemy quiet except for Trench Mortar activity round the Brickstacks. Fired during day & night at the targets. Fired C of the LA BASSEE CANAL was relieved	
	25/11/16		The nine guns South of Company by 71st Machine Gun Company	
	26/11/16		The four guns North of the Canal are relieved by 16th M.G. Coy.	
	28/11/16		The Company move to billets in BETHUNE. The Company move to rest billets near ESSARS.	

R.H. Acton Capt
Comdg 95. M.G. Coy
Nov 30th 1916

95th Brigade.
5th Division.

95th BRIGADE MACHINE GUN COMPANY

DECEMBER 1916

Army Form C. 2118.

WAR DIARY
or
INTELLIGENCE SUMMARY.
(Erase heading not required.)

95TH Coy Machine Gun Corps

REFERENCE MAP – BETHUNE Combined sheet
Sheets 36 A. S.E. / 36 A. S.W. / 36 B. N.E. / 36 C. N.W.

Vol / 2

Instructions regarding War Diaries and Intelligence Summaries are contained in F. S. Regs., Part II. and the Staff Manual respectively. Title pages will be prepared in manuscript.

Place	Date	Hour	Summary of Events and Information	Remarks and references to Appendices
SLOANE SQARE X11.b.3.3	1-12-16		95th Bn. M.G. Coys. in rest billets — Hdqrs. at SLOANE SQ. — Transport at NESPLAUX X.14.b.	
LES 8 MAISONS R.2.d	4-12-16		The Coy. relieved the 13th M.G. Coy. in the line between NEUVE CHAPELLE and RICHEBOURG L'AVOUÉ. 13 guns in position in the trenches, with 3 guns in reserve abart 800 yds behind the line. All the 13 guns except one were employed in covering gaps between strong posts in the front line — the guns being placed between 300 and 600 yds from the front trench. The Coy. Hdqrs. was stationed in a farm about R.2.q.d.7. Between 4-12-16 and 20-12-16 the line was quiet; no indirect fire was carried out during this period. The enemy machine guns were inactive. There was trench mortar activity fairly regularly.	
R.35.6.4.9.	20-12-16	abart 3pm	The 111th Inf. Bde. took over our Coy. Hdqrs., which moved to-day to R.35.6.4.9. There was considerable hostile artillery & trench mortar activity against our left & centre trenches abart S.5.a. 1 O.R. was wounded — he belonged to the section holding the left sector. (evacuated by trench mortar.)	

WAR DIARY or INTELLIGENCE SUMMARY.

(Erase heading not required.)

95th Coy. Machine Gun Corps Army Form C. 2118.

Place	Date	Hour	Summary of Events and Information	Remarks and references to Appendices
BEUVRY	22nd		The Coy was relieved by the 111th and 112th M.G. Companies; the 111th Coy. taking over 8 positions in the line, & the 112th — 4 positions	
		6pm	32 O.R. were billeted in BEUVRY — The men being in huts at F.20.c.2.8, where was also the Coy. Hdqrs.	
	29th		The Coy. remained in rest until the 29th. Training was carried out after X'mas. The Coy relieved the 13th M.G. Coy. in the trenches between GIVENCHY (inclusive) and LOTHIAN Rd TRENCH in S.27.c. 15 guns were in the line, 1 gun in	
GORRE			reserve at Coy. Hdqrs. at F.4.c.5.5. The line was quiet except for trench mortar activity near GIVENCHY	
	30th		Our guns fired about 400 rds. each night on to areas behind enemy	
	31st		line e.g. CANTELEUX + VIOLAINES.	

R.J. Gitkins/Lieut for Capt.
Comdg. 95th Coy. M.G. Corps.

5th Division
15th Infy Bde

95th Machine Gun Coy
~~Fr Dec 1917~~
1917 JAN — 1917 NOV.

To ITALY DEC 1917

95th MACHINE GUN COMPANY

95th BRIGADE

2nd DIVISION

APRIL 1917.

Army Form C. 2118.

WAR DIARY
or
INTELLIGENCE SUMMARY.
(Erase heading not required.)

of 95TH Coy. MACHINE GUN CORPS.
from 1st Jan to 31st Jan (incl) 1917

Vol 13

Place	Date	Hour	Summary of Events and Information	Remarks and references to Appendices
GIVENCHY (Sector)	1-1-17 to 3-1-17		Company in the trenches with 15 guns. Coy. HdQrs at GORRE. F.4.c.4.7 (Sheet 36.b NE.) Situation quiet - normal; trenches in poor condition in night wet weather. All guns within 700 yds of the front line - 5 being employed to cover gaps between posts in front trench. Indirect fire carried out at night on points, tracks, tramways & stray lines.	
	4-1-17	7 pm	A mine was blown by us tracks at A 9 b 15.40 (Sheet 36.c N.W. 7500) in conjunction with an artillery bombardment. 8 guns fired indirectly from LE PLANTIN and front trench line	
			WINDY CORNER in co-operation - one gun swept German parapet of MACHENSEN trench. Enemy retaliation was not heavy. 3 O.R. wounded by shrapnel.	
	5-1-17		1 O.R. wounded by fragment of hostile trench mortar.	
	5-1-17 to 13-1-17		Fired at night on points behind enemy's line including SAINTELEUX, VIOLAINES, CH. LE ST ROCH, RUE du MARAIS. During this period, with exception of trench mortar fire and a few complacements. Enemy's machine guns generally inactive.	
	14-1-17		Company was relieved by 13th M.G. Company.	
BEUVRY Sheet 36 b NE 14/16	14-1-17 to 31-1-17		Company received billets in BEUVRY, Company HdQrs at F.14.a.8.2. Remained in billets & carried out training in this area. 1 gun and team 1 on in duty each night against hostile aircraft. No attacks were made.	

Army Form C. 2118.

95th Coy. Machine Gun Corps

SUMMARY

(Erase heading not required.)

Instructions regarding War Diaries and Summaries are contained in F.S. Regs. and the Staff Manual respectively. Title will be prepared in manuscript.

Place	Date	Hour	Summary of Events and Information	Remarks and references to Appendices
	21.1.17	5pm	9 guns relieved 9 guns of 15th M.G. Coy. in the trenches in the CUINCHY sector. Situation normal. Ground roads knee deep frost.	
LE PREOL	22.1.17 to 29th	10 am	Coy. Hdqrs moved to LE PREOL at F.16.d.0.4 & relieved Hdqrs of 13th M.G. Coy. Indirect fire was carried out each night on points in rear of enemy's lines including AUCHY - LES - LA BASSEE, DISTILLERY etc. Enemy machine gun activity below normal. Hostile fire every day & night. Disposition of guns — 3 in BRICKSTACKS, 2 in CANAL EMBANKMENT, 3 between CANAL and GIVENCHY, 1 in STAFFORD REDT in LA BASSEE Rd. 2 employed for indirect fire purposes.	
	31.1.17			
	26.1.17	7.15	Information having been received of a hostile relief, 11,000 rds. were expended in	
		11.30pm	sweeping enemy approaches, roads & tracks.	

[signature]
Major Comdg.
95th Coy. M.G. Corps
31.1.17

Army Form C. 2118.

WAR DIARY
INTELLIGENCE SUMMARY
(Erase heading not required.)

of 95th Coy. Machine Gun Corps February 1917

Reference Maps 36 B N.E. 1/20000
36 C N.W. 1/20000

Vol 14

Place	Date	Hour	Summary of Events and Information	Remarks and references to Appendices
CUINCHY Sector.	1-2-17		Coy. Hqrs. situated at F.16.&.1-2, LE PREOL. Transport lines at F.16.a.9.7. Eleven guns in position in the trenches on the CUINCHY Sector viz. STAFFORD REDT (1) BRICKSTACKS (3) EMBANKMENT (2), SPOIL BANK. (1) ORCHARD (1) MANE REDT (1) and 2 guns employed for indirect fire at CEMETERY (A.21.a.8.5) and ORCHARD A.15.a.A.8.55. Situation quiet, enemy machine guns inactive. Construction of 2 sheets proof emplacements in front line about A.15.5.9.5. commenced. Points in rear of our lines were engaged every night by indirect fire. AUCHY, LA BASSÉE Rd., DISTILLERY, SIDINGS, CANTELEUX, being among the targets engaged.	
	6-2-17	8.30pm	A raid was carried out by the 12th D.C.L.I. regt. on the enemy trenches between the BASSÉE Rd. about A.22.a.1.2. Our guns had machinery before zero to zero none of our usual from 8.30 to 9pm placed barrage on trench 200 x S.E. of mine-crane, were on W. LA BASSÉE Rd.	
	9-2-17		2 sets emplacements at A.15.b.9.5. completed.	
	16/17.2-17	12 mn	2 mine shared by us N.W. of RED DRAGON CRATER, the enemy did not on retaliate.	
	18.2.17	8pm	The enemy blew a mine N of RED DRAGON CRATER, but took no offensive action beyond a slight shelling.	

Army Form C. 2118.

WAR DIARY
or
INTELLIGENCE SUMMARY.

(Erase heading not required.)

of 95th Coy.
Machine Gun Corps

Instructions regarding War Diaries and Intelligence Summaries are contained in F. S. Regs., Part II. and the Staff Manual respectively. Title pages will be prepared in manuscript.

Places	Date	Hour	Summary of Events and Information	Remarks and references to Appendices
GUINCHY Sector	20.2.17	night	In view of recent prisoners statements that none of tanks N.E. and S.E. of CANTELEUX were quite ready the enemy at night, several thousand rounds was fired on the tanks this night & succeeding nights. Burst at A.17.d.7.6 were also engaged for some nights.	
	24.2.17 to 28.2.17		Stretcher squad from 24th Division working + machine guns were constantly more active than in the early part of the month.	
	28.2.17		Kent 4000 rds were fired on targets every night. 1 O.R. wounded (slightly) by shell fire at MARIE REDT.	

N. W. Parr
Major commanding
95 M.G. Coy.

No. 95
MACHINE GUN
COMPANY.
No. ....
Date 28-2-17

Army Form C. 2118.

WAR DIARY
or
INTELLIGENCE SUMMARY. 95th Machine Gun Company

(Erase heading not required.)

Nov 15

Place	Date	Hour	Summary of Events and Information	Remarks and references to Appendices
Guinchy	1st		Four machine guns in battle position in the line two machine guns in indirect fire position, indirect fire being made each night on selected targets. Whilst the enemy lines an average of 5,000 rounds being expended nightly.	
	6th		A successful raid was carried out by 13th Bn Glouc Regt, four machine guns took part, using indirect fire, 10,000 rounds being expended.	
	16th		203rd Machine Gun Company are attached for instruction.	
	18th		203rd Machine Gun Company returns 95th Machine Gun Company in the line	
Béthune	19th		The Company in billets in Béthune for the night	
	20th		The Company marches to Burbure	
Burbure	23rd		The situation is now on a post billets + firmount training is taking place 32 men from the Battalion are attached as ammunition carriers for the coming operations.	
	23rd /25 31st		All training continues	

S.H. Harewood Major
Commanding 95th M.G. Company

WAR DIARY or INTELLIGENCE SUMMARY

Army Form C. 2118.

of No. 5 Company Machine Gun Corps.

APRIL 1917.

Place	Date	Hour	Summary of Events and Information	Remarks and references to Appendices
BURBURE	April 1st 2nd 3rd 4th 5th		Company in billets in village of BURBURE & carrying out Reconnaissance carried out of gun positions for covering advance of 1st Cav. Divn.	
			No. 3 & 4 Sections marched to ESTREE-CAUCHIE arriving by 9 p.m. These sections are now under the orders of the 1st Cav. Divn. & attached to the 2nd Can. M.G. Company.	
	6th		Hqrs, No. 1 & 2 Sections at BURBURE — No. 2 Coy. remained in billets at ESTREE-CAUCHIE. Hqrs, No. 1 & 2 Coys. moved to HAILLICOURT. No. 3 & 4 Section from ESTREE-CAUCHIE in the morning & march to ECOIVRES, where Hqrs was with 2nd Can. M.G. Coy. until 6 p.m. These sections take up their 8 gun positions	
	7/8/17		during the night at A22.c.4.6 (sheet 57 B.) in the GRAND COLLECTEUR trench.	
	8th		Some strong shift into found in the trench and occupied. Hqrs, No. 1 & 2 Coy. marched from HAILLICOURT to VILLERS-AU-BOIS when they halted. Drew for the advance. Five horses laid in early morning by a section in the line.	
	9th	3.65 a.m.	Due to a continued hostile whiff shower fire was carried out in barrage lines.	
		5.30 a.m.	Our artillery opened barrage & infantry went forward to the attack.	

Army Form C. 2118.

WAR DIARY
or
INTELLIGENCE SUMMARY.
(Erase heading not required.)

95th M.G. Coy.

April 1917

Instructions regarding War Diaries and Intelligence Summaries are contained in F.S. Regs., Part II. and the Staff Manual respectively. Title pages will be prepared in manuscript.

Place	Date	Hour	Summary of Events and Information	Remarks and references to Appendices
A 12 c 5.6. (57 B)	April 9th	5.45 a.m.	Hostile artillery retaliated + m. heavy was shelled fairly heavily until 6.30 a.m. when shelling slackened off + became intermittent. No damage was done to guns on teams and the shelter of the shafts + dug. mt. One dug was hit and rendered unserviceable. Bivvi. was hit in several places.	
		6.51 a.m.	Our 7 machine guns opened fire + continued until 9.57 a.m. in accordance with machine gun fire programme in substance sent to the Can. Corps. Fire was supported by one gun from A17 b and d, A18 a, + c. Barrage moved off 8.52 a.m.	
		7.15 a.m.	An H.E. shell pitched in trench + severely wounded 2 O.R. – m of whom has since subsequently died. The wounded were quickly removed by stretcher bearers of 31st Divn + taken to our advanced ref. str.	
		8.0 a.m.	All hostile shelling of no positions ceased – proving to thin the enemy sent no chlorine gas shells which produced caused no casualties.	
		9.57 a.m.	Our M.G. fire barrage ceased. Guns were left ready for S.O.S. once.	
		7 p.m.	Orders received to rejoin remainder of the Coy. at VILLERS AU BOIS.	
	9/10th night		3 + 4 sections unwounded their positions + marched to ECOIVRES.	
	10/	afternoon	3 + 4 Sections marched to VILLERS-AU-BOIS and rejoined the Coy.	

Army Form C. 2118.

WAR DIARY
or
INTELLIGENCE SUMMARY.
(Erase heading not required.)

of 95th M.G. Coy.

April 1917.

Place	Date	Hour	Summary of Events and Information	Remarks and references to Appendices
VILLERS-AU BOIS	10/11/12		Company rested in billets at VILLERS.	
	13	Afternoon	The 95th Bde. proceeded to take over the line in the GIVENCHY-EN-GOHELLE area. Enemy has just been driven from GIVENCHY and his position is uncertain 4 guns go forward with battalions — 2 with 1st DEVONS on right and 2 with 1st D.C.L.I. on left.	
	13/14	night	During the night these 4 guns were in position in GIVENCHY. 8 guns relieve 8 guns of 10th Coln. M.G. Coy. at CABARET ROUGE + occupied positions intended for indirect fire at S14 c.1.9. It is believed that the enemy has retired beyond range of these guns. 4 guns held in reserve in QUARRY at S8 b.3.8. Coy. Hdqrs. established at S13 d.9.9 (CABARET ROUGE).	
	14	dawn	Transport line remain at VILLERS AU BOIS. 2 guns moved forward from QUARRY + put in position about S3 b.5.0 in support of 1st D.C.L.I. 2 guns took up position in captured enemy trench at S10 d.4.4 and S10 b.6.9. — 2 guns in trench at M34 d.4.3. situation very quiet.	
		day	The 2 guns at S3 b.5.0 moved forward + placed in trench near M3 d 4.3 — N° 2 Section with 1st D.C.L.I. on left and half of N° 1 with 1st DEVONS on right. Good shelter obtained for gun teams in captured dug-outs.	
	15	day	Remaining 2 guns in QUARRY and 2 guns from Coy. Hdqrs. moved into positions	

Army Form C. 2118.

WAR DIARY
or
INTELLIGENCE SUMMARY.

of 95th M.G. Company
April 1917.

(Erase heading not required.)

Instructions regarding War Diaries and Intelligence Summaries are contained in F.S. Regs., Part II. and the Staff Manual respectively. Title pages will be prepared in manuscript.

Place	Date	Hour	Summary of Events and Information	Remarks and references to Appendices
near S.3.b.50	16th		and S.3.d.8.8. — 2 to support 1st DEVONS and 2 to support 1st D.C.L.I. Situation quiet. 2 guns moved from area S.3.b.50.4 but in position about S.2.b.2.5 - firing along South Side of BOIS DE L'HIRONDELLE. 1 O.R. severely wounded. G's have subsequently moved	
	17th		2 Guns moved from Bois Hugo. It appears 2 guns moved yesterday from S.3.b.5.0. 12 guns now in position and 4 in Batt. reserve. Situation quiet. Enemies hostile artillery activity.	
	18, 19, 20			
	21st		1 O.R. wounded g.s. Ammo issued for M.G. fire barrage by 14 of our guns and 10 of 13th M.G. Coy. to cover attack of 1st Devons & 1st D.C.L.I. on 23rd inst. on CENTRAL ELECTRIC GENERATING STATION at M.36.b.7.7.	
	21st/22nd night		6 gun positions prepared & occupied in houses at M.29.d. & 9.b. 8 gun positions dug in the open at S.5.b.7.4.	
	22nd		Our artillery bombarded the enemy's position during the day.	
	23rd 3 am		8 gun positions at S.6.b.7.4 occupied. During the night 21/22 13th M.G. Coy. 12 positions at M.34.d.6.3 and 4 at S.5.c.5.6. 1 O.R. wounded near S.5.b.7.4. (2 guns both in position) Gunning at M.36.d.4.7.	
	4:45 am		In conjunction with artillery 14 of our guns + 10 of 13th M.G. Coy. opened an intense barrage which moved in 5 stages in front of the attacking infantry across area of CENTRAL	

2353 Wt. W2544/1454 700,000 5/15 D. D. & L. A.D.S.S. Forms/C 2118.

WAR DIARY or INTELLIGENCE SUMMARY

(Erase heading not required.)

Army Form C. 2118.

95th M.G. Coy
April 1917.

Place	Date	Hour	Summary of Events and Information	Remarks and references to Appendices
ELECTRIC GENERATING STATION, LA COULOTTE, BREWERY, ELEU DT LEAUVETTE, AVION, & Gardens S.W. of AVION — a wintering ground between these points.	April 23rd	5:15am	4 O.R. killed as result of hostile artillery retaliation on right + 2 O.R. wounded near M.29.c.9.6. Hostile artillery barrage of heavy H.E. shells was seen in sight during the attack, this shelling continued during the morning. Reports came in at 8am that the 1st D.C.M. have been held up with hostile M.G. fire – another barrage of our M.G.'s asked for. This barrage was fired on line by 12 of 2/13th M.G. Coy that 6 guns of our guns at M.29.c.9.6. were close by after 8am. on S.O.S. barrage line. 2 guns of our guns at M.36.c.4.4 were intermittently firing to rest of the day. Many lights were fired in rear of about LA COULOTTE & trenches immediately S.W. Many lights were fired in rear of the enemy which accounted in the a[...] of our men to our being the day. Both enemy machine gun & trench mortar were silent & several rifles were seen saving them. During the day 3 guns were kept up firing of H.E. shells – 2 howitzers were similar.	
		9 pm	8 guns at S.S. & T.4 withdrawn to tire horse summ. from S.14.c.8. to S.10.c.4.a.	

Army Form C. 2118.

WAR DIARY
or
INTELLIGENCE SUMMARY.
(Erase heading not required.)

95th M.G. Coy

April 1917.

Instructions regarding War Diaries and Intelligence Summaries are contained in F.S. Regs., Part II. and the Staff Manual respectively. Title pages will be prepared in manuscript.

Place	Date	Hour	Summary of Events and Information	Remarks and references to Appendices
	April 23rd	night	Slow fire (indirect) carried out throughout the night on barrage lines by 16 guns of 13th M.G. Coy & 6 guns of one at M29c9.7.	
	24th	day	Situation whole artillery quieter. Our 2 guns in the Quarry at M35 c.m.7. continued to harass & inflict casualties on the enemy throughout the day. Another gun was hit hard, but was 'knocked out'.	
		11pm	Crew received fr relief by 10th Can. M.G. Coy to night.	
		night	Whole Coy. was relieved by 10th Can M.G. Coy, who occupied 4 positions in even buts between S14B8 & S10A0, 2 positions in Quarry at M36 c.4.7, and 6 positions in houses at M29 c.9.7.	
	25th to 30th		Coy. marched to huts in camp at CHATEAU DE LA HAIE. Coy remained in billets & carried at training daily.	

S.H. Moore Major
Comm'dg 95th M.G. Coy.

Army Form C. 2118.

WAR DIARY
or
INTELLIGENCE SUMMARY.
(Erase heading not required.)

of 95th Company
Machine Gun Corps.
for May 1917

Vol 17

Place	Date	Hour	Summary of Events and Information	Remarks and references to Appendices
CHATEAU DE LA HAIE [W12 central Sheet 36 B]	May 1st		Coy. Strength = 11 Officers, 166 O.R.	
	to 3rd		The Company is billeted and is daily training attention being paid to Bayonet fighting, training mechanism & immediate action instructions. 2 O.R. reinforcements received from M.G. Base.	
	3rd	2 pm	The Company marched to the BIENTATA TUNNEL A15 (Sheet 57B N.W.) & stays there during the night; transport at A15 also. Orders received to relieve 16 guns of 3rd and 10th Can. M.G. Coys in the line, FRESNOY Sector, on night of 4th/5th.	
	4th	7 pm	Sections leave camp independently to relieve, guides being met at COMMANDANTS HOUSE.	
	5th	3 am	Relief of the Canadian M.G. Coys. complete. Disposition of Coy. is as follows. No. 2 Section (4 guns) in FRESNOY at (Sheet 57B N.W.) C1a.4.1, (Sheet 36 c S.W.) U25 c B.1, T30 d 9.9 U25a 1.4, generally about 100 yds. behind the front line, which were approximately from (Sheet 57B N.W.) C1 c 5.7, though C1 central (Sheet 36 c S.W.) U25 d 0.5, U25 a 2.1, U19 c 2.3. These guns situated in shell holes with practically no cover. No 3 Section in trench about B6 c 0.20 (Sheet 57B N.W.) - 4 guns - with excellent field of direct fire to the S.E. including OPPY WOOD + village, ground N and N.E. of OPPY. No 4 Section in trench between T29 d 9.0 and T29 d 1.8 (Sheet 36 c S.W.) - ARLEUX LOOP trench. These guns have a field of direct fire on enemy front line & area behind in U19. & command valley running	

Army Form C. 2118.

WAR DIARY
of 95th M.G. Coy
INTELLIGENCE SUMMARY.
(Erase heading not required.)

for May 1917.

Instructions regarding War Diaries and Intelligence Summaries are contained in F. S. Regs., Part II. and the Staff Manual respectively. Title pages will be prepared in manuscript.

Place	Date	Hour	Summary of Events and Information	Remarks and references to Appendices
FRESNOY Sector.	May 5th		Between ARLEUX and FRESNOY and ground line W and N.W of FRESNOY. The primary duty of M.Gs guns, however, is a S.O.S. barrage indirect fire about 600 yds. E and N.E. of FRESNOY through U26.c0.3 and U25.b4.5. No 1 Section in reserve in dug outs in VILLERVAL, near Coy. H.Qrs, which is situated at B3.d.8.3. Enemy shelled heavily with lachrymatory gas shells during the night. 1 O.R. wounded by shell-fire. FRESNOY shelled heavily during the whole day, especially twice, about 10 p.m. Enemy artillery active over whole Bde area. Strafing carried out by No 3 Section on enemy working in OPPY area — hits observed. Orders issued for 4 guns in FRESNOY to be withdrawn on account of the extremely heavy hostile shell-fire, and 4 guns of No 1 Section to advance & take up position on high ground of ARLEUX LOOP in T29.6 to command N.E. of FRESNOY.	
	6th	10 p.m.	No 2 Section successfully evacuate their position during a Quiet period, & return to reserve in WILLERVAL. No. 1 go forward & take up 4 positions in trench at T29.b+2 (2 guns) and T29.6.6.6 (2 guns) these guns now command by area of fire enemy lines in front of our front line from U25.d.0.6 to U19.2.5.0 (approx). The normal fire S.O.S. barrage	

WAR DIARY of 95th M.G. Coy

INTELLIGENCE SUMMARY for May 1917.

Army Form C. 2118.

(Erase heading not required.)

Place	Date	Hour	Summary of Events and Information	Remarks and references to Appendices
FRESNOY Sector	May 6th		which now forms a continuous line from C.2.a.6.3 (Sheet 57B.N.W) to U.19.d.1.0 (Sheet 36.c S.W) Sniping continued by No 3 Section. Enemy aircraft one constantly over our frontline — our guns have constantly engaged them both from the positions S and N of ARLEUX. 1 O.R. wounded by piece of A.A. shell	
	7th		Very heavy hostile shelling all day, especially S of No 3 Sect, in front of Pde, in our sight. One gun at B.6.c.2.1 hit by shell fire rendered unserviceable. Slightly rising ground about B.12. central with a view to placing guns there to sweep S side of our salient round FRESNOY by direct fire. Field of fire from here in this direction is found to be only moderately good and whole area round B.12. central is constantly heavily shelled by the enemy's heavies — no cover besides shell holes available. 3 O.R. wounded by shell-fire	
	8th	3.30am	Intense barrage put down by the enemy in FRESNOY, trenches N and S, also in ARLEUX and the ARLEUX LOOP.	
		4.30am	Information received from forward infantry companies that enemy had attacked + practically overrun FRESNOY. No S.O.S. Signal made. On account of the few light, smoke & thick dust, which enemy's shells were raising in + all round FRESNOY	

Army Form C. 2118.

WAR DIARY of 95th M.G. Coy.

INTELLIGENCE SUMMARY. for May 1917.

(Erase heading not required.)

Instructions regarding War Diaries and Intelligence Summaries are contained in F. S. Regs., Part II. and the Staff Manual respectively. Title pages will be prepared in manuscript.

Place	Date	Hour	Summary of Events and Information	Remarks and references to Appendices
FRESNOY Sector	May 8th	3 a.m.	Section officers in touch with forward battalions received orders that further firing on S.O.S. barrage line was of little use, owing to the enemy having re-occupied FRESNOY + a large portion of FRESNOY WOOD. Known to be covered for which guns stood by.	
		day	No movement of enemy was seen either by guns covering W of FRESNOY or by guns covering OPPY + to the N.	
		7 a.m.	1 gun at T29 A.1.9 blown up by a H.E. shell — 1 attached O.R. (1 D.C.L.I) killed and 1 O.R. wounded at the gun position.	
		day	ARLEUX, ARLEUX LOOP, + all trenches in area severely shelled during whole day — several local counter-attacks were undertaken by 1st D.C.L.I. and 12th GLOUCESTERS in area T30 b and d. No targets presented to our 7 guns in FREUX LOOP. Situation obscure, the enemy did not attempt to advance out of FRESNOY WOOD or through T30.	
		2 p.m.	Orders received that a counter-attack would be made at 2 a.m. 9th, with our original front line as the objective. 1st DEVONS + 1st NORFOLKS to attack.	
		5 p.m.	Situation much quieter throttle artillery activity has 10 guns in action, 4 in reserve.	

Army Form C. 2118.

WAR DIARY
INTELLIGENCE SUMMARY.

of 95th M.G. Coy
for May 1917.

(Erase heading not required.)

Instructions regarding War Diaries and Intelligence Summaries are contained in F.S. Regs., Part II. and the Staff Manual respectively. Title pages will be prepared in manuscript.

Place	Date	Hour	Summary of Events and Information	Remarks and references to Appendices
FRESNOY Sector	8th		4 O.R. wounded by shell fire.	
	9th	2 am	Our artillery barrage opened – our machine guns did not co-operate owing to the small safety angle on the heads of our troops advancing from the A.R. LEUX LOOP across T.30. Hostile artillery opened up a barrage in retaliation over B1 & 2.1 heavily shelled with H.E., 2 guns hit here, but only penetrated in the barrel casing & repairable. 1 O.R. killed and 2 O.R. wounded.	
		morning	Our troops reached the objective, but were unable to maintain their position owing to an unsupported flank. Situation quieter.	
			Orders received for relief by 15th M.G. Coy.	
		night	15th M.G. Coy. placed 12 guns in line & positions occupied by Nos. 3,4,1 Sections, 200 4 in reserve at WILLERVAL.	
	10th	2 am	Relief complete. Company withdrawn from the line to occupy a bivouac camp at A.28.b.2.9 (Sheet 57.B. N.W.) – Transport at A.28.a.2.4. Company remained in camp, re-organised & carried out training the necessary for new form of incident fire drill especially for the men was fair. A comparatively few will	

WAR DIARY

INTELLIGENCE SUMMARY

of 95th M.G. Coy for May 1917.

Army Form C. 2118.

Place	Date	Hour	Summary of Events and Information	Remarks and references to Appendices
CAMP	May		was adopted as a standard throughout the company, the men practised in it.	
ECURIE.	14		2 guns & teams posted at A.17.B.5.9 for anti-aircraft duty, guarding NINE ELMS ammunition dump.	
	16, 17, 18		Company remained in camp. Anti aircraft guns obtained no targets — hostile machines came over from time to time, but kept always at to great a height to be engaged by machine guns. 8 O.R. reinforcements received from M.G. Base & 6 from 6th M.G. Coy.	
	18.		Orders received to put 10 guns on the line — 4 at B.11.a.5.5 to relieve 4 guns of the 15th M.G. Coy.) & 6 in CORPS line, E. of WILLERVAL, in B.2.c. and B.10.a.	
		12 noon	10 guns in position. No 2 Section at B.11.a.5.5 — duty of these guns is S.O.S. barrage on line W. of FRESNOY — positions in the open, fairly well dug in. No. 4 Section guns at B.10.d.1.0, B.10.c.5.4, B.10.a.8.0, B.10.a.7.7, half No. 1 Section at B.2.c.5.2. and B.2.c.5.4. Lines of fire were arranged for these 6 guns for enfilade zones fire along CORPS line from B.10.d.1.0 to trench in B.2.c. Open emplacements were made. R.E.'s are constructing deep dug-outs in this trench — these are not yet ready for occupation. All these 10 guns come under direct orders of O.C. 13th M.G. Coy. — D.M.G.O. situation quieter. Hostile shelling much less, but enemy is aircraft still very active over our lines.	

Army Form C. 2118.

WAR DIARY
or
INTELLIGENCE SUMMARY.

of 95th M.G. Coy

for May 1917

(Erase heading not required.)

Instructions regarding War Diaries and Intelligence Summaries are contained in F. S. Regs., Part II. and the Staff Manual respectively. Title pages will be prepared in manuscript.

Place	Date	Hour	Summary of Events and Information	Remarks and references to Appendices
CORPS line	May 20th		One gun hit by piece of H.E. Shell at B.2.c.5.4. – damage reparated. Gun still in action. 10 O.R. reinforcements arrived from 13th M.G. Coy.	
	21st	10 pm	No 3 Section relieved No 4. Half No 3 relieved half No 1 in Corps line.	
			No 4 Section returned to camp.	
	22nd	9 pm	Two guns of 10th D.C.L.I. relieved our 2 guns on anti-aircraft duty at A.17.f.5.9.	
			These guns have had no targets.	
		11 pm	Four guns of 2nd Cav. M.G. Squadron relieved No 2 Section on barrage work at B.11.a.5.5.	
		12 mn	Relief complete. No 2 Section returned to camp – quiet night for relief.	
			Orders received for relief of 6 guns in Corps line by 5th and 99th M.G. Coys.	
	23rd	10 pm	Section of 5th M.G. Coy relieved the 4 left guns in Corps line.	
		11 pm	2 guns of 99th M.G. Coy relieved running 2 right guns in corps line. These 6 guns teams returned to camp.	
	24th		Company engaged in cleaning limber strip guns & ammn. Gear. During the last few days, alternative have been made to the Winter hole on the tripod, so that zero & points have been moved to right zero. This alteration has been	

Army Form C. 2118.

WAR DIARY of 95th M.G. Coy.
INTELLIGENCE SUMMARY. for May 1917.
(Erase heading not required.)

Place	Date	Hour	Summary of Events and Information	Remarks and references to Appendices
ECURIE	May 24th	11 am	has been found necessary in order to use the dials accurately conveniently for No 2 on the gun. 6th M.G. Coy arrive to take over our camps.	
		2 pm	The company marched to ANZIN and billets there in the CHATEAU.	
ANZIN	25th to 31st		The company & transport remain in billets & carry out training daily. Special attention is being paid to points of bayonet training between 16's and 18's. Instrumentation of 50 are supplied daily by the company for employment on roads.	
	27th	6	O.R. arrive as reinforcements from the M.G. Base. LIEUT. H. Du H. ALLIX has been mentioned in despatches for good work during the operations on the SOMME, Aug–Sept 1916. Notification that 7730 SGT. T. COLMAN of this company has been awarded the military medal was received. Sgt. Colman showed great coolness and personal courage while in the front line opposite LA COULOTTE (sheet 36 c S.W.) in the QUARRY at M 36 c 4.7 on April 22–24th. Heavy enemy rifle & shell fire and hostile activity after our attack at 4.45 am on April 23rd. He personally works his gun were responsible for obtaining many hits on enemy parties in COULOTTE	

WAR DIARY

of 95th M.G. Coy. Army Form C. 2118.

INTELLIGENCE SUMMARY.

for May 1917

(Erase heading not required.)

Instructions regarding War Diaries and Intelligence Summaries are contained in F.S. Regs., Part II. and the Staff Manual respectively. Title pages will be prepared in manuscript.

Place	Date	Hour	Summary of Events and Information	Remarks and references to Appendices
	May			
	31st		Trenches to W & N.W. also for the silencing of a hostile machine gun & trench mortar. This amount has been of the same courageous & active throughout the recent operations. Coy. strength 11 Officers and 183 O.R.	

B.H. Horn Major
Commanding 95 M.G. Coy.

Army Form C. 2118.

WAR DIARY

INTELLIGENCE SUMMARY of 95th M.G. Co.

for June 1917

(Erase heading not required.)

Instructions regarding War Diaries and Intelligence Summaries are contained in F.S. Regs., Part II. and the Staff Manual respectively. Title pages will be prepared in manuscript.

Place	Date	Hour	Summary of Events and Information	Remarks and references to Appendices
Comblain Châtelain	June 1st	11 p.m.	Coy. Strength 196. Officers 11. O.R. 184. Coy. at ANZIN and proceeded to C.C. by motor bus & occupied billets vacated by 13th M.G.Co. Transport & equipt. marched by road.	
do	1st – 8th		Coy. remained in billets & carried out training. Special attention was paid to training in Indirect fire, elementary tactical handling & great deal of interest was stimulated & initiative in gunners sports. A Coy. football league was drawn up & played. Spent. Horse Shows &c.	
	9th	6 a.m.	Coy. left C.C. & proceeded by motor bus & took over camp from 15th M.G.Co. at ECURIE. Transport proceeded by road.	
	9th - 15th		Coy. remained in camp. Working parties supplied daily – Q. The remainder training. Works on limbers for Divn. Rhoms?	
	15th		Orders received for relief of 6th M.G.Co. in ARLEUX sector. Arrangements for relief made with M.G. Co. in the line. 8 guns in position in ARLEUX loop, 4 guns indirect fire, 1 in reserve at WILLERVAL. 5 guns in ARLEUX loop. Aliases T2.9 central, 1 T29 d. D5. 10.0. 1 gun B5 a.4.5. 1 gun B c 20.05. 1 gun B6 c.4.4. central 4 T29 d. D5. 10.0. 1 gun B5 a.4.5. 1 gun B c 20.05. 1 gun B6 c.4.4.	
	15th/16th	11 p.m.	4 guns indirect fire at B5 c.4.4.	

WAR DIARY or INTELLIGENCE SUMMARY

Army Form C. 2118.

Place	Date	Hour	Summary of Events and Information	Remarks and references to Appendices
ARLEUX Sector	16.11.17		Ground reconnoitred with a view to placing guns on right & left in suitable positions for direct fire on enemy front line & trench W. of Tunney's Trench North. On night no position was found to afford this direct fire, so left 2 guns were moved further to left on higher ground at T.29.b.6.6 & T.29.d.65.95 whence direct fire was obtained on N. of Tunney's Nook. Enemy trench in T.30.d. 5 guns on left were known in position to sweep by direct fire the enemy front line from T.30.b.4.3 to C.1.a.1.1. Remainder of enemy first line in dead ground, is covered by S.O.S. barrage line of 2 indirect fire guns. 1 gun at C.5.a.4.3 from C.1.a. 05.40 to C.1.c.30.25.	
	19.20.17	night	No. 4 Section relieved No. 1 in right positions of Arleux Loop	
	23.11.6	all night	No. 1 Section returned to reserve at Willerval	
	24.11.	3 a.m.	No. 1 Section relieved No. 2 in left of Arleux Loop	
			No. 2 Section arrived in Willerval. For 3 days not the relief by No. 1 Section having been carried out with no mishaps.	
	24th		Enemy Willerval shelled by 4.2" & 5.9" in seemingly counter battery work against our field batteries in the village. Our troops in the line were still very quiet. Enemy continues to shell Oppy-Arleux village. We have no troops in these villages.	

2353 Wt. W2544/1454 700,000 5/15 D.D. & L. A.D.S.S./Forms/C. 2118.

WAR DIARY or INTELLIGENCE SUMMARY

Army Form C. 2118.

Place	Date	Hour	Summary of Events and Information	Remarks and references to Appendices
Athuis Redon	24th	afternoon	Quiet on the enemy's part. Our artillery carried out heavier barrages at various intervals through the day on Spy Wood & vicinity.	
		night	Very quiet. Enemy aeroplanes active over own trenches. We fired at them without much effect.	
	25th	forenoon	Willerval again shelled by 4.5" & 5.9". Knocked about quiet. Our artillery continued with harassing bombardments.	
		afternoon	Reconnoitred ground B 6 d & B 6 c to find positions for 4 guns which were to keep in a barrage for situations on the 26th. Positions finally picked at B 6 c 4.0.	
		night	Reserve section No 2 carried ammunition up & worked at positions in B 6 c 4.0. Night quiet, weather dry & warm.	
	26th	all day	Continued shelling of Willerval by enemy artillery. Our artillery active over enemy front line system of enemy.	
		night	No 2 again working at B 6 c 4.0. No 4 section carried ammunition to B 5 c 3.2 which the 4 guns of No 3 were going to march in barrage scheme for situations on R. 28 t.	

WAR DIARY or INTELLIGENCE SUMMARY

Army Form C. 2118.

Place	Date	Hour	Summary of Events and Information	Remarks and references to Appendices
Army	27/5	noon	Air gun positions and line shelled very quiet	
		afternoon	Enemy artillery active on Villerval barrage on our front line in front of Oppy. B6 & 10 No 2 which had been in reserve relieved No 3 Section which proceeded to position in B6 & 10.	
	28th	morning	Positions for the first time for several days in Villerval. Seven enemy planes were very low over Arleux kept firing machine guns.	
		afternoon	Gas war dense off Villerval by our guns. Particularly heavy barrage in front side Oppy-Villerval. Villerval received severe attention.	
		evening	Our 15th Bde delivered an attack at 9.10 pm on the enemy front line after an intense artillery & machine gun barrage. Own barrage was sufficient by 3 guns the H guns of B6 & 10 2 lt H guns at B5 c 32 of own Company now in the barrage scheme, the objectives were entirely successful several hundred prisoners & several machine guns were captured.	
		night	During night all own guns maintained a slow rate of fire on the enemy's barrage line.	

2353 Wt. W2544/1454 700,000 5/15 D. D. & L. A.D.S.S. Forms/C 2118.

Army Form C. 2118.

WAR DIARY
or
INTELLIGENCE SUMMARY.
(Erase heading not required.)

Place	Date	Hour	Summary of Events and Information	Remarks and references to Appendices
Aubers	28th	night	An distinct enemy counterattack on our red lines was completely dispersed by our own guns.	
	29th	all day	Quiet in the morning on our own front. Much activity on Wilrawe by enemy heavy artillery.	
	30th	do	Quiet in all parts of our sector. Heavy rain the whole time, becoming very muddy.	
		night	No 3 Section withdrawn from barrage position at B6 = 40.5 relieved No 4 Section in right part of Aubert Sect., this relief was exceedingly carried out.	

Callinghan Major
Commanding 95th Machine Gun Company.

Army Form C. 2118.

WAR DIARY
or
INTELLIGENCE SUMMARY

(Erase heading not required.)

of 95th Machine Gun Company
for July 1914.

Vol 19

Instructions regarding War Diaries and Intelligence Summaries are contained in F. S. Regs., Part II. and the Staff Manual respectively. Title pages will be prepared in manuscript.

Place	Date	Hour	Summary of Events and Information	Remarks and references to Appendices
ARLEUX Sector	July 1st		Company Strength: 12 Officers 183 O.R. Coy. in the line near Arleux. Distribution as follows:- Coy Hd. Qrs. and 1 Section in reserve in Villerval at B3d33 (Sheet 51bN.W.) 1 Section of guns at B5a+3, 1 gun B6c 20.05, 1 gun B6c 4.4 and T29d 05.40 (Sheet 36c S.W.) 1 Section of guns – 2 at T29 central, 1 gun at T29d 6.6 and 1 gun at T29d 65.95. 4 guns for indirect fire & barrage S.O.S. at B5c+ 4. Arrangements for M.G. Defence of Sector similar to that noted in diary for June 16th/14th. Transport lines Beuvin.	
	2nd.		1 O R. evacuated sick.	
	3rd.		1 OR reinforcement from C.C.S.	
	4th.		1 OR reinforced and from C.C.S.	
	10th & 11th		Situation quiet. Company remained in positions as above. Orders received for relief of Coy by the 13th.	
			M.G.Coy. on night of 6th/14th 95th Bde. relieved by 13th Bde.	
	6th/14th	night	Relief of Coy by 13th M.G. Coy successfully carried out. Company marched to camp at St. Austin: the last Section arriving about 4 a.m.	
	9th.		Lieut J.S. Wilson M.C. appointed 2 i.c. in command of the 95th M.G. Coy left St. Austin and carried out training daily.	
	9th/14th.		Coy. Hd. Qrs. & Coy remain at St. Austin and carried out training daily.	

Army Form C. 2118.

WAR DIARY
or
INTELLIGENCE SUMMARY.

of 95th Machine Gun Coy
for July 1917.

(Erase heading not required.)

Instructions regarding War Diaries and Intelligence Summaries are contained in F. S. Regs., Part II. and the Staff Manual respectively. Title pages will be prepared in manuscript.

Place	Date	Hour	Summary of Events and Information	Remarks and references to Appendices
	4th/14th		Instructions in Indirect fire Pine Ridge was again given to all ranks. Special attention was also paid to Coy. close order drill. Orders received for 8 guns to take up position in Arleux sector, to take part in a machine gun barrage to cover a raid on Drocourt trench from T.30.d.95.20 to T.30.d.6.9 (3.6 + 5m.) on night 13th/14th at 2 a.m.	
	10th		2OR seventh reinforcement rejoined.	
	12th		Ground reconnoitred by officers for gun positions for the indirect barrage fire. 8th reinforcement until 14/15th — 3 a.m. 1OR reinforcement from C.C.R.S.	
	13th	night	No 1 and 2 Sections proceeded from St Aubin to take up positions. No 1 occupied + indirect fire gun positions built by the Coy. during June 2, since vacated by the 13th M.G. Coy.; 2 new positions at P.5.c.2.0 (5.1.N.W.) 2 positions at P.5d.2.2 dug & occupied by No 2 Section. Weather fine, & hot. Rain fell heavily all night.	
	14th	evening	Rain fell heavily all night.	
	15th	3 a.m.	8 gun barrage opened fire on their barrage line for the raid. 1OR wounded by hostile M.G. fire (indirect). Barrage consisted of 1 lift direct barrage 3 to 3.6 on U.25.c.6.4 to U.25.a.2.2, second barrage 3.6 to 3.45 on U.25.c.8.6 to U.25.a.4.3. Rain fell heavily during whole time of firing — every shelter for belt-filling &c completely flooded out. An unusual number of stoppages were experienced — due to wet belts, it was found practically impossible to fire, and was very half more than once.	

WAR DIARY
INTELLIGENCE SUMMARY.
(Erase heading not required.)

Army Form C. 2118.

of 95th Machine Gun Company
for July 1917.

Place	Date	Hour	Summary of Events and Information	Remarks and references to Appendices
	15th	3 a.m.	The need for ammunition to be pressed to Machine Gun Companies already packed in hills & water bottles was most severely felt. Under war conditions it is practically impossible to get ammunition in hills supply by means of existing arrangements for attempting to fire hills in the field. Practically no batteries of artillery opened fire at zero hour — 3am.	
		4 am	Instructions received to cancel operation. This message was received by telephone at Batt. Hd Qrs. in B10t. where a runner from each section stayed.	
		5 am	Orders received from D.M.G.O. to retire to camp. About half of the men withdrew.	
		10 p.m	Remainder of Nos. 1, & 2, Sections withdrew with guns & gear, & marched back to camp at St Aubin.	
	15th		Orders received to relieve portions of 190 & B.M.G. Corps in the Sling sector on night of 17th/18th.	
			Arrangements for relief & handing over of trench stores between Companies made.	
	16th/17th		95th Inft. Bde. took over section from South of Oleog to South of Arleux	
	17th	2.30 p.m	The Company marched to hand out lines at Fosseux & that tea.	
		8 p.m	Coy. moved off by Sections to take up positions in the new sector.	
	17th/18th night		Coy. relieved 5 guns of 190th M.G.Coy. & 4 guns of 13th M.G. Coy. Relief complete 3 a.m. Disposition of Coy :- Coy Hd Qrs & No 2 Section at P.15 central (51bN.W.) No 3 Section with 5 guns on right. No 1 Section with 4 guns on left. No 1 Section with 3 guns & transport at Berwin.	

Army Form C. 2118.

WAR DIARY
of 95th Machine Gun Company
for July 1916

INTELLIGENCE SUMMARY
(Erase heading not required.)

Instructions regarding War Diaries and Intelligence Summaries are contained in F. S. Regs., Part II. and the Staff Manual respectively. Title pages will be prepared in manuscript.

Place	Date	Hour	Summary of Events and Information	Remarks and references to Appendices
Offy Sector	17th/18th		No 3 Section 5 guns at B.6.d.4.2., B.12.d.1.1, B.11.d.8.7, B.11.d.9.1, B.12.a 9.2. No 1 " " " B.12.d.7.3, B.6.d.4.4, B.5.d.7.1, B.5.a.65.15. Situation quiet, trenches wet.	
	18th		Deduced these two guns in position as part of Divn. M.G. Defence Scheme.	
	18th/22nd		Pn. 13th Bde. M.G. Defence established in attached scheme. 4 weeks guns from transport lines put in position.	
	20th		Major E.A. Watson D.S.O. Commanding 95th M.G. Coy. received orders to proceed to Franklin no reason assigned. He left the Coy. on the 21st. after having commanded it continuously since March 1916. All ranks very deeply regret his departure.	
			No 1 Section relieve No 3. No 2 relieve No 1. No 3 withdraw to Coy. Hd. Qrs. No 3 to Reserve.	
	21 st.		1 O.R. evacuated sick.	
	20/23rd		1 O.R.	
			Situation Quiet. All ranks working hard in the line to provide cover from weather & shell fire. The small left of elephant were found very useful for providing rapid cover from weather & fig in shells.	
	23rd		No 3 Section relieve No 1. No 1 Section relieve No 2. No 1 withdraws to Coy. Hd. Qrs. No 2 to reserve.	
	24th		1 O.R. wounded by hostile M.G. fire. wound in arm.	

2353 Wt. W2544/1454 700,000 5/15 D. D. & L. A.D.S.S. Forms/C 2118.

Army Form C. 2118.

WAR DIARY
or
INTELLIGENCE SUMMARY

(Erase heading not required.)

of 95th Machine Gun Company
for July 1916

Place	Date	Hour	Summary of Events and Information	Remarks and references to Appendices
	29th	day	Our guns this barrage is on an average 350 to 400' in front of the front line – in many cases in NO MANS Land. Thus a complete barrage can be put down along the front on the S.O.S. rate – in addition, should the enemy break through the wire run up against belt after belt of direct M.G. fire. Situation quiet. Work on improving & building new shelters for gun crews in position taken in hand commenced.	
	29th/31st		During the month the return of the Indirect Fire Direc. instituted in the Coy. have again been undoubtedly proved. In count of/Elinonates for guns is urgently needed. It appears also that the longest light test of each gun about the machine that was will are of from a form of indirect fire calculations have been standardised in the Coy; it is considered that it would be a benefit if more were utilised throughout the Corps – this would greatly facilitate work + tend for more accuracy. Unable indirect M.G. fire at night has accounted 3 O R of the Coy during fortnight. This casualties received severe hundred yards behind front line + are to prove that in a harassing fire indirect is worth work the necessary expenditure of ammo. Coy Strength 10 Officers 178 O.R.	

A.G. Gittins Lieut
Commanding 95th Machine Gun Company.

Army Form C. 2118.

WAR DIARY
of
INTELLIGENCE SUMMARY.
(Erase heading not required.)

of 95th Machine Gun Company
for July 1917

Instructions regarding War Diaries and Intelligence Summaries are contained in F. S. Regs., Part II. and the Staff Manual respectively. Title pages will be prepared in manuscript.

Place	Date	Hour	Summary of Events and Information	Remarks and references to Appendices
	23rd/29th		Work proceeding well. No 1 Section providing working parties every night. The assistance of 1 R.E. Cpl. & 12 sappers & 20 infantry being obtained from 25th to 28th. This assistance proves invaluable. The R.E.'s are constructing 2 deep dugouts, one at B.12.a 38.25 for a Section Hd. Qrs. & for gun team shre, one at P.b.7. 38.40 & for gun in Britannia Trench. Situation quiet. Weather fine which are in short storms.	
	26th		10 R. wounded by enemy indirect M.G. fire.	
	28th		15th Bde. relieve 95th Bde. Orders received for 15th M.G. Coy. to relieve 95th M.G. Coy. which is to occupy 12 forward positions in new in accordance with Opn. Scheme of M.G. Defence.	
	29th	day.	15th M.G. Coy. relieve by Sections at various intervals during day. We take over 12 positions vacated by 15th Coy. Disposition of Coy. after disengagement - Coy. Hd. Qrs. sites at B.5 enteral. 4 guns of No 3 Section in Rec Line behind the (mor) 15th Bde. Sector. 4 guns of No 1 in Kent P.S. Duke St. 4 guns of No 2 as follows - one in machine gun town in tramway tunnels, 20 B from junctions with Kent Rd. 2 guns at B.M.C. 3.9. No 1 Section resting at Gervin. The Defence of the Div. Sector is very strong in M.G.'s. About 3 successive belts of fire have been arranged behind the front. Un guns engaged in this Opn. Scheme in addition to having fire lines along Kin. defensive flt, have also a small Indirect Fire S.O.S. Barrage - about 150 x or less	

Machine Gun Defence.

The Divn front is defended by 48 machine guns echeloned in depth of which 26 are in action in the 95th Bde. Sector.

Behind the front line there are 4 successive belts of M.G. fire arranged across the Divisional Sector, to comprise the Divisional M.G. Defence Scheme.

The forward belt is arranged on an average 500ˣ behind the front line. The rear most belt is formed by guns in position in the Red line.

95th M.G. Coy has 11 guns in action, 4 in support at Coy. Hd. Qrs, 1 in reserve at Ecurie.

A. By Indirect Fire Barrage from Div.
 Scheme guns.
B. By Direct Fire from Bde guns.

A/ 6 guns of the 95th M.G. Coy form part of Div Defence Scheme & are shewn in blue on attached map. No 1. at B18c 3.1 No 10 at B18c 65.40 No 11 at B18c 30.95. No 20 at B12a 40.30 No 21 at B5d 43.15. No 22 at B5d 42.24.

The 3 first provide Southern part of foremost Divisional belt of fire, the 3 last are sited specially to defend the South side of ARLEUX VILLAGE.

No 1 gun also sweeps by direct fire No MANS land from B12 b 85.45 to B12c 25.40.

These 6 guns, also all other guns forming part of Div. M.G. Defence, are laid on S.O.S. barrage lines, on which they fire in case of hostile attack on S.O.S. signal being sent up. This K.O.S barrage is shewn in blue, actual area swept shaded blue; this extends from 300ˣ to 500ˣ on an average in front of our front line. Thus 20 M.G's cover the Bde front by an indirect barrage – about 150ˣ per gun.

In event of a successful enemy attack all Div. guns cease fire on their barrage lines, & engage the enemy by direct fire along their respective belts of fire as laid down.

B/ In addition to the above indirect fire barrage, the whole of the Bde front line is covered by direct fire by 5 Bde guns: 2 of Bdes on left & right : 1 Div Scheme gun.

The line of which are shown in red. These guns open fire immediately the enemy is seen to advance, or the S.O.S. signal is observed.

Gun at B.18.d.5.2 (M.G. Coy on right) covers front to house at B.13.a.c.b/

Gun near OPPY WOOD at B.18.b.4.1 fires mainly on Bde area on right, crossing fire with gun of Bde on left at B.18.d.5.2

Gun in BARON TRENCH fires on direct enfilade line from house to B.12.d.4.4 (enfilade).

Gun in BABY TRENCH fires on enemy front line from OPPY CRUCIFIX to 200' south of junction of CRUCIFIX LANE and FRESNOY TRENCH.

Gun at end of KENT Rd enfilades front of FRESNOY TRENCH from B.12.b.4.2 to C.7.a.4.9

Gun in OUSE ALLEY fires directly on NO MANS Land from B.12.a.85.45 to C.1.c.25.40 (enfilade)

Gun in BRITTANIA TRENCH of M.G. Coy on left covers from bank in C.1.c. to right edge of FRESNOY WOOD.

Gun in BRITTANIA TRENCH at B.6.d.4.4 covers from right edge of FRESNOY WOOD at B. d.4.4 as a line to FRESNOY VILLAGE. These two last guns cross fire.

Coy. Hd qrs & support section situated at B.15.d.0.8
Right Section Hd Qrs . at B.11.d.7.45
Left Section Hd Qrs . at B.12.a.4.3

WAR DIARY or INTELLIGENCE SUMMARY

(Erase heading not required.)

Army Form C. 2118.

of 95th Machine Gun Company for August 1917.

Vol 20

Place	Date	Hour	Summary of Events and Information	Remarks and references to Appendices
OPPY-ARLEUX SECTOR	Aug 1st		Company in the new M.G. Area of the sector. 16th Inf. Bde. holding the sector. 12 guns in position. Section of four guns at No.12 position. (B18a 3.9) No.13 (B11d 95.10) No.14 (B11d 6.7.3) No.15 (B11c 6.5.50). Section Hd. Qrs. at B11d 85.65 in Kent Trench. Section at position — Indirect fire (B17d 40.25) 10A (RED LINE) 2 & 3 position (B17c 3.9) Section Hd. Qrs. at 10A gun position. Remaining Section at 5 position 7A (B18a 9.9) in Red line. 6A & 9A (B16b) in Red line. No.1 of position 20yds North of Tommy Trench. No.5. 20yds South of Machine Gun Trench. Both these latter positions being about 200yds from junction of trenches with Kent Road. Coy Hd Qrs situated in dug out near cross-roads B15 Central. 1 Section working at transport lines at Bavin. All these 12 guns except the L.R in positions form part of Divisional M.G. Defence Scheme; as shewn in July diary the Divn M.G. Defence is very strong. These 8 Divn Guns this new M.G. section are laid on S.O.S. line so close as possible infront of own front line, on which they have orders to fire as S.O.S. are from infantry rapid fire — They also open slow fire if enemy fools down a barrage on own front trenches. They are aided to harrass successional back of M.G. fire about enemy front through. Each gun has an S.O.S. barrage of slightly less than 150	

WAR DIARY or INTELLIGENCE SUMMARY

Army Form C. 2118.

of 95th Machine Gun Company for August 1917.

Place	Date	Hour	Summary of Events and Information	Remarks and references to Appendices
	Aug 1		Barrage firing arranged in order to get benefit of oblique fire as much as possible. Considerable amount of work to be done in positions & emplacements. Situation generally quiet. Hostile Artillery not very active, enemy M.G. fire quite normal & slightly less than his usual during July. His aircraft busy in the evenings.	
	1-5		Worked on M.G. emplacements & shelters. About 300 rds indirect firing carried out nightly — chiefly on enemy S.area C.18.1. and position of Merveine C.8.c.4.3. & area & similar localities. Weather very stormy & wet.	
	5/6	night	Targets as above were fired on – also Offey Support Trench. Neighbourhood of gun position was shelled with 5.9 – possibly in retaliation to damage inflicted by our fire.	
	6th	1.30am	Enemy suddenly bombarded our front trenches in Albery again extremely heavily. One minute later P.O.S. green lights were sent up mainly in front of Albery & also from front line trenches took. Practically all the machine guns of the Bn opened rapid fire on the P.O.P. lines simultaneously & nearly 5 mins before our artillery opened fire. A few of our guns did not fire on account of these guns covering an further front to effective area. Among the guns firing was Machine Guns used by hostilities 2, 8, 17. Situation was again normal at 2.5 am. Casualties nil	

WAR DIARY of 95th Machine Gun Company

INTELLIGENCE SUMMARY. 1st August 1917

Army Form C. 2118.

(Erase heading not required.)

Place	Date	Hour	Summary of Events and Information	Remarks and references to Appendices
	Aug 1st	morning	It appears enemy attempted a raid on our positions about 13L to but did not succeed in entering our trenches or in passing through our wire. During bombardment enemy sent down numerous gas shells + phosgene gas and trench of R.W. Batt. of 151st Bde holding trenches F.6 of Orient.	
	1st	night	No 4 gun fired 3500 rds on tracks from C9a 8.3 to C2C0.1, C9a 8.36 & C8d 0.5. New limited targets. Day duty support. Work being done on 4, 5, 3, 2, 3 positions in order to improve good shells from weather. Getting out to 4 & 5 positions proceeding. Weather generally more favourable.	
	1/2	9.30pm to 1 am	Targets as above, also LAMBERT ALLEY + tracks from C13b 6.5.5b & C8d 0.3 & 14 & 65. to C13b 9.1 + track on - Hood L4 extended. In addition No 3 gun fired at intervals on C9a 0.9 in No Man's Land, where enemy two advanced new posts of late + two posts from time to time a M.G.	
		3.40 am	Heavy bombardment in R.N. Div sector No 10A + No 13. guns opened slow rate of fire During 25 rds did the enemy fire an answering flat own detachments unaffected. Hostile M.G's slightly more active. Usual indirect firing - tasks - carried out	

WAR DIARY of 95th Machine Gun Company

INTELLIGENCE SUMMARY.

(Erase heading not required.)

Army Form C. 2118.

for August 1917

Place	Date	Hour	Summary of Events and Information	Remarks and references to Appendices
	Aug 11th		Gun changed K.C.I.C. Enemy aircraft unusually active. Orders received to be especially on the alert during the night. Relievement of our new transport lines started by a T.30.b.6.15 cm H gun about midnight.	
	11/12	night	1000 rds fired on enemy moving near Recon Trench. T.30.b.6.6 & back from C.4.a.05.15 & C.6.a.0.5.	
			2nd Lieut Y. Vitali granted 10 months leave to S. America left today. 3 Anti Aircraft positions have been finished at 21 position (B.5d.1) 20 (B.12a.to 0.25)	
	12th	day	1 (B.19c.3.1) 500 rds fired on hostile aircraft. Indirect fire during night on T.30.b.6.6 & 8.(3.) (reported sunk of activity.	
	13th	day	Lee He Oro 2 Cam dugout 115ft deep completed at 16.20 position. dugout in B.Maria trench also being worked on, also repairs to under B road dugout at 23 position at B.5d.40.35 being carried out.	
		night	T.30.b.6.6, C.20.d.6, U.26.a.o.5. fired on - 2000rds expended.	
	14th	day	Too No fired at hostile aircraft.	
		night	2000 rds on T.30.b.60 (Recon junc.) T.30.b.6 K.b.2, C.6.6.5 K.U.26.b.0.3	
	15th	day	3 hulls at hostile aircraft & none night firing	

WAR DIARY or INTELLIGENCE SUMMARY

Army Form C. 2118.

95" Machine Gun Company for August 1917

Place	Date	Hour	Summary of Events and Information	Remarks and references to Appendices
	Aug 16		A quiet time of work. Dug-outs being carried on. Enemy position is being completed with 2 Dug-out shelters at head. Guns in Nevers Trench moved 60' into Baron Trench. (B.12.a.6.5) - Same duties. This gun has been moved on account of very close shelling of Nevers Trench 16 which hostile artillery has paid special attention.	
		day	500 A.A. against hostile aircraft, one plane turned back to hostile line.	
		10.45pm	Orders received for as many guns as possible to fire on tracks etc observed on account of enemy relief in Otfroy Sector (information from a deserter)	
		11.50pm	15/50th fired from 25.21.20.1.T.11 (B.18.a.55.00) on tracks & trenches E of Otfroy & W of Neuviereux, (Sambre Alley, tracks junk trenches trenches etc. Dyn artillery	
		2am	also carried out harrasssing fire.	
	17"		Have firing against E A & tracks & trenches. Situation quieter than usual the last few days.	
	18"		Work were forward & teams much more comfortable. Have day & night firing. Enemy aircraft turned back on one occasion.	
	19"	5pm	Orders received for 21-22 guns to barrage 7.30a.29.16 7.30b 75.00 U.25c4 & K V.25a.3.0 in order to operate with a gas bombardment by 16 Sussex Regt R.E.s at 12.30am.	

Army Form C. 2118.

WAR DIARY of 95" Machine Gun Company
or
INTELLIGENCE SUMMARY. for August 1917

(Erase heading not required.)

Place	Date	Hour	Summary of Events and Information	Remarks and references to Appendices
	Aug. 9th	Day	95K Coy. relieved 15" K.O.S.B. in the sector. We relieve 15" K.M.G.Coy tomorrow.	
		night	Weather fairly 4 work on Nos 2,3, 4 +5 positions greatly improved by putting in small trench shelters of curved segments. Work done on 12, 13 +15 positions 4 Repairs to for Dun shelter post in rear have proved to be quite comfortable for the teams. Most of the emplacements in the static have been modified to give standing room for No 2. when the gun is in action — this providing of room for No 2 seems very essential.	
	10th	day	Relief of 15" K M.G.Cny complete by 9.30 pm. 15 casualties we have had for past 12 days. Ripotition of Coy after this exchange – Coy HdQuarters at B.15. Gake 5 sections in the line holding 11 positions viz. Platomore scheme with July Dpara., 1 team 4 guns at Coy Hd.Qrs., 1 section of transport lines at Cannes. No indirect firing carried out on account of relief. Owing to slight unrest on part of own Bn troops last night No.1 Gun at B.18.C.3.1 turned out & Ren. covered fire owing to shelling & not being heavy enough to warrant carrying on. Arrangements made for placing guns at Coy Hd.Qrs in position in Queen trench (disused) at B.12.q.9 in order to complete direct fire defences of Bn front — this gun to have by directfire enemy front line in c.7.a.+c. Firing of guns of BABY trench	
	11th			

Army Form C. 2118.

WAR DIARY of 95 Machine Gun Company

or

INTELLIGENCE SUMMARY. for August 1917

(Erase heading not required.)

Place	Date	Hour	Summary of Events and Information	Remarks and references to Appendices
	Aug. 19th	12.35am	5/50 rds fired in accordance with instructions. Enemy retaliated heavily especially near 20.2, T.2.2 positions. No casualties. Hostile M.G.'s more active during the operations.	
	20		Situation normal – usual firing – no suitable aeroplane target.	
	21		15th Bde relieved 95th Inf Bde.	
	22		15th & 95th M.G. Coy's exchange places during disposition of Coy K same as previously when in position. New M.G. Sector (29th July k16th Aug) Relief complete by 10 pm. 12 Guns in position. Coy H.Q. B.15 central. 1 Section 2 Guns in reserve at Sewri.	
			Own 2000 yds fired at hostile aircraft – usual nightfiring. Heavy bombardment some distance on our left on our sector Quiet.	
	23rd	day	Normal situation. AA position at YA empties. 2 news one of 10A commenced. No firing against BA. 2000 rds fired on road from Otpry to Pervaise New work E.13c 60.45.5 in frenory loop.	
	24th		Work on new horse & mule standing at Kerosene line proceeding well, but no material yet available. Brick standings have been put down.	

WAR DIARY of 95th Machine Gun Company

INTELLIGENCE SUMMARY for August 1917

Army Form C. 2118.

(Erase heading not required.)

Place	Date	Hour	Summary of Events and Information	Remarks and references to Appendices
			Keeping such a record of stoppages were search already	
			gives us hints (at factory) I packed in a lot similar to present PAA lot	
			about 50% of stoppages would be avoided if the ammunition b/be used	
			for M.G. work were more carefully selected & packed as about 75% of ordinary	
			stoppages would not occur. Rectifying can be carried out successfully	
			in a good dugout, which is not always to hand, but certainly cannot	
			be successfully done under ordinary trench conditions. On one	
			occasion after firing during a severe storm several guns were almost	
			out of action due to the impossibility of keeping the belt dry in order to	
			enable it feed through a machine gun	
			Bittew Captain	
			Commanding 95th Machine Gun Company. 31.8.17.

WAR DIARY of 95 Machine Gun Company

Army Form C. 2118.

INTELLIGENCE SUMMARY.

for August 1917

(Erase heading not required.)

Place	Date	Hour	Summary of Events and Information	Remarks and references to Appendices

4 Rein M.G. teams occupied by Friday has worked very well the S.O.S. barrage being put down by the M.G's promptly on the area Batteries cover must be taken over drawing up many alternative permanent positions for these S.O.S. lines & Defence lines (which are switched on & should enemy force a successful advance on our positions.

Sights alternative, 1 Vain Guns are urgently required. We have not yet received other to about to be authorised.

A careful record of stoppages has been kept during the month's daily nightly firing. It shows a large percentage of No 1 stoppages, ½ in stoppages being mainly No 3. The No 4's are undoubtedly due to inferior Ammun — not of any serious nature. The No 3's are due mainly to keep firing which is not done of course when the hot sections in a trench, Best firing machines have produced 30 doubtful overs. A rather large proportion of thick rimmed cartridges & freak rings with faulty caps have been encountered. Stoppages due to gun have been extraordinarily rare, all guns have been tested by firing a few bursts every other night. The conclusion drawn from

WAR DIARY or INTELLIGENCE SUMMARY

Army Form C. 2118.

of 9th Machine Gun Company for August 1917

(Erase heading not required.)

Place	Date	Hour	Summary of Events and Information	Remarks and references to Appendices
	Aug 24		Hostile aircraft 5 am. were back by firing too 10 108. Casualty wounded.	
			by M.G. fire from hostile aeroplanes. Hostile artillery very active on Cobourg Trench St Kts	
	25th		Situation & shelling Quiet. Hurrie firing by enemy M.G. unusually active on left flank	
	26/31st		Situation Quiet. If we are firing has been carried on during daylight against S.A.	
			Patrol 2.500 who for might have been forced. Knolls & areas behind enemy lines.	
			Been known to the establishment in the Artillery widow arrangement by Kr.	
			P.M.Q.O. Others have visited Ovops Hd. Qrs. the shape has been dry & the	
			Artillery showing the extent & limits of own intrenching	
			Further work carried on & own standing for transport. A span Bow hunt force	
			has saved T in a process of erection & nearly completed of the new line.	
			General Situation normal during month. Enemy M.G. not very active	
			are carried out harassing fire every night = 10000 who on air currents firing	
			fired by the 4 M.G. Corps in the line in the am. A device who came over & our	
			line near Offey reported several casualties inflicted by our indirect M.G. fire.	
			The formation of S.O.S. line & Barrage for all guns as applied in the forwards	

WAR DIARY of No 95th Machine Gun Company

INTELLIGENCE SUMMARY for September 1917

Army Form C. 2118.

(Erase heading not required.)

Place	Date	Hour	Summary of Events and Information	Remarks and references to Appendices
Achiet le	1st		Company Strength 18 O.R. Officers 11. Company dispositions: new machine gun sectors as detailed in diary for Aug 31st. Situation normal. Hence indirect & Anti Aircraft fire being carried out.	
	2.		Positions 1a, 2a, 9a, 2 & 3 relieved by 15th M Coy. 7.10 a.m. & 7.13 relieve by 18th M.G. Coy. No 1 & 2 Anti aircraft guns & Bay H.gs at 8.15 p.m. No 3 & 4 holding positions H. 5. 14. 7.15. Minor night firing.	Vide O.O. No 15
	3.		Carried out. During the last two nights swung round positions had been carried out at such positions so were the high bay relieving Division. No 1 & 2 Sects from Coy. H.Qrs. No 3 Sect from R. Humfront relieve 3 Sections 13th M.G. Coy. in North Advent Sects Lt.H.gs of Company took place successfully in accordance with O.O. No 16. Disposition of Company is in time table.	O.O. No 16.
	3/4 night	10.0.16.	Passed quietly. Relief our contact by 8 p.m. 3500 rounds were fired indirectly. An antiseme. howard. k.h. possibly was brought down at K. 20 from in field of division on our left. Ojar & Mother Artillery active about midnight. (1 O.R accidentally wounded — self inflicted injury — revolver bullet wound in hand.)	

WAR DIARY

of 95th M.G. Coy

INTELLIGENCE SUMMARY for September 1917.

Army Form C. 2118.

(Erase heading not required.)

Place	Date	Hour	Summary of Events and Information	Remarks and references to Appendices
MEUX Sector.	Sept 4th	night	No 2. Sect. took up places with No 2 Lieut 205th M.G. Coy. Manoeuvre firing carried out.	Vide O.O.No.16
	4/5			
	5th	day	New scheme of fire orders for lines of fire of the Company's guns positions which have adjusted Formulas made out. 16 guns of the Company in position.	
	6		All positions except Pill No. 3 position relieved by the 94th M.G. Coy. on receipt of the 95th M.G. Coy is relieving No.3 position tomorrow. This position was completely in the Company's withdrawn to Mallerive of Camp near ECURIE	Vide O.O.No.7
	7		Company clothes & cleaned all guns in the morning. A new case parade was held in the afternoon. Remaining of No.3 section of No.3 position were relieved by 8am. The whole relief took place [illegible] without casualties.	
	8		9.30am Company & transport & mules to breeze at A.C.Q. arriving by 12.30pm	
	9		Company paraded at 6.45am & marched to Villers-sur-Simon (about 5½ km) arriving by midday. The health of the Company in fairly good.	

WAR DIARY of K 95th M.G. Company

INTELLIGENCE SUMMARY for Septr 1917.

Army Form C. 2118.

(Erase heading not required.)

Place	Date	Hour	Summary of Events and Information	Remarks and references to Appendices
	10		Parade from 9am K 12.15pm & 2pm K 3.30pm. Dismounting, Knowing parts of gun drill, mechanism were carried out.	
	11		Company marched to VIGNEREUIL & billeted. Learnt had been attached by R.G.O.@ (to the Company) who is the N.K. instr. on account of sufficient support of the NEWS.	
	12		In the morning practice in Ammunition supply, limber driven, direct open sight fire were carried out. In the afternoon the new Barrage Indirect fire drill was practised for the first time	
	13		Company parade from 6 K 12.30pm & 2 K 3pm. Ammunition supply, with back mules, Barrage fire & was practised.	
	14		Training continued. Pulling on elevation by large straight barrage drive, practice in harassing & shooting was carried out	
	15		Indirect attack of Indirect fire practised also Barrage Fire.	
	16		Company Parade for Divine Service.	
	17		Company carried out a practice attack action for machine Gunn.	Very heavy O O No 1.
	18		Instruction in defence against gun by the Co. N.C.O.	

WAR DIARY
or
INTELLIGENCE SUMMARY.

of K 95th M.G Company for Sept 17.

Army Form C. 2118.

Place	Date	Hour	Summary of Events and Information	Remarks and references to Appendices
VILLERS-SIR-SIMON	18		Remained morning were stood in taking officers Barrage driver.	
	19	morning	Barrage Runs, elementary hanging & gun cleaning	
	20		Company practised machine Gun advance Guard & afternoon attack. Battalion were worked for a period during a march. Disposures	
			for the afternoon to Knight 21/22nd. Officers reconnitred the ground ready	
	21/22		GRAND RULLECOURT in the afternoon evening	
			To parade with with H am when Company marchd to Grand	
			Rullecourt area, took up positions laid down & moved for the night.	
	22		The operation. B.R.) Seen as in training. OO. No 3. Company arrived took	
			in Breech by 10.20 a.m.	
	23		Company attacked Divas twice. Didure received for leaving Rue Oren	
			& retraining at LIGNY	
LIGNY	24		Company paraded 12.45 pm & marched to Ligny arriving at 7.15 pm	
			throughy was successfuly carried out Rair detrained 6.10 pm.	
	25		Coy detrained at AUDRIGQ (5 miles HAZEBROUCK SP) at 12.30 a.m. travelled to	
MENTQUE			MENTQUE, arriving at 5 a.m. Coy was billeted here & spent the day resting.	

WAR DIARY or INTELLIGENCE SUMMARY

of 95th M.G. Coy for September 1917

Army Form C. 2118.

Place	Date	Hour	Summary of Events and Information	Remarks and references to Appendices
MENTQUE	Sept 26th	morning	Coy checked all gear to provide of recent training were repeated.	
	27th	9 am	Parade for full exercise — three outposts on TOURNEHEM side of MENTQUE. Coy marches to TOURNEHEM at 1pm for baths in the first.	
		3 pm	Orders received for immediate move to MOUILLE.	
		6 pm	Marched to MOUILLE & billeted there. G.S. wagon did not travel with us; a doable journey has to be made by one limber to carry certain stores left for transport to haspa. Arrived MOUILLE at 8.15 pm. Comfortable but scattered billets.	
SERQUES		9 pm	Mile outside — nr. SERQUES.	
NIEPPE	28th	8.30 am	Coy paraded and marched to NIEPPE (about 27), arriving at 1 pm. Billets consisted of huts. Recommendation for New Years Honours first were asked for today, and the form was put forward.	
			LIEUT. ANDREW SCOTT NICOLL for gallant and continuous good service and untiring devotion to duty. This officer joined the company 9 months ago, after being on service for over 20 months, and his conduct has always been an example of gallantry and determination to all, this was especially the case during the open	

Army Form C. 2118.

WAR DIARY
or
INTELLIGENCE SUMMARY.
(Erase heading not required.)

of 95th M.G. Coy for September 1917.

Place	Date	Hour	Summary of Events and Information	Remarks and references to Appendices
NIEPPE	Sept. 28th		ations in front of THELUS (April 9th) and LA COULOTTE (April 23rd), when he commanded his guns with conspicuous coolness & courage. Recommended for the Military Cross.	
			LIEUT. ANTHONY PERCIVAL, for his gallant conduct when in charge of two guns in the front line West of LA COULOTTE on April 23rd. Although this position was subjected to persistent heavy shelling, he was instrumental in inflicting a number of casualties on the enemy by his skill & courage in handling his guns. Recommended for "mention in despatch".	
			7728 C.S.M. McARA, JAMES for continuous good work & devotion to duty. This warrant officer has been in service with the Company since its formation & has at all times rendered distinguished good services. Recommended for the Meritorious Service Medal or "Mention in Despatches".	
			31959 PTE. PHELAN, KEVIN. For the tenacity & courage with which he worked his gun under an extremely heavy hostile barrage on April 23rd in front of LA COULOTTE. The gun emplacement was hit by 2 Blind Shells & the vicinity of his position was under a violent fire for some hours. This man kept very	

WAR DIARY

INTELLIGENCE SUMMARY

of 95th M.G. Coy
for September 1917.

Army Form C. 2118.

(Erase heading not required.)

Place	Date	Hour	Summary of Events and Information	Remarks and references to Appendices
NIEPPE	Sept 28th		Frequently been in charge of a gun team in action, has displayed on all occasions a splendid example of coolness & having carried with consistent good conduct, this teams. Recommended for "Mention in Dispatch". 53556 Cpl. ANDERSON, WILLIAM. For gallant conduct and continuous good service. This N.C.O. distinguished in a very gallant manner & carried out his duties of supervising the firing of the guns of his sub-section in the most praiseworthy manner during considerable hostile artillery fire on April 9th. This conduct has been of a similar high standard on all occasions. Recommended for "Mention in Dispatch".	
	29.	8.30am	Coy. paraded & marched to METEREN. Halt from 12.50 to 2pm for dinners. Although no cookers were available, the Coy cooks managed to provide tea in 40 mins in time. Arrived at billets at 4.25 & FL.3 at 4.30 pm. Found comfortable quarters. Hostile aircraft over billets during the night.	
	30	10am	Parade for checking telescopic fan. 2 to 3pm practise barrage drill. Hostile aeroplanes over active.	

WAR DIARY of 95th M.G. Coy

INTELLIGENCE SUMMARY. for September 1917.

Army Form C. 2118.

(Erase heading not required.)

Place	Date	Hour	Summary of Events and Information	Remarks and references to Appendices
			The march discipline of the Coy. has greatly improved during the past few days marching. On the 29th many of the men had sore feet but none fell out.	
			The greater part of the month has been spent in training which has been exceedingly beneficial. Much attention has been paid to musketry in & practice of all ranks in Lewis's Fire., the new Barrage Drill as set out from CAMIERS Small Arms School has proved very sound & is a great improvement on anything previous. The method has been well tested in the various of practice for training purposes. T shaped bases for tripods have been made for all guns.	
			The signalling personnel establishment of the Coy. has been increased, by training some men from the sections as signallers. These men have picked up the work very well & have enormously assisted in solving the different problems of communication & control within a M.G. Coy. They have been taught telephone both in all its branches, flag signalling etc. A fullaphone has recently been issued to the Coy.	

WAR DIARY
OF 95th M.G. Coy
INTELLIGENCE SUMMARY.
(Erase heading not required.)

For September 1917.

Army Form C. 2118.

Instructions regarding War Diaries and Intelligence Summaries are contained in F.S. Regs., Part II. and the Staff Manual respectively. Title pages will be prepared in manuscript.

Place	Date	Hour	Summary of Events and Information	Remarks and references to Appendices
	Sept.		The painting of all vehicles has been finished, in many cases has been two coats of paint; etc. Reinforcements which arrived appear to have had little training in the more advanced portion of M.G. work; consequently much have had to be trained in laying lines in lorries firing etc. Whilst less time is available for "open warfare" practice. In addition to this the extra supplies, special instruction has been given to range-takers, men chosen for snipers, & all asked men from the regiment of this Bde.	
METEREN	30th		Orders received for relieving 23rd Div. in the line near GHELUVELT on Oct 1st & 2nd. Coy. Strength 10 officers, 177 O.R. 2/Lt. J.F.B. WINDER was Divn. Claims Officer was struck off the strength of the Coy. on Sept. 21st.	

R.F. Sutton Capt.
Comdg. 95 M.G. Coy.

95th Machine Gun Company.
Operation Order No 15 by Captain R.J. Cuttor M.C. Commanding.

1/ Positions 7A, 8A, 9A, 2 & 3, 10A, 12, & 13 occupied by the 95th M.G. Coy will be relieved by 15th & 189th M.G. Coys tomorrow 2nd inst. Relief will take place in accordance with attached time table.

2/ No 2 Section teams after relief at 7A, 8A & 9A will relieve 2 teams of No 1 Section at 14 & 15 positions. Sec Hd Qrs will be at Kent Rd. No 2 will send 1 gun & gear of No 4 Sect. (at No 15 position) to Coy. Hd Qrs.

O.C. No 2 Section will arrange that only his 4 guns & gear are retained by him after relief.

3/ On relief No 1 & 4 Sections will withdraw with guns & gear & will be billeted at Coy Hd Qrs for night of 2/3rd previous to their relieving Sections of the 13th M.G. Coy.

4/ 6 belt boxes will be handed over at 2, 3, 7A, 8A & 9A positions & 8 belt boxes at 12, 13 & 10A positions: extra boxes will be brought to Coy Hd Qrs. Tripods will be handed over at all positions. All other gun gear will be brought out with sections.

5/ All maps, fire orders, range cards & other particulars will be handed over. 1 patrol tin full of water will be handed over at each position & Sec. Hd Qrs; surplus tins will be brought to Coy Hd Qrs.

Receipts for all gear handed over will be taken & sent to Coy. Hd Qrs on completion of relief.

6/ O.C. No 2 Section will report completion of relief to Coy. Hd Qrs.

7/ Acknowledge.

Cuttor Captain
Commanding 95th Machine Gun Company

1.9.1917.

Time Table of Relief (to accompany O.O.15)

Section	From	Relieved By		To	Relieve		Guide, Remarks etc.
		By	Time			Time	
No 1	No 12 position " 13	2 teams (169th M.G.Coy)	11 am	Coy H.Qrs.	1		Guides for Relieving 169th M.G. Coy to be furnished by 2nd Lieut TYNE ALLARYS at 11am. Bulk storage of 169th will be in KENT RD
Half of No 2	" 14 " 15	No 2 Sect. QA	(about) 3pm	do	1		Guides for No 2 Section at 7A dugout at 3pm
	7A 8A 9A	3 teams of S.S.	(about) 11pm	(14 15	3 teams (about) of No 1	3pm	No guides necc. (15) M.G. Coy Section Station of No 2 Sect. will be in KENT RD
4	10A " 2 " 3	1 team 159th 1 team of S.S.	3pm 8.15pm	Coy H.Qrs do do	1		Guides for teams of 159th to be at junction of House and TYNE ALLEYS at 3pm Officers of 159th M.G.Coy will take over at 10A dugout
3	Remains at transport lines until reliefs until 3rd inst.						

P.F.Fitzsimmons Capt. 1/11/17

SECRET

95 Machine Gun Coy.
Operation Order No 16.

1. The 95th Inf. Bde is now holding the ARLEUX Sector. On the night of the 4th inst, 16 guns of 95th Machine Gun Coy will be in position in that sector.

2. Tomorrow 3rd inst, No 1 Section will relieve No 3 Section 13th M.G. Coy in right forward sector (positions 1,2,3,4. Section H.Q. T29d1.7) No 3 Section will relieve No 2 Section 13th in left forward sector (positions 5,6,7,8. Section H.Q. T29d1.7) No 4 Section will relieve No 1 Section 13th in support (positions 9 (Divn 23), 10 (Divn 24), 11 & 12. Section H.Q. B5 C7.8). Relief will be in accordance with attached time table.

3. 8 belt boxes only and no other gun-gear per position will be handed over by 13th M.G. Coy. 96 belt boxes will be delivered to 13th Coy Transport Lines morning of 3rd inst.

4. On 4th inst at dusk, No 2 Section 205th M.G. Coy will relieve No 2 Section 95th M.G. Coy in positions W.5. 14 & 15. No 2 Section (95th) will occupy positions of No 2 205th (Divn Nos 8, 9, 18 & 19). Four half teams of No 2 Section (95th) will be at No 2 Section (205th) Hdqrs dugout M.G.2 (B4 C6.5) at 6 P.M.; these half teams will be conducted to their new positions and one man from each will subsequently guide teams of 205th to present positions of No 2 (95th) & afterwards guide their own remaining half teams & guns to new positions.

5. No 2 Section will hand over & receive no other gun gear, except following unless otherwise ordered. 8 belt boxes & tripod per position - the trench stores, 2 full tins of water (per position & Section H.Qrs), 5 boxes S.A.A. (per position). All maps, all particulars of Indirect Fire etc will be handed over. No teams will leave present positions until all orders are thoroughly understood by relieving teams.

6. All movement will be by trenches as far as possible; No 3 Section will use limbers as far as "RIDGE" end of TIRED ALLEY, and will carry from there.

7. O.C. No 2 Section will carry out indirect firing nights 2nd/3rd & 3rd/4th from No 15 position. O.C. No 4 Section will arrange to carry out indirect firing on night of 3rd as handed over to him.

8. O.C. No 2 Section will arrange to hand over 95th Coy stores at BANK DUMP to O.C. No 2 Section 205th.

9. Receipts for all gear and stores handed over and lists of all gear and stores taken over, will be sent to Coy H.Q. as soon after reliefs as possible.

10. Coy H.Q. will close at B15 central at 4.30 P.M., 3rd inst and will reopen at that hour at M.G.2 dugout. Rations will be brought to B4 C5.7 (where RED LINE cuts WILLERVAL – ARLEUX road) by 9 P.M. 3rd inst and subsequent nights.

11. Acknowledge.

Captain
Commanding 95th M.G. Coy.

2/9/17.

Time Table to Accompany O.O. 14

SECTION	FROM	RELIEVED BY TIME/DATE	TO	IN RELIEF OF TIME & DATE	GUIDES etc. REMARKS
No 1	Coy. H.Q. B15 Central	—	Bdi No 1 Position B16 60.30 2. B6a 92.68 3. B6a 65.43 4. T30c 35.40	No 3 Sect 13th M.G.C.	2.45 pm 26 3 inst.	Guides from 13th will be at junction of TIRED ALLEY & RED LINE at 2.45 pm.
No 3	CAMP	—	5. T30c 4.9 6. T30a 6.3 7. T30a 05.35 8. T30a 05.27	No 2 Sect 13th M.G.C.	3.0 pm 3rd inst.	Guides from 13th will be at junction of TIRED ALLEY & RED LINE at 3.0 pm. Officers i/c of 4 & 8 positions will go along with guides for T30 65.43 & T30 65.27 to Shemako entrants.
No 4	Coy. H.Q.	—	9. B5a 60.60 10. B5a 62.65 11. T29b 65.55 12. T29b 66.70	No 1 Sect 13th M.G.C.	3.15 pm 3rd inst.	Guides from 13th will be at junction of TIRED ALLEY & RED LINE at 3.15 pm.
No 2	No 4 Position (Compy Sap) B11a 52.72	No 2 Sect 13th M.G.C.	8. B4a 35.90		6.0 pm 3rd inst.	Guides from Lieutenant of No 2 Section (45+) will heal before relief.
	5 (M.G. TR SAP) B11a 36.10		9. B4 b 15.30			
	14 B11d 62.75		18. B5a 25.35			
	15 B11a 63.35		19. B5a 15.90			

SECRET.

95TH. M.G. COMPANY.
Operation Order No 17.

1. The 95th Inf. Bde. now holding sectors C2 & C3 (i.e. ARLEUX & SEVERN ALLEY) sectors will be relieved by 92nd Inf. Bde. on 7th inst. On completion of relief 95 Bde. will concentrate in ROCLINCOURT area prior to marching to ACQ area on the 8th to training Area LE CAUROY on the 9th.

2. The 95th M.G. Coy. will be relieved in some positions by the 94th M.G. Coy. on the evening of the 6th inst. & will vacate remaining positions which are not relieved.

3. No 1 Section will be relieved by 1 team of 92nd M.G. Coy. at No 3 position, and will vacate positions 1, 2, 4 without relief.

4. No 2 Section will be relieved in Divn position 8 & 9 by 2 teams of 'C' Section 94th M.G. Coy. & in Divn position 18 & 19 by 2 teams of 'A' Section 94th M.G. Coy. O.C. No 2 Section will also arrange to hand over positions 1A (B4a.4.2) & 2 (B4c6.50) in RED LINE to 'C' Section 94th. No belt boxes will be handed over to 2 last positions.

5. No 3 Section will be relieved in Bde positions 7 & 8 by 2 teams of 'B' Section 94th. & will vacate Bde position 5 without relief. No 6 Bde position may be relieved by a Lewis gun team of 94th Inf. Bde. in which case further orders will be issued.

6. No 4 Section will be relieved in Divn positions 23 & 24 by 2 teams of 'A' Section 94th M.G. Coy. & will vacate Bde positions 11 & 12 without relief.

7. Orders for relief of signallers will be issued later.

8. Arrangements have been made for 1 man per relieving team of 94th M.G. Coy. to be at respective gun positions at 3 p.m. 6th inst. for purpose of reconnaissance. These men will subsequently act as guides to their own teams.

9. All relief & vacations of positions will take place in accordance with attached time table. On relief Company will withdraw to MARLBOROUGH CAMP. Coy. H. Drs. will move from M.G.2 dugout in RED LINE on completion of relief.

10. Limbers will be at following places & time. No leads will be used.

    No 1 Section No 1 limber (empty) at B5a.1.3 (road) at 10.30 p.m.
    " 2   "   No 4   "   "   B4b3.1 (where Plumer Ln. joins road) at 9.0 p.m.
    " 3   "   No 7   "   "   B5a.1.3 (road) at 10 p.m.
    " 4   "   No 10   "   "   B5a.1.3 (road) at 9.30 p.m.
                  S.A.A.   .   Coy. H. Drs.   at 8.30 p.m.

11. At each position to be relieved there will be handed over; fire orders, range cards, gun team rough maps, 8 belt boxes, 10 boxes S.A.A., 2 tins full of water, alternative position (complete with sticks correctly placed) & all trench stores. No gun gear will be handed over. O.C. Sections will hand over & thoroughly explain, copies of all fire orders, maps, orders for pursuit, particulars of Indirect firing etc. All belts will be overhauled & inspected before handing over, & no team will leave position until all orders have been thoroughly understood by relieving teams. Lists of stores will be made out in duplicate, 1 list to be handed over & 1 list receipted to be handed into Orderly Room by 12 noon 7th inst.

12. Written reports of relief complete to be handed in at Coy. Hd. Drs. by Section Officer on their way down.

13. Acknowledge.

                                    (sgd) Littler Captain
                                Commanding 95th Machine Gun Company

5.9.1917.

TIME TABLE of RELIEF to ACCOMPANY O.O. Nº 17.

SECTION	FROM.		RELIEVED BY	TIME	VACATE AT	REMARKS.
Nº 1 SECT. H.Q. T29 d 1.7	BDE Nº 1 POSITION	B4 b 05.30	—	—	8 pm	Arrangements for guides to meet be'arrivee labs.
	" 2 "	B6 a 16.68	—	—	8 pm	
	" 3 "	B6 a 11.41	93rd M.C. Coy will be notified later			
	" 4 "	T30 c 16.90			8 pm	
Nº 5 SECT. H.Q. T29 d 1.7	" 5 "	T30 c 13.90	—	—	8 pm	Arrangement for guides to meet be'arrivee labs.
	" 6 "	T30 a 58.32	Bn Comr will be turn Qr notified 9t Bn later			
	" 7 "	T30 a 00.25	B Sec 9t lt	8 pm		Advance gunners of 9t lt will act as guides
	" 8 "	T30 a 04.28	-do-	8 pm		
Nº 2 SECT. H.Q. B4 c 65.50 COY. H.Q.	DIV " 8 "	B4 d 46.85 } B4 b 15.48 }	C Sec 9 t lt	8 pm		
	" 9 "					
	" 10 "	B6 a 23.30 } T29 c 2.3 }	A Sec 9 t lt	8 pm		
	" 19 "					
	M.G. 1 RED LINE	B4 a 4.3				Steam'e C' section 9 t lt overlay M.G. 1 (B4 a 4.3) F
	M.G. 2	B4 c 65.50				M.G. 2 (B4 c 65.50) RED LINE.
Nº 4 SECT. H.Q. B5 c 45.65	DIV " 23 "	B5 a 45.63	A Sec 9 t lt	8 pm		[Sect Ha Qrs of 9 t lt M.G. Coy will probably be as follows
	" 24 "	B5 a 60.65	-do-	8 pm		for 4 r 8 guns (T29 d 1.7) (B5 c 45.85)
	BDE " 11 "	T29 b 65.50	—	—	8 pm	DIVN 23. 24. 18 c 19 (B5 c 45.85)
	" 12 "	T29 b 64.75	—	—	8 pm	M.G. 1.2. DIVN 8 c 9 (B4 c 65.50

Training O.O. N°1.   Ref. Map 51C. NE
                                1/20000

Information.
1. The 95th Inf. Bde. is holding front line from D19a20.95, D13a0.0.
D14c0.0. facing due north. Hostile front line runs through D13c2.3,
D13d0.4, D13d5.4 – facing due south.
   95th M.G. Coy. is in position in Bde. sector, with Coy Hq. at D19d8.2
(300 south of STRIP WOOD)
   The 95th Bde. is attacking the enemy's positions due north on Z
day at zero hour.
   Boundaries for attack.
        East.   D25b2.6, D19b4.4, Crucifix (incl)
                D8a0.7 Tower (incl) D2b5.9
        West.   D25a2.5, D19a2.0, D13c1.0, D13a2.0,
                D7c2.0, D7a3.0, D1d4.0, D1a6.9.
   Objectives. First Yellow.
                D13a2.8, D13b0.8, D13b7.6
                Second Blue.
                D1a4.3, D1b0.3, D2a2.3.
   Yellow objective. Attacking troops. 1st/5th Surreys on right & 12th
        Gloucesters on left. D.C.L.I. in support. Devons in reserve.
   Blue objective. D.C.L.I. on right, 1st Devons on left, 1st/5th Surreys
        in support of Gloucesters.
   The attack will be covered by M.G. Barrage fire only. All details
   regarding infantry assault are attached in Appendix 2.

2. **Action of M. Guns – General**
   95th M.G. Coy. is reduced to 12 guns organised in 3 Sections N°1, 2 & 4.
   95th Coy is to cover left half of Bde frontage in the attack
   & defence. 205 Coy. with 16 guns will cover the right half.
   95 Coy will send forward 1 Section to defensive
   positions to defend final objective.

3. **Detail action of 95th Coy.**
(i) N°1 Section will take up barrage positions at D19c4.4.
   They will be ready to fire by zero – 5 mins.
   Fire will be in accordance with Barrage table.
(ii) After firing barrage, N°1 will move forward & take
   up defensive positions to defend Blue objective. Positions
   to be not more than 600 behind Blue line & nearer, if
   possible.
(iii) N°2 & 4 Sects will be in position ready to advance in our
   present support trenches at D19a5.5 by zero – 15 mins. At
   zero N°2 & 4 will advance with 30" intervals between
   guns to Barrage positions at D13a7.2 & D13a40.25
   respectively. They will be ready to fire a Barrage as in
   table by zero + 55 mins.
(iv) After capture of Blue line, N°2 Sect will move forward
   & take up barrage position D7b0.0 & N°4 will move
   forward & take up Barrage position at D7a4.0.
   N°2 will move at zero + 155 & be in position & guns
   laid on S.O.S. barrage (as below) ready to fire by zero +
                  200.

2

No 4 will take on No 2's S.O.S barrage as well as his own from Zero + 155 to Zero + 200. No 4 will move at zero + 200 + ● in position + guns laid on own S.O.S barrage ready to fire by Zero + 245. From Zero + 200 to Zero + 245 No 2. will cover S.O.S barrage of No 4 as well as their own.

4. Watches will be synchronised on parade at 7.55 am.

5. Lateral intervals between teams during advance will be at least 50 yds. Pack mules may be used for each advance up to a position not closer than 300 x from gun positions to be taken up.

6. Coy H.Q. will be at D.19.a.8.3 from time of capture of 1st to time of capture of 2nd objective.
After capture of 2nd obj! Coy H.Q. will move forward to D7c.5.0.

7. Immediately after having taken up defensive positions on Blue line, No 1 will send up the S.O.S signal which is 1 White Very light.

A S Nivell Lieut for Capt
Comdg 95th Machine Gun Coy

Appendix A.

Water Rations. 48 hours water & rations will be dumped at D.19.b.25.00 by 6 pm on Y day.

Ammunition. There will be a dump of 60.000 rounds S.A.A. at D.19 Central.

The Transport officer will be responsible for having the following. 10.000 rounds S.A.A. at Gun position at D.19.c.Y.Y before Zero hour —15 min. Z day.

20.000 rounds S.A.A. (10.000 each to Nº 2 & 4 Sec) at Gun positions at D.13.A.y.2 & 40.25 by Zero + 45 min. also 5000 rounds to each section by 0 + 120. 10.000 rounds S.A.A. at D.7.a.25.40 by Zero + 2½ hours.

With each consignment of S.A.A., 4 full petrol tins of water will be sent up & empty tins returned by returning mules.

Appendix B.

Communication. Communication between Coy H.Q. & Sections will at first be by visual signalling then by telephone at every stage. The signalling Cpl will be responsible for arrangements. Signallers will accompany each section & lay out lines as they advance. By Zero —15 there will be a telephone exchange at H.Q., Nº 1 section & also a telephone at our present support line to Nº 2 & 4 Sect. Exchanges & telephones for 2 & 4 Sect. will be advanced with those sections at Zero.

On Nº 1 section advancing the signallers will lay out line with this section & connect up with the exchange at Nº 2 & 4 Sect. As Coy H.Q. move forward, Coy exchange will move with H.Q. & rear lines pulled in. Runners will not be used in this operation.

Appendix C.

Transport. On morning of Z day all sections will unload limbers on road at D.25.a.95.72 D.19.a.95.30.

At the conclusion of operations the limbers will be loaded at the following point.

Nº 2 & 4 Sect. on road at D.13.c.95.70
Nº 1 Sect on road at D.7.a.20.85.

Appendix D.

Equipment. Kettles will be used to cool the M.G. Batteries in action.

S.d. Nicoll Hanft. Capt.
Comdg 98ᵗʰ M. Gun Coy

Firing Table

Section	Guns	Position	Barrage	Time mins	Rate of fire (rds per gun per min)
1	4	D.9.c.7.7	D.13.c.30.78 to D.13.c.90.82 D.13.a.23 to D.13.c.95.45 D.y.c.8.0 to D.y.c.95.10 D.y.c.3.8 to D.y.c.95.80	0 to 15 15 to 30 30 to 45 45 to 60	— " —
2	4	D.13.a).2	D.y.4.60 to D.y.14.58 D.1.c.85.42 to D.1.a.25.38 D.1.a.9).23 to D.1.6.38.20 D.1.6.10.98 to D.1.6.46.98 And on S.O.S. Call	60 to 85 85 to 105 105 to 130 130 to 150	— " — rapid
4	4	D.13.a.40.25	D.y.a.32.61 to D.y.a.74.60 D.1.c.4/5.45 to D.1.c.85.42 D.1.a.55.24 to D.1.a.9).23 D.1.a.62.98 to D.1.b.10.98 And on S.O.S. Call	60 to 85 85 to 105 105 to 130 130 to 150	— " — rapid
1	4	Forward Area	No Man's Land in front of Blue line Direct fire	S O S Call	rapid

SECRET

95th M.G Company Training D.O.2.   Reference MAP.
                                    enlarged 1/10000 scale from 5/6.

A. **General Idea.** Our forces moving from S to N have captured Guard Rullecourt & the
enemy's line 6 & N of it. (The 5th Divn on our Bdes front is consolidating a line
N of Guard Rullecourt in O3c & d6 (very nearly a line along the wire fence.). The
enemy's front line of a trench system is southernmost trench in O3A & b.
The advance is to be continued.

B. **Special Idea.** During the early morning of the 22 inst the 95th Bde will attack & capture
the German trench line system from the Guard Rullecourt J6 in 133d (incl)
to Western boundary of square 133 c.
  1st E Surreys (RIGHT) & 1st D.C.L.I. (LEFT) will attack & capture the
first (BLUE) objective.
  1st Devons (RIGHT support) & 12 Glosters (LEFT support) will pass through
the first 2 Bns at Blue objective & will attack & capture final (GREEN) objective.
  After capturing Green objective the Bde will push forward posts on
to the Pincourt & Avesnes Rds. with the object of obtaining observation towards
the North.
  The boundaries between Bns will be approx. a line drawn due S from
road junction at 133 Central.
  The jumping off line will be taped out during night 21st/22nd.
  The attack will be carried out as follows:—

    o   Infantry move forward from jumping off line
    o + 5   enter German front line
    o + 9   capture Blue objective (10 mins halt)
    o + 19   advance from   "   "
    o + 22   capture German 3rd line
    o + 24   leave   "   3rd "
    o + 26   capture   "   4th "
    o + 28   leave   "   4th "
    o + 30   capture Final (Green) objective.

The Arty. barrage (represented by signal flags) will move at rate of 50ᵡ
per min. Bn.H.Q of DCLI & E. Surreys will not move, but Hq. of Devons & Glosters
will move forward as soon as the Bns pass through Blue objective. Advance
Bde Hq will be in Orchard at Ogb 15.50.   95th T.M. Bty will move when ordered.
  All prisoners will be sent under escort to Bde. H.Qrs. S.O.S
signal is White very lights fired in rapid succession with a few Golden
Rain rockets.
  Watches will be synchronised at Coy. H.Q at 4.15am. The 95th M.G Coy will
send forward 2 guns with each of the Devons & Glosters to consolidate
final objective.   Remainder of guns will provide a M.G barrage.

C. **Detail Action of 95th M.G.C.**
  (1) Nos 3, 2 & 1 Sections will provide M.G. Barrage to the batteries A.B & C.
respectively. Positions will be taken up & targets engaged as on attached
barrage table. These sections will take up their positions on arrival on
ground. All guns will be correctly laid before dusk & left mounted
during night.
  (2) No 4 Section will provide 2 guns to advance & consolidate Green line
with 1st Devons on right & 2 guns to advance & consolidate with
12th Glosters on left. These guns will be placed in positions approx as
follows:—
    No 1   at 133 d.2.4 approx in front line to fire WNW.
    " 2   at 133 c 3.)   "   "   " to cross fire with No 1
    " 3   at 133 d.2.1   "   "   " to fire on S.O.S in front of green line at
                                                133 c.2.8 & area.
    " 4   at 133 c 3.4   "   "   " to fire on S.O.S. in front of green line at
                                                133 d. 3.4 & area

  3 & 4 guns are to have a "stop line" allotted in front of old German
3rd line.
O.C. No 4 section is to apply to O.C. 1st Devons & 12 & Glosters for the co-operation
of 2 & 3 Lewis guns respectively & to co-ordinate the fire of these L.Gs in accordance
with pre-arranged scheme.

No. 4 Sections guns will advance with the infantry advancing to reoccupy area of their gun positions. 30" intervals depth between guns Nos of teams will be kept during advance of at least 100 laterally between teams. Guns will be carried in manner so similar to that of carrying rifles adopted by the infantry. Any opportunities of engaging the enemy during the advance or after having taken their objective will be exploited to the fullest extent.

Gun positions of No. 4 Sect. should be outside any present German trenches & sited in shell holes etc. in inconspicuous positions. Guns are to be so sited that arc of fire obtained in event of hostile attack. Men from other Sects. will be lent to No. 4 Sect. in order for 14 belt boxes & 2 tins of water to go forward with each gun. These men will be returned after gun positions have been taken up with the object of them taking up S.A.A. to No. 4 positions later.

O.C. No. 4 Sect. will send in to Coy H.Q. a brief situation report & rough map of his dispositions as soon as [?] after Green Line positions have been taken up. He will state his requirements.

(4) All sections will report "OK" by telephone or runner ½ hour before zero.
(5) Coy. Hd. Qrs. will be at & remain throughout operation at O3a.7.0.
(6) Sect. Hd. Qrs. will be as near as possible to their directing guns.
(7) Watches will be synchronised at [?] at 12.30 am & 4.30 am.
(8) Arrangements for Defence. In event of hostile counter attack No. 4 Sect. guns will fire as allotted to Btys A.B.C. will open rapid fire on S.O.S. lines on receipt of S.O.S. In event of heavy hostile bombardment or own rifle fire a slow rate of fire on S.O.S. line will be carried out by Btys. A.B.C. In event of a hostile attack succeeding in [?] degree No. 4 Sect. will fire on stop lines & Btys A.B.C. will be ready to lower their barrage immediately on to any previous barrage line as notified.
(9) Zero hours will be notified later.

Barrage Table.

Ref. maps.
1/5000 enlarged from 1/10000.
1/10000 S.I.C.

Battery	Sec.	Guns	Location	Barrage	Time	Rate of Fire	Remarks
A	No.3	4	O10b.35.82	O3b.18.86 to O3a.56.82	0 to 3		
				133b.22.08 to 133c.55.06	3 to 8		
				133a.48.55 to 133c.48.55	8 to 19	Slow [?]	
				133b.12.12 to 133c.52.80	19 to 24		
				133b.12.12 to 133c.49.98	24 to 28		
				133b.18.33 to 133a.49.24	28 to 35		Also on S.O.S. calls Rapid Fire
B	No.2	4	O10a.93.24	O3a.56.82 to O2b.98.99	0 to 3		
				133c.55.06 to 132b.49.01	3 to 8		
				133c.48.58 to 133a.q.5	8 to 19	Slow	
				133c.52.80 to 132a.93.88	19 to 24		
				133c.49.98 to 132b.92.07	24 to 28		
				133a.49.24 to 132b.9.4	28 to 35		Also on S.O.S. calls Rapid Fire
C	No.1	4	O8.8.8	O3b.46.72 to O3b.18.81	0 to 3		
				O3b.46.92 to 133a.22.08	3 to 8		
				133a.46.38 to 133a.18.55	8 to 19	Slow	
				133a.42.42 to 133a.14.91	19 to 24	Rate of fire	
				133a.41.14 to 133b.12.12	24 to 28		
				133b.49.09 to 133b.18.33	28 to 35		Also on S.O.S. Rapid Fire

N.B. Line of directing guns (i.e. following barrage lines) is to be laid on corresponding limits of first barrage.

D. Sutton Capt.

Information	The Coy will take part in operations July tomorrow morning.
Parade	The Coy will parade at 3.45 p.m. today.
Dress	Marching orders with the following articles in pack.
	Mess Tin
	Water Bottle (Full)
	Iron Ration
	Waterproof Sheet
	1 Pair Socks
	Knife, Fork & Spoon
	Box Respirator in "Alert" position
	All pistol ammunition will be collected on Parade & a Certificate will be given by each Section Officer his section is not in possession of any ammunition.
Transport	One Fighting limber will accompany Each Section to carry Guns & Gear. No belts or boxes will be taken by Nos 1, 2, & 3 Sections. No 4 Section will take 5 it "Empty" belt boxes. 1 Empty S.A.A. limber will accompany Coy. O.C. No 4 will be responsible for seeing that these boxes are empty. The Transport Officer will arrange the necessary feeds and forage for the horses.
Spare Kit & Great Coats	The Great Coats & Spare Kits of men will be folded up & left in billets.
Rations	The unexpended portion of 1 days rations & tomorrow's breakfast ration will be carried on pack.
Bivouac	Sections will march direct to their positions and will bivouac for the night in positions allotted. No 4 Section will be with Coy H. Qrs.
Water	Each Section will carry 5 petrol cans of water on fighting limber for drinking & cooking purposes & 2 cans of water for the guns.

Appendix B.

Coy H. Qrs.	Coy H. Qrs will be about O.3.d.70.00.
Communications	The Signalling Corpl. will lay lines between Bde. H. Qrs. & Coy H. Qrs. & from there to A. Battery on right & connecting with B. Battery on the way, also line from Coy H. Qrs to C. Battery on left. There will be an exchange at Coy H. Qrs. 2 Signallers will be detailed to each Battery H. Qrs. 2 Signallers will accompany No 4 Section in the attack & will lie in lines (imaginary) with empty reels & 1 telephone. The Signalling Corpl will remain at Exchange after he has got in communication with the Batteries. Communication with forward section will be by Visual & the trench signalling lamp. Discs etc. will be taken. All signallers will carry flags in the event of wires being cut & if so signallers will be posted in positions so as to get in touch with Coy H. Qrs.
S.A.A. Supply	There will be a dump of 80,000 rounds S.A.A. & 48 hours water rations at O.3.d.4.0. The Transport Officer will deliver 20,000 rounds S.A.A. (imaginary) to each of A., B., & C. Battery Positions by midnight 21st inst. The mules will do the requisite number of journeys with drivers and the Transport Officer will insure that a report will be sent to Section Officers when their dumps have been completed. This S.A.A. will be drawn from Bde Dump at O.9 central.

Appendix C.

Technical Notes	1. All Guns will be laid by the Compass method. i.e. Compass in front of guns.
	2. Gun Intervals will be roughly 30'.
	3. Emplacements. At each gun position a "V" type emplacement would be dug. The digging will NOT be done, but the outline of the excavation will be shown at each position by cutting round with a shovel.
	4. Special attention will be paid to regular & frequent pulling through of barrels & filling up with water.
	5. Guns will be relevelled & Elevation dial adjusted at least every 2 belts.
	6. Guns will be tested, & tripod allowed to settle by firing about 1 belt between 10 P.M. & 4 am on the final barrage line. Testing will be at different intervals.

Army Form C. 2118.

WAR DIARY
INTELLIGENCE SUMMARY
(Erase heading not required.)

of the 95th Machine Gun Company
for October 1917.

Instructions regarding War Diaries and Intelligence Summaries are contained in F.S. Regs., Part II. and the Staff Manual respectively. Title pages will be prepared in manuscript.

Place	Date Oct.	Hour	Summary of Events and Information	Remarks and references to Appendices
METEREN (SHEET 27)	1st	7 a.m.	Company Strength. 10 Officers. O.R. 177. Four Sections and Headquarters, embussed and proceeded to RIDGEWOOD (Sheet 28) taking over billets from 191st M.G. Coy. in N.5.a. Transport proceeded by Road. Afternoon — Sector of 69th M.G. Coy. reconnoitred, with a view to Relief on the 2nd inst.	See O.O.R.
	2nd	1.30 a.m.	Hostile Aeroplane dropped 2 Bombs on Transport lines at N.3.c. & 5. (approx) which inflicted severe casualties to our Animals, resulting in 30 Animals being killed and 18 seriously wounded. 2 O.R. (Including one attached).	
		11 a.m.	Half No. 3 Section left billets and successfully relieved half of 17th Section left of M.G.Coy. at J.15. d.37. (Sheet GHELUVELT 20000). Remainder of Relief was successfully carried out in accordance with Time Table.	GHELUVELT.
		4 p.m.	Remaining sub sections of No. 3. placed in positions at J.14.c.57. Disposition of Company as follows — 2 guns No. 3 Section in "Pill Boxes" J.15.d.37. protecting right of Brigade front in neighbourhood of the REUTEL BEEK. by direct fire. Three positions are through behind the front line. Remaining 6 guns in action (2 guns No. 1 Section at J.14.d.5.6. 2 guns J.14.d.57. 2 guns 1/No. 3. J.14.c.57.) are protecting the left 2/3rds. of Brigade front, as far North as track South of POLYGON WOOD, by an indirect S.O.S. Barrage line of 100 yards per gun. Coy. H.Q. at J.13.d.85.k. Nos. 1 + 2 Sections and Transport at N.3.c. Relief of 69th M.G.Coy. was complete by 2 p.m.	

WAR DIARY

Army Form C. 2118.

of the 254th Machine Gun Company
for October 1917.

INTELLIGENCE SUMMARY.

(Erase heading not required.)

Instructions regarding War Diaries and Intelligence Summaries are contained in F.S. Regs., Part II. and the Staff Manual respectively. Title pages will be prepared in manuscript.

Place	Date	Hour	Summary of Events and Information	Remarks and references to Appendices
NIEUWPOORT SECTOR.	November 3rd Oct. 3rd	7 p.m.	Both Artillery's extremely active. 2 O.R. killed. Lieut: A.C. MILLS & Lieut: A.C. MILLS slightly wounded. (S.S.) Heavy intermittent shelling throughout the night on whole of Bile Sector. S.O.S. Signal sent up some distance on our right.	
		Morning	3 O.R. killed.	
		5.20 am	2360 rounds on S.O.S. Barrage on S.O.S. call on right part of Bile Sector	
		Day	Intermittent heavy shelling. N°s 1 & 2 Sections proceeded from Camp to take up Barrage Positions near BLACK WATCH CORNER. Their right guns together with right guns of the 15th M.G.C. formed D & E Btys of N°2 Group which was commanded by LIEUT: NICOLL of this Company. Position of this Group soon in charge of BLACK WATCH CORNER. Instructions as to the targets for this Group were issued by the D.M.G.O.	VIDE O.O. 1999
		4 p.m.	N°s 1 & 2 Sections arrived at CLAPHAM JUNCTION, whilst they were interring their gear the enemy Besisted a dump close by inflicting about 12 Casualties, O.R. (wounded). N°s 1 & 2 Sections proceeded to their gun positions, an extremely heavy hostile barrage was put down along the route. LIEUT: A.P. NEWMAN was wounded together with 3 O.R., 2 O.R. were killed.	
		Night	Lines of N°s 1 & 2 Sections Guns laid. N°4 Section vacated their position and moved to the vicinity of their "Jumping-off" points. The enemy put down several sharp Barrages during the night. LIEUT: FISHER O.C. N°3 Section assumed command of the right subsection of N°4 in place of LIEUT: MILLS.	

WAR DIARY
of the 75th Machine Gun Coy.
INTELLIGENCE SUMMARY for October 1917.

Army Form C. 2118.

(Erase heading not required.)

Instructions regarding War Diaries and Intelligence Summaries are contained in F.S. Regs., Part II. and the Staff Manual respectively. Title pages will be prepared in manuscript.

Reference Sheet - GHELUVELT 1/40,000

Place	Date	Hour	Summary of Events and Information	Remarks and references to Appendices
REUTEL BEEK SECTOR.	Oct 4th	4 am	2/Lieut W.G. FAULKE wounded (G.S.), this officer gallantly remained at duty.	
		5.30am	An extremely severe barrage was put down by the Enemy across the whole front.	
		6 am	Our troops attacked the Enemy's position.	
		6.15am (approx)	17th Section followed the Infantry. On the right strong resistance was experienced at POLDERHOEK CHAU. On the left our troops met with slight Resistance. Hostile barrage by guns of all calibres was heavy; machine guns from the CHATEAU succeeded in holding up our advance.	
		Morning	Situation resumes. 1No. 2 Group carried out the M.G. barrage.	
		Afternoon	Right 2 guns 17th Section have taken up position in strong point captured from the Enemy, at J.16.c.7.5.- 5 left guns J.16.a.2.1. #	
		11am	2/Lieut W.G. FAULKE wounded for the 2nd time, by a Sniper from the CHATEAU. Right 2 guns of 17th Section under LIEUT. W. FISHER inflicts considerable casualties on the Enemy's parties in the CHATEAU WOOD. A counter attack moving just north of the CHATEAU was dealt with most successfully before it developed.	
	4/5 night		S.O.S. firing carried out by No.2 Group. No counter attacks developed on our front. 1 OR died of wounds 2 OR (including 1 attached) wounded.	
	5th	Morning	Situation very quiet. 2 left guns of 17th Section moved to positions in pillbox J.16.100× north (on higher ground) J.16.a.2.1. 1 nin of 17th Section had to cover the Blue Front by direct fire.	

WAR DIARY

or

INTELLIGENCE SUMMARY.

(Erase heading not required.)

Army Form C. 2118.

of the 95th Machine Gun Coy. for October 1917.

Place	Date	Hour	Summary of Events and Information	Remarks and references to Appendices
REUTELBEEK SECTOR.	Oct 5th	Morning	Hostile M. Guns active from North of CAMERON (COVERT) of left Battalion more strongly. Orders received for withdrawal of No 1, 2 & 3. Sections tonight through CAMERON COVERT to North East corner, thence along Road E.N.E. Casualties 1 day nil.	R/f Map GHELUVELT 1/10,000
	5/6	Night	Nos 1, 2 & 3 Sections successfully withdrew.	
	6th	Day	Nos 1 & 2 Sections arrived at Tpt from N 3 C; No 3 Section withdrew to BEDFORD HOUSE (SHEET 28). Situation was very quiet. Casualties nil. No 4 Section remained in the line, with 2nd Lieut. Evans in Command.	VIDE OP. 20
	7th	Morning	Situation remained the same. Casualties 1 O.R. killed, 1 O.R. attacked from S.E., D.C.O. (?) Lieutenant O/C 13th M.G. Coy Guns was killed and the 2 Guns were taken over by 1/14th Section, until a new officer arrived. Some active targets were obtained in the morning.	
	"	Day	Several small parties of the enemy were seen and fired on with good results. Walker Conditions were very bad, rendering communication very difficult.	
	8th	Morning	No 3 Section relieved No 4 Section in forward positions. No 4 Section withdrew to BEDFORD HOUSE. Relief was carried out safely. Casualties 1 O.R. killed. Very little movement by the enemy.	VIDE O.O. 21

WAR DIARY
INTELLIGENCE SUMMARY

of the 95 Machine Gun Company
for October 1917.

Army Form C. 2118.

(Erase heading not required.)

Instructions regarding War Diaries and Intelligence Summaries are contained in F. S. Regs., Part II. and the Staff Manual respectively. Title pages will be prepared in manuscript.

Place	Date	Hour	Summary of Events and Information	Remarks and references to Appendices
REUTELBEEK SECTOR	8th	Morning	No 2. Section left Tel Fries this morning under Lieut Percival and took up the following position Approx. from J.16.c.7.5. to J.16.a.5.6. This operation was successfully carried out.	VIDE O.O. 22 Ref Map GHELUVELT 1/10,000
	8th	Day.	Heavy Shelling all day. 1 Officer & 21 OR left for CALAIS to bring back 110 Remount mules.	
	8th	Night	No 3 Section moved to gun position J.15.d.3.7. for Barrage purposes. Night was spent in carrying ammunition to new positions.	
	9th	Morning	1st S.A. Brigade attacked the POLDER HOEK RIDGE. No 3 Section went forward with the Bde. No 3 Section covered the advance by Barrage fire. The attack was not successful and all had to retire to original positions. Very little enemy Artillery fire during first phase of attack, but later it was very heavy. Casualties 1 Officer (Lt Percival) who severely wounded, also 1 O.R. Intermidate.	
	9th	Day.	Positions were heavily shelled all day. 2 Reinforcement Officers arrived from Base Depot.	
	9th	Night	Positions still being heavily shelled. Proportion of Gas Shells were used.	
	10th	Morning	Situation unchanged. Enemy kept up Bombardment all night. It was difficult in getting up Rations and Ammunition. Casualties Nil.	
	10th	Day.	Enemy Artillery Quietened down.	

WAR DIARY or INTELLIGENCE SUMMARY

Army Form C. 2118.

Place	Date	Hour	Summary of Events and Information	Remarks and references to Appendices
REVELSBEEK SECTOR	25th	Day	Balance of Company moved to Camp in RIDGE WOOD AREA.	
	25th	Night	During the night hostile aeroplane dropped bombs on Camp casualties 1 Officer LIEUT POWELL, badly wounded and 1 O.R. wounded.	
	26th	Day	No 1 4th Sections in the line, 13th Inf Bde attacked in the morning capturing many prisoners. Casualties 1 O.R. killed. Hostile artillery very active on Back Areas. Infantry Captured POLDERHOEK CHATEAU. Part had to Retire to original positions later in the day. Situation unchanged. No 1 4th Sections in same positions.	
	27th & 28th		2 Guns withdrawn from FRITZ CLARENCE FARM, and 2 from VERBEEK FARM. No 3 Section which the Remaining 4 guns. No 2 Section relieves 9 Gs at CRRUISE FARM Nos 1 & 4 Sections withdrew to Camp at RIDGE WOOD. Casualties 1 O.R. wounded. Situation unchanged. Hostile aircraft over Camp. Bombs were dropped but no damage was done at Camp.	
	29th		Information has Received that Corps Commander has granted the Military Medal to the following: No 31989 Bgde Phelan J.	
			No 5 " Pidgely A. } for Gallantry in Action 4/5th October 1917.	
			No 61 " Woods W.	

Army Form C. 2118.

WAR DIARY
or
INTELLIGENCE SUMMARY.
(Erase heading not required.)

8th Coy. C/S Machine Gun Corps
of October 1917

Instructions regarding War Diaries and Intelligence Summaries are contained in F.S. Regs., Part II. and the Staff Manual respectively. Title pages will be prepared in manuscript.

Place	Date	Hour	Summary of Events and Information	Remarks and references to Appendices
REUTELBEEK SECTOR	11th	Morning	Situation unchanged. Everything very quiet. We were now able to get up a good supply of ammunition.	R/Map GHELUVELT 1/10,000
	11th	Eve'g	Situation still the same. No Remount (Mules) arrived to-day from CALAIS.	
	11th	Night	Enemy shelled CAMPER or COVERT very heavy. 1 Reinforcement Officer arrived.	
	12th	Morning	The Company was Relieved by the 143rd M.G. Coy. Relief was carried out safely for us, but relieving Coy. had several casualties going in. After Relief, Coy. moved to Camp in the RIDGEWOOD AREA. Weather conditions were very bad. Company remained in Camp overnight.	VIDE O.O. 23
	13th	Aft.	Company moved to Rest billets in Curragh Camp, VESTOUKE Area. Received draft 5 + O.R. 1 Reinforcement Officer arrived from Base Depot. Two Officers were slightly wounded on upwards journey by front dropping. A.He Remained at duty.	R/Map No. 28 1/40,000
	22nd	Eve'g	Coy. at Curragh Camp carried out programme of training including Barrage Drill.	
	23	Afternoon	No.1 + 4 Sections moved to Camp in RIDGEWOOD area. previous to going in the line.	
	24th		No. 4 Sections moved into the line to positions at VERBEEK FARM. arrived all safe	
	25th	Morning	No. 1 Section moved into the line to positions at FITZ CLARENCE FARM arrived all safe. Three 3 Sections formed "D" Battery for Barrage Purposes under command of Lt DADD

WAR DIARY
— OR —
INTELLIGENCE SUMMARY.
(Erase heading not required.)

Army Form C. 2118.

of the 95th Machine Gun Company for October 1917.

Place	Date	Hour	Summary of Events and Information	Remarks and references to Appendices
NEUVE BEER SECTOR.	30th	Day.	Nos 1 & 4 Sections relieved two sections of the 15th Coy. in the right and left forward positions respectively. Lt. HAMPTON assumed command of No.1 Section. The relief was very bad owing to the standing over by the 15th Coy. The work had apparently been done at the Emplacements by that Company, and no positions were handed over without any ammunition whatever. No. 2 Section remained in same positions at CARLISLE FARM. No. 3 Section went into Reserve at TOR TOP. Casualties 3 OR wounded.	
	31st	Day.	There was heavy bombardment of back areas and large numbers of gas shells were used. At night Company H.Q. were moved from CLAPHAM JUNCTION to old H.Q. of the 205th Coy. at STIRLING CASTLE. One Reinforcement Officer reported for to MG Base. Casualties NIL. Company Strength Officers 10 OR 187.	

Henry Evans Lieut for
O.C. 95th Machine Gun Company

WAR DIARY
or
INTELLIGENCE SUMMARY

Army Form C. 2118.

95th Machine Gun Company

From 1st April 1917

Place	Date	Hour	Summary of Events and Information	Remarks and references to Appendices
REUTELBEEK Sector	1	morning	Company Strength Officers 6 O.R. 199. The Company in the line of Hotel POLDERHOEK CHATEAU. With 1 Section of 15 M.G. Company attached for Barrage work.	
		day	Enemy artillery very active	
		night	Enemy artillery still active. Enemy fairly quiet. Barrage gun fire on selected targets. Casualties 1 Officer wounded 1 O.R. Reinforcement 1 O.R.	
	2	morning	Enemy very quiet. During getting ammunition forward, but very difficult owing to E/a	
		day	State of the ground. Enemy still quiet.	
		night	No 1 Section was relieved by 1 section of 13 K.M.G.Cy. Casualties 1 O.R. wounded	
	3	morning	Heavy shelling by the enemy. Enemy constructs new frontline. Working party returned by forward guns. Remainder of Company were relieved by 13 K.M.G.Cy. the morning. Relief successfully carried out. No casualties. On relief Company embuses Kemp at RIDGE WOOD.	O.O. No 26
	4		In Camp. Cleaning Guns & equipment.	
	5		Company left camp at noon & proceeded to the line 2 relieved 13th M.G.Cay. Reinf subsequently carried out Casualties 1 O.R.	O.O. No 27

WAR DIARY

95th Machine Gun Corps — Army Form C. 2118.

INTELLIGENCE SUMMARY

For **Nov. 1917**

Place	Date	Hour	Summary of Events and Information	Remarks and references to Appendices
	5	night	The Company was disposed as follows:— No. 4 Section on left front in CAMERON COVERT. No. 1 " " in front line. Two guns of No. 3 Section 123 a. 40. 45 firing up SEHERBEEK VALLEY. " " " " " at JUT FARM No. 2 Section in reserve at CLAPHAM JUNCTION. H.Q. STIRLING CASTLE. Reinforcements received 1 officer 60 O.R.	O.O. 27
	6	day	At 6 a.m. our troops attacked the POLDERHOEK CHATEAU. The 1st D.C.L.I. with 2 Coy. 1st Devons carried out the attack. Two companies Royal Surreys in support & B Companies 12 K(illegible)in reserve. The objective was the line J.16.c.4.0. to J.16.d.0.2. The Chateau donor to REUTELBEEK about J.16.d.30.25 incl. P.G. posts in advance of this line in immediate donor of Chateau. Advance was covered by artillery & M.G. barrage. No. 1 Section with 4 guns advanced which D.C.L.I. to which on the left its No. 1 Section was attached. The enemy heavy hostile machine gun fire so a good trap to which is engaged stating point. The attack on the right met successful. The 1st Devons Regt captured the mound on right of Chateau. 1 gun got into position on the mound, the other gun was awaiting further fire when going forward. The gun on the right the enemy counter attacked during the following without success. Its got stranded tonight & accounted for a large No. 2 gun of No. 3 Section at 132 a.d.40. As got defended tonight & accounted for a large body of the enemy, enemy again & later attacked in force precurs & the same 3 guns did efficient work in breaking up the attack. Casualties. Killed 3 O.R. (wounded) 17 O.R. 1 gun destroyed	

WAR DIARY
or
INTELLIGENCE SUMMARY.
(Erase heading not required.)

Army Form C. 2118.

Place	Date	Hour	Summary of Events and Information	Remarks and references to Appendices
	6	night	Enemy artillery very active against our position.	
	7	morning	British unchanged. Situation quiet. No 3 ducks from enemy retrn N° shots in the line. No 1 Section withdrawing to move at CLAPHAM JUNCTION. Relief carried out successfully. Two guns of No 3 Section at JUT FARM move into Camp. K Section at CLAPHAM JUNCTION.	
		day	Situation unchanged. Hostile shelling active.	
		night	Enemy barraged CAMERON COVERT for 2 hours. Hostile M.G's very active during the night. Casualties 3 O.R.	
	8		Situation unchanged. Position quiet.	
			Situation unchanged. Position quiet.	
		day	Situation unchanged. Position very quiet. Casualties 1 O.R.	
		night	Situation quiet except for enemy M.G. which were very active. Casualties 1 O.R. Killed. 3 O.R. Wounded	00.28
	9		the Company was relieved by the B's M.G. Company. Relief completed by 11 am. Casualties 16 O.R. killed. On relief Company withdrew to camp at RIDGE WOOD.	
			In Camp at RIDGE WOOD. Cleaning guns & gear.	
	10		Company move from RIDGE WOOD to (CONQUEROR CAMP) in WESTOUTRE area	
	11		Company skies at same Camp. Cleaning Cannot be down owing to move being to day.	
	12		Company skies in camp. Transport moves off ahead of the Company with ks for the	
	13		night in MAPLE Area. Map HAZEBROOK 5A	
	14		Left CONQUEROR Camp 2.45 from & marched to OUDERDOM & entrained at Dickebusch C Station for NIEPPE -LES - BLEQUIN where we detrained about 1.30 am	

Army Form C. 2118.

WAR DIARY
or
INTELLIGENCE SUMMARY.
(Erase heading not required.)

Instructions regarding War Diaries and Intelligence Summaries are contained in F. S. Regs., Part II. and the Staff Manual respectively. Title pages will be prepared in manuscript.

Place	Date	Hour	Summary of Events and Information	Remarks and references to Appendices
	15	1.30 am	Battalion at NIELLES was warned out and placed in readiness to the day's march. The Company marched to billets at WATERDAL. The men only got in at 3 o'clock & most were too tired to take food.	
		11.30 am	Company marched off from Waterdal & marched to billets at BRUMEMBURG.	
			Ref: map CALAIS 1/3 100,000. 4 miles SE hills of Sr—	
BRUMEMBURG	16		Company fitting & resting at Brumemburg.	
	17	afternoon	Church parade	
	18	morning	Training & Company & Platoon drill etc. park & YUKON park	
		afternoon	Revised practice on range	
	19	morning	Specialators practice. Bomb & Lewis gun	
		afternoon	Officers drill	
	20	morning	Training exercise at Passing Over a Strong defence	
	21	"	Practice Stopping Armoured Attack. Inspection by Brigadier	
		afternoon	Training in Infantry duties	
	22	morning	Company paraded under Brig Gen KCB for Cr. Rivers	
		afternoon	Specialaters for Rifle Rifles.	

WO 95/1580/4

5th Division

95th M.G.C.

~~January~~ TO ~~March~~

~~T9 & S~~

1918 APR

95th

9th Brigade.

5th Division.

95th MACHINE GUN COMPANY

APRIL 1918.

Confidential

Register No
Part No
Volume No

War Diary
of
95th Machine Gun Company
for the month of
April 1918.

R. Daniel Capt. & Major
Commanding 95: Company
5th Batt. M. G. Corps.

30.4.1918.

Army Form C. 2118.

WAR DIARY
or
INTELLIGENCE SUMMARY.

(Erase heading not required.)

Instructions regarding War Diaries and Intelligence Summaries are contained in F. S. Regs., Part II. and the Staff Manual respectively. Title pages will be prepared in manuscript.

Place	Date	Hour	Summary of Events and Information	Remarks and references to Appendices

(A7092). Wt. W12859/M1293. 75,000. 1/17. D. D. & L., Ltd. Forms/C.2118/14.

WAR DIARY or INTELLIGENCE SUMMARY

Army Form C. 2118.

95th Machine Gun Company

April 1918

Place	Date	Hour	Summary of Events and Information	Remarks and references to Appendices
LONGARE	1st April		Company strength 9 Officers 190 O.R.	
	2nd		Company preparing to move to FRANCE	
	5th		Two Sections left and entrained at VISENZA for FRANCE	
	4/5		Two Sections moved (Today), one section entrained at VISENZA and at TAVERNELLA	
	6th		Company in the train	
IVERGNY	7th		Nos 1 & 4 Section detrained at PETIT HOUVIN and marched to IVERGNY where they were billeted.	
	8th		Nos 3 & 1 sections detrained at MONDICOURT & FREVENT respectively & went up to IVERGNY	
	9th		No 2 Section detrained at FREVENT & went up to IVERGNY. Company now complete at IVERGNY	
GRINCOURT	10		Company paraded at 9.30 am & marched via LEUCHEUX & MONDICOURT to GRINCOURT	
	11th		Both sides to go into the line. Company owing to off rations going about four miles were ordered to return to PARIS	
			The transport left here at 6am & marched to PARIS and the company with fighting limbers marched to MONDICOURT where they rejoined train left at 6.30 pm	
	12th		Travelled most of the night & detrained at THIENNES & afterwards marched to PARIS station	FRANCE Sheet 36A
			Sections formed into actions at 12:30 & moved to LEPACE then proceeded to take up a line VIGNETTE, & PERNAGE, TOURANT-DACK & LES LAURIERS CHATEAU. The line was taken up about	
			Coy H.Q. was established with village of LA PETITE VIN Three sections eventually the line were distributed as follows No 1 Section with 1st DEVONS on the right. No 3 Section with 1st DCLI & ack left. No 2 Section being in close support with 1st R. Berks	
In Line	13th		No 4 Section was fighting rear in the Bois de VACHES. The guns were all sides in points around the enemy situation. The enemy were much distressed and pushed forward in small parties during the night. The enemy attacked the left flank of our line about 11am formed from our right. The movement was quickly checked by machine gun fire.	

Army Form C. 2118.

WAR DIARY
or
INTELLIGENCE SUMMARY.
(Erase heading not required.)

Instructions regarding War Diaries and Intelligence Summaries are contained in F. S. Regs., Part II. and the Staff Manual respectively. Title pages will be prepared in manuscript.

95th Machine Gun Company
April 3rd 1918

Place	Date	Hour	Summary of Events and Information	Remarks and references to Appendices
FORET DE NIEPPE	/3		Our left was forced back a little & the Left Company of No.223 M.G. Coy was in danger of being cut off and the line refused to conform with the line. Enemy fired during afternoon when the gun was put out of action & one man speared and wounded. Casualties 1 Officer (since wounded) T. B. R. Company left behind & the crew escaped & were destroyed by shell fire.	
Do	14		The enemy made an attack by the summer. At 11.30 AM enemy attacked right company of left Battalion. He attacked in fine weather during the attack was successfully broken off by machine gun fire. The supply of S.A.A. at this time was getting serious, but the scarcity of ammunition. A system of filling belts at Battalion Headquarters was adopted and found most useful to this company from support gun fillers belts — reassumed them forward as required. On and about 11 further attacks on most of the guns in support was noticed & formed rebel. Two specific positions there. In the afternoon a concentration on ESPINETTE was ordered. This was watched broken up by machine gun & artillery fire. During the attack on the farm on our front above 2700 rounds will not a pieces S.A.A & more fell and apparently packs broken up the enemy into the shelter of the contour. Gun up and the dusk movement on gun was directed by Shell fine column. On the afternoon the enemy made a small attack against Left Battalion Right Brigade, but this was ineffectually dealt with by two of our guns. They were all 15 over the gun known Range & our gun was unable to bring up & indirect fire on enemy. The enemy gun were successful in putting two Lewis M.G. teams out of action. The evening was fairly quiet except for a slight bombardment upon line by the enemy. Aircraft continuously flying low examining machine gun area from this Nos 2 & 11 M.G.	

Army Form C. 2118.

WAR DIARY
or
INTELLIGENCE SUMMARY.
(Erase heading not required.)

95th Machine Gun Company
April 1918

Place	Date	Hour	Summary of Events and Information	Remarks and references to Appendices
FIRET du NIEPPE	15th		The night was quiet, no action important, many enemy shells during the day tho' enemy guns were put out of action by a piece of shell. There were small parties of enemy men and aircraft. Casualties 3 OR.	
Do	16th		The night was again quieter but the barrage was continually shelled. Enemy trench mortars were very active during the day. Hostile artillery was very active by night on our line. A good deal of movement seen today behind enemy lines.	
Do	17th		The day very quiet. Hostile artillery trench mortars very active during the day. The Company was relieved in the front line by the 151st M.G. Coy in the evening. 8 guns are in the barrage line as follows 2 guns at J26d7/8 = J26d5/2 J20d 2/5, 2 guns in support at J11d5/8 2 at J11d6/2 at J11d5/8. Coy HQ at J20d2/5. The men are splendid during their tour in the line. They all did exactly what was expected of them when our troops temporarily retired until relieved the system of keeping guns in pairs is strongly recommended. Coy still in Reserve.	
Do	18th		Coy still in Reserve. Officers reconnoitering the back area. Reinforcements 1 Offr 19 OR	
Do	19th		Brigade Reserve. Reinforcements received 1 Officer 19 OR	
Do	20		Coy still in Brigade Reserve. Orders received to relieve 13th M.G. Coy in Right sector.	
Do	21		The Company moved into the line this evening and relieved the 13th M.G. Coy.	
Do	22		relief was reported at 11.30 pm	

WAR DIARY or INTELLIGENCE SUMMARY

Army Form C. 2118

95th Machine Gun Company   April 1918

(Erase heading not required.)

Place	Date	Hour	Summary of Events and Information	Remarks and references to Appendices
FOREST DE NIEPPE	22nd	cont'd	No casualties during relief. The Company had 16 guns in the front line and 8 in support. Coy. HQrs were in the Forest at J.16.c.7/1.	
Do L1+L2 def Sectors	23rd		The night was fairly quiet. There was a good deal of gas shelling in the Forest. The support positions were heavily shelled during the afternoon. In the morning the enemy positions opposite our Centre were shelled (ref. 10.D.18 (Bn.))	
Do	24th		The night was very quiet. Enemy batteries opposite our operations withdrew to their former position.	
Do	25th		The enemy positions were shelled early the morning. Counter Battery work was going to answer, but afternoon shelling our support lines and the front was heavily shelled during the afternoon. It was very quiet in our front. Heavy shelling of the forest and defences being thought by our lines was answered and from hostile guns tonight. At 9.30 p.m. an activity opened along on enemy positions down opposite us at J.15.d.1.12 & J.15.d.6.7. L.O.E. Lumego commenced. The operation was most successful, carried out by 1st & 2nd Aus. (1st Aust. Division) + 2nd Aus. division) went forward and took up the new line. Coy HQ Lahore Canadian during the operation. The guns went forward through positions very rapidly. The new positions were attained by 1st Cdn division 2nd LIEUT EVANS & 4 O.R's support position and occupied the positions reached by our front line them giving close support and maintaining supply line.	Reference Group B.M.95.915 J.2.14.15.57.34.7 95th Bde G.S. No 327
Do	26th		N26a N26.a.9/0 K26c 6.0/7 K20d o/o K21 8.9/1 K26c.1/4 N26a 1/10 K31 Central. A barrage was put down on 1st B&ET Village by four guns in support covering the advance of troops. Hostile trench was fairly light enemy put positions not working to position, 3 machine guns was repaired. The night was quiet in front but a lot of gas shellfire on the front during the night. Casualties 1 Officer & OR wounded. all day	

Army Form C. 2118.

WAR DIARY
or
INTELLIGENCE SUMMARY.
(Erase heading not required.)

9th Machine Gun Company. April 1918.

Instructions regarding War Diaries and Intelligence Summaries are contained in F.S. Regs., Part II. and the Staff Manual respectively. Title pages will be prepared in manuscript.

Place	Date	Hour	Summary of Events and Information	Remarks and references to Appendices
L1 & L2 Subsectors	26th contd		Our machine Gun Battalion has now been formed coming into force from to-day. This Company now becomes B Company 5th Battalion M.G. Corps. Major CUTTING the present O.M.G.O. has been appointed 2nd i/c B. Battalion. Coy Commanders have been appointed as follows 4 2nd in command Lonsdale appointed as Captain, the Headquarters has been formed, neither any two applied the Regt Sergt Major or Signalling Sergt. The Enemy kept up a heavy Bombardment on the dummy this morning.	
Do	27th		Heavy shelling of our positions during the night. Smoke screen down to enemy means a half hearted attack on our front but the attack was successfully resisted by the fire guns of our Section. Heavy shelling of our front line and support areas kept the night guns in L.2. Sub Section busy. Moved about much and did the Brigade front was continuous tonight some 600 - and 14 this night guns in L.2. Sub Sector were moved table left. We were some successfully covered out and on was sealing during the night on the front. There were much heavy gas shells. Hostile aircraft very busy bombing our area and our line between communicated lines guns and shells etc in Nos 1 & 3 Sections changed position tonight thereby unexpectedly carrying out the Right front Section. Their conceal during move away hostile gas lines.	
Do	28th			
Do	29th		Enemy aeroplanes were busily active during the night. Intermittent shelling all day. Hostile aircraft active.	
Do	30th		Night very quiet but heavy shelling of front during the night. Intermittent shelling of rear positions all day.	

A.S. Nicoll Major
Comdg B. Company
5th Battalion Machine Gun Corps

WO 95/15805

~~3 Army Troops~~

5 DIV 95 Bde

95

TRENCH MORTAR BTY

1915 Oct to 1915 Dec

(1254)

3rd Army

9

26 Bde 12/7333

Hogs Trench Mortar Batty.

Oct 15

WAR DIARY

of 95th Trench Mortar Battery

for October 1915

95th French Mortar Battery

No.	Unit	Rank	Name	Service	Trade or Calling

WAR DIARY or INTELLIGENCE SUMMARY

Army Form C. 2118.

Place	Date	Hour	Summary of Events and Information	Remarks and references to Appendices
	1915			
Vadheureux 12th Army Trench Mortar School	3/10	1.30pm	Left Vadheureux with 95th Trench Mortar Battery in two motor lorries into two School Trench Mortars & tubes for 65th Brigade, 22nd Division. Arrived Halloureux S/c. Guns and reported arrival to Brigade Major. Billeted in Halloureux. No ammunition.	A/effective experience for each of troops 382
Halloureux	5/10	6.30 a.m.	Under Brig. Major's order left for Tancourt with 14th Kings own Liverpool Regt - the men of battery remaining at Halloureux.	
Tancourt	6/10 - 12/10		Occupying trenches in Brigade frontage.	
Tancourt	13/10		Ammunition arrived at Tancourt. Who remainder of Battery were told that Ammunition in accordance with order of Brigade Major - & billets these, the	
Halloureux	14/10		Remainder of Battery remaining at Halloureux.	
Tancourt	16/10 - 22/10		In accordance with order of Brig. Major arrived at Tancourt. Battery then met by 65th Brigade on 19/10. Battery trench being carried on until 22/10	
Guillacourt	22/10		Under orders from Div. Hqrs., Battery moved at Guillacourt, 22nd Div. Hqrs. being reported there	
Dornart	25/10		Transport (wagons, lorries) & Transport officer into order, arranged battery to Dornart where he reported at headquarters of 365 (West) Division - Battery billeted at Dornart	

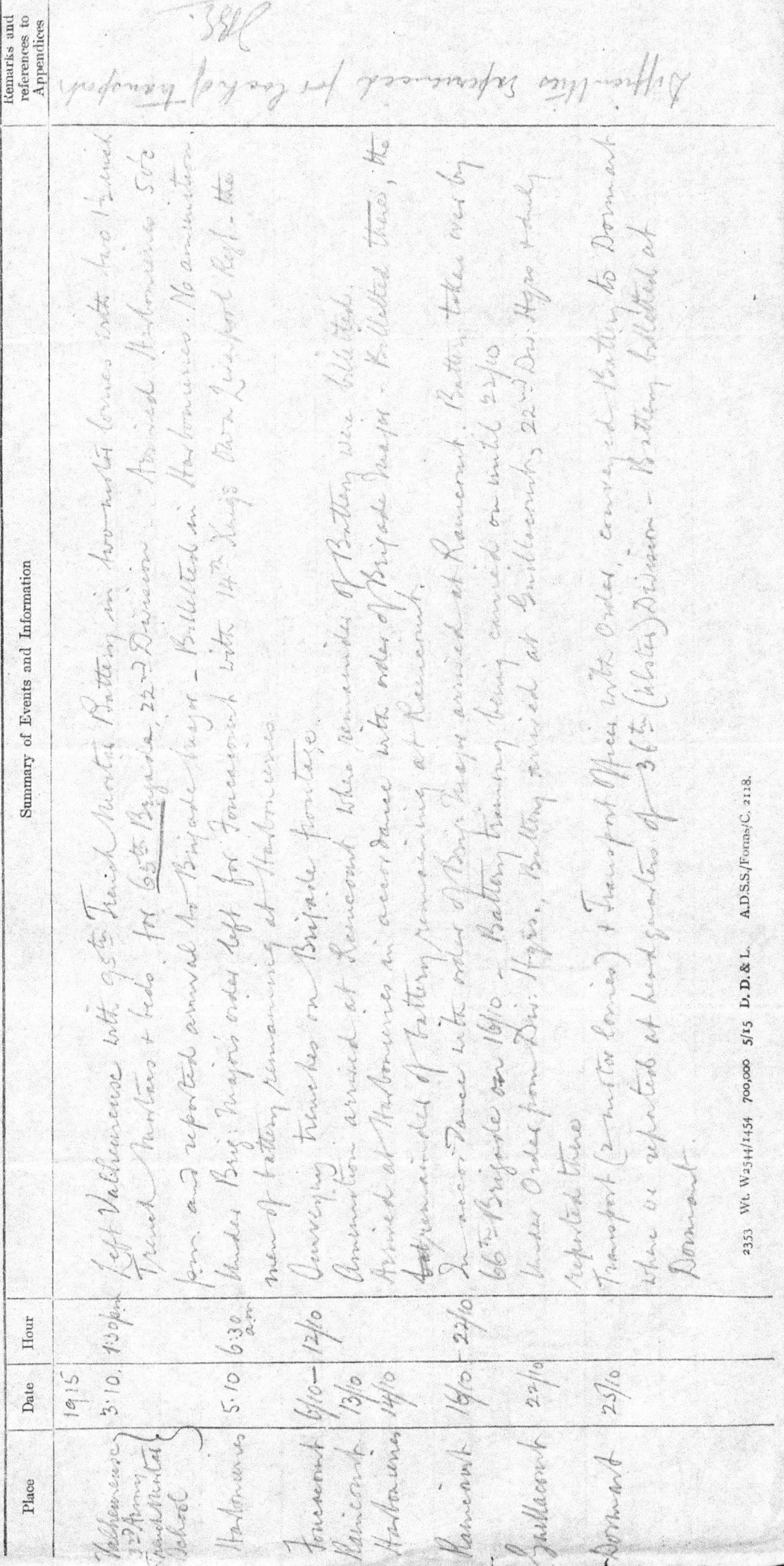

Army Form C. 2118.

WAR DIARY
or
INTELLIGENCE SUMMARY.
(Erase heading not required.)

Instructions regarding War Diaries and Intelligence Summaries are contained in F. S. Regs., Part II. and the Staff Manual respectively. Title pages will be prepared in manuscript.

Place	Date	Hour	Summary of Events and Information	Remarks and references to Appendices
Denmark	25/10	10 am	Under B.O. of 35th (Ulster) Division Battery proceeded to Spesempo & early reported to Brig: Genjl of 108th Brigade at Rosenwerf - Battery billetted at Spesempo	

J Bryan Schad
n/o OC 95th French Mortar Battery

B.a.R. 9

26 Bde

21/7604

Jenet
95, Morier Battery

Nov. 1915

Vol II

WAR DIARY or INTELLIGENCE SUMMARY.

Army Form C. 2118.

95th TRENCH MORTAR BATTERY

Place	Date	Hour	Summary of Events and Information	Remarks and references to Appendices
EPECAMPS	1915 June 10th to June 15th		Divisional Training.	
	June 15th		Mortar Brigade Orders started first Class of instruction in the 1½" Trench Mortar, its class being composed of 2 N.C.O.s and 8 men. The idea of class is to enable the Battery to replace its Infantry casualties with men (infantry) of the Brigade who have some knowledge of Trench Mortar work.	
"	June 20th		Class of Instruction completed with satisfactory results	
"	June 23rd June 24th June 25th		First consignment of L.S. Stokes Trench Mortar (25 in Bin) arrived. Total came + found they worked well. Having received Brigade Orders to move to a given point making necessary arrangements thereto. 8 a.m. left Epecamps for Neuville via Bernaville and proceeded to St. Sauveur as per Orders. Arrived at 9½ R. gate and Battery billetted there	
"	May 16th June 30th		Weather rainy ... ... later snow and frost being prevalent also much rain	

J. Byron Sherid 2/Lt
O/c 95th Trench Mortar Battery
108th Brigade
36th (Ulster) Division

9

95th Jamaica Natan Batty

Do

Vol III
26 Bdle

Army Form C. 2118.

WAR DIARY
or
INTELLIGENCE SUMMARY.
(Erase heading not required.)

Instructions regarding War Diaries and Intelligence Summaries are contained in F. S. Regs., Part II. and the Staff Manual respectively. Title pages will be prepared in manuscript.

Place	Date	Hour	Summary of Events and Information	Remarks and references to Appendices
BERNEUIL	1/2/15		On L.G.C. unit. 108th Brigade 36th (Ulster) Division	
ST RIQUIER	15/2/15	10.00a	108th S.M. Bnd 108th Brigade 36th (Ulster) Division t arrived at Frévillé.	
FRÉVILLE	14/2/15	11.30a	107th Brigade attached to Brigade - Billets here.	
FORCEVILLE	29/4/15		We proceeded and the General Mentioned 7 days furlough to England.	
			During the month 11th April 1915 we received the remainder of the new pattern trench mortar, consisting of one Mark I, Mark II trench mortar (hitherto longer tails) eight large (500 lbs) & seven small (8 pattern) and seven (No 12) trench charges. The trenches were accordingly to the crews ammunition.	
			According to the longer tails to the Bombs (to the effect in) the longer the range of the mortar (each furlong), by 80 yards (light lands) a 41/2 yards	
			Trial: No practised a bit of light through the 5in at the enemy (carried out by the 1st line from Frévillé) twenty & holmshuts.	

J P. [signature]
95th Trench Mortar Battery

WO 95/1580/6

BEF

5 Div.

95 Bde

95 Trench Mortar Bty

1916 July

Army Form C. 2118.

WAR DIARY
or
INTELLIGENCE SUMMARY

(Erase heading not required.)

95th T.M. Battery

95 TM Bty
Vol 1

Instructions regarding War Diaries and Intelligence Summaries are contained in F. S. Regs., Part II. and the Staff Manual respectively. Title Pages will be prepared in manuscript.

Place	Date	Hour	Summary of Events and Information	Remarks and references to Appendices
WALLY	1/7/16		Quiet day. Very few prisoners. Day engagements at night.	
	2/7/16		Shelled all day in trenches and in Wailly. Mess Room and good part of battery form destroyed. One girl killed. Moved partly by lorry and partly by rail to ETREE-WAMIN.	
ETREE-WAMIN	3/7/16		Arrived ETREEWAMIN about 7 a.m.	
	4/7/16		Drill and General training	
	5/7/16		do	
	6/7/16		do	
BERNEVILLE	7/7/16		Marched to Berneville – arrived about 8.30 p.m.	
	8/7/16		Drill and General Training	
	9/7/16		do	
	10/7/16		do	
	11/7/16		do	
	12/7/16		do	
	13/7/16		Marched from Berneville to Beaudricourt. Arrived about 10 pm	
BEAUDRICOURT	14/7/16		do do Beaudricourt to Candas	5 pm
CANDAS	15/7/16		do do Candas to Herissart	3 pm
HERISSART	16/7/16		do do HERISSART to BRESLE	12 noon
BRESLE	17/7/16		do do BRESLE to BECORDEL	6 pm

Army Form C. 2118.

WAR DIARY
or
INTELLIGENCE SUMMARY

(Erase heading not required.)

Of A T.M. Battery

Instructions regarding War Diaries and Intelligence Summaries are contained in F. S. Regs., Part II. and the Staff Manual respectively. Title Pages will be prepared in manuscript.

Place	Date	Hour	Summary of Events and Information	Remarks and references to Appendices
BECORDEL	18/7/16		Shellock occasionally by very long range guns. Went to our trenches.	
do.	19/7/16	11 p.m.	Half Battery went up to trenches with 4 guns. Casualties 3 O.R. wounded heavily shelled going in — Battery caught in enemy barrage.	
LONGUEVAL	20/7/16		Shelling all day by enemy. Carrying party of Seuforts torn up about 250 rounds of ammn. No ammn expended as batty was in position to repel a counter attack by enemy. Remainder of batty went up to trenches. Enemy shelled valley with weeping shells. Batty Hdqrs. moved from valley to trenches occupied by B.L. seige Battery. Fired at point 1119.D.1.9 Enemy were seen to run out of their position and along a main road. Our men returned and their hurry a machine gun was shot by their fire.	
	21/7/16		Button moved to PONT ST in order to enentuate fire on enemy points, four guns were placed in PONT ST and three in between — had about 5 H.C.S.'s. Great difficulty was experienced in getting ammn to batty so all horse arms to trenches bringing ration and 20 free ammn. It was found impossible to get more than 230 rounds up. All were shelled out of this location.	
	22/7/16		CORNWALLS and SURREYS attacked about 340 A.M. The batty fired in support of attack. @ B.9 and S.11.D @ 3.3 and S.11.D.2.5 @ 3.40 A.M. aero quat about 320 rounds were fired	
	23/7/16	3.40 A.M.		

WAR DIARY or INTELLIGENCE SUMMARY

Army Form C. 2118.

95th T.M. Battery

Place	Date	Hour	Summary of Events and Information	Remarks and references to Appendices
LONGUEVAL (South)	23/7/16	3-0 am	Some ammn. was destroyed by shell fire.	JL
		6 AM	Strong German counter attack repulsed. The battery put out a barrage, but ammn. was very scarce owing to difficulty in getting it up to the guns. Also scarcity of crews from 2nd Lt. FITCH, killed, 2nd Lt. R.HOSEGOOD (wounded) and Lt. R. HOSEGOOD (2nd in command I.O.R. killed B.O.R. wounded) LONGUEVAL CHURCH (VDC 2.1 ALL TMP)	JL
	24/7/16	7 p.m	Heavily bombarded by enemy for about ½ hour. But we unable to get guns into action. They two guns were in a position where the enemy could see two strong points from the orchard about S.11 D 05. The battery opened up and put a barrage in front of the advancing troops. Owing to smoke and darkness it was impossible to see what happened. About 160 rounds were fired. Headquarters shelled out and moved into a bit. See map Field Office. 2nd Lt N.G. RIVER. wounded. 1 O.R. killed. 7 O.R. wounded.	JL
	25/7/16		Quiet day. Relieved about midnight by 15th Bucks. Headquarters in ten position again shelled. A quantity of material such as 2 revolvers, about 60 Box Respirators, No. 14 Grenades, 1 Bicycle and a quantity of machinery were fired over destroyed completely.	JL
	26/7/16	6 pm	Capt. SCOTT-LORIMER, one officer and an orderly went up to trenches with reinforcements from 13th Bucks.	JL
	27/7/16	6 am	NORFOLKS, CHESHIRES and BEDFORDS attacked. The Battery known army points. Casualties 1 O.R. wounded of the battery. Ammn. still coming up to	JL

Army Form C. 2118.

WAR DIARY
or
INTELLIGENCE SUMMARY
(Erase heading not required.)

95th T.M. Battery.

Instructions regarding War Diaries and Intelligence Summaries are contained in F. S. Regs., Part II. and the Staff Manual respectively. Title Pages will be prepared in manuscript.

Place	Date	Hour	Summary of Events and Information	Remarks and references to Appendices
LONGUEVAL	27/9/16		difficulty in getting it to guns	
	28/9/16		Large enemy party of about 90 brought up short 300 rounds of ammunition. We open fire on enemy patrol before the GLOUCESTERS attacked.	
	29/9/16		Battery withdrew to POMMIER REDOUBT	
	30/9/16		Site at Pommier Redoubt. Shelled fairly heavily about 11 pm	
	2/9/16		Shelled during day at odd intervals. Men dug trench to take shelter in.	
			No casualties.	

J.C. Donaldson Capt
O.C. 95th T.M. Battery.

Army Form C. 2118.

WAR DIARY
or
INTELLIGENCE SUMMARY

(Erase heading not required.)

Instructions regarding War Diaries and Intelligence Summaries are contained in F. S. Regs, Part II. and the Staff Manual respectively. Title Pages will be prepared in manuscript.

Place	Date	Hour	Summary of Events and Information	Remarks and references to Appendices
	30/10/16	10.4 a	Enemy sent over 18 H.E. time (30) "whizz" (?) rounds opposite 95 Trench at the same time they sent some 9/2s opposite 98 Trench. All pits were lifted & retained by 4/57th Battery.	Opp.
		6 pm	Enemy again active sent kniesenpers and Granatz. We used our trench mts. D 17.2 gun. Opp. enemy Grand side. Weather very fine - artillery gun's quiet.	

2449 Wt. W14957/M90 750,000 1/16 J.B.C. & A. Form/C.2118/12.

95 INFANTRY BRIGADE.

12 BN GLOUCESTERSHIRE REGIMENT.
1915 NOV TO 1918 OCT.

95 BRIGADE MACHINE GUN COMPANY.
1916 JAN TO 1918 APR.

95 TRENCH MORTAR BTY
1915 OCT TO 1915 DEC.
AND 1916 JULY.

1580

95 INFANTRY BRIGADE.

12 BN GLOUCESTERSHIRE REGIMENT.
1915 NOV TO 1918 OCT.

95 BRIGADE MACHINE GUN COMPANY.
1916 JAN TO 1918 APR.

95 TRENCH MORTAR BTY
1915 OCT TO 1915 DEC. AND 1916 JULY.

158D

www.ingramcontent.com/pod-product-compliance
Lightning Source LLC
Chambersburg PA
CBHW080816010526
44111CB00015B/2566